Early Massachusetts Marriages

Prior to 1800.

As found on the official records of

Worcester County.

FIRST BOOK.

EDITED BY

Frederic W. Bailey,

ED. "EARLY CONN. MARRIAGES," DESIGNER BAILEY'S PHOTO-ANCESTRAL RECORD, "THE RECORD OF MY ANCESTRY." MEMBER AMERICAN HIST. ASSO., CONN. HIST. SO., NEW HAVEN COLONY HIST. SO., N. Y. GEN. & BIOG. SO., SONS OF THE AMERICAN REVOLUTION (MASS.), MANAGER BUREAU OF AMERICAN ANCESTRY.

Southern Historical Press, Inc.
Greenville, South Carolina

This volume was reproduced
from a personal copy located in
the Publishers private library

All rights reserved. No part of this publication may be reproduced,
stored in a retrieval system, transmitted in any form, posted
on the web in any form or by any means without the
prior written permission of the publisher.

Please direct all correspondence and book orders to:
SOUTHERN HISTORICAL PRESS, Inc.
1071 Park West Blvd.
Greenville, SC 29611

Published 1897 by:
   Frederic W. Bailey
ISBN #978-1-63914-657-4
Printed in the United States of America

CONTENTS.

	PAGE
PREFACE,	iv
WORCESTER,	1, 165
MENDON,	13
UXBRIDGE,	18
RUTLAND,	22
DUDLEY,	24
STURBRIDGE,	30
LUNENBURG,	33
BOLTON,	40
UPTON,	48
HARVARD,	52
LEICESTER,	58
SPENCER,	62
HOLDEN,	68
SOUTHBOROUGH,	72
GRAFTON,	75
SHREWSBURY,	78
WESTMINSTER,	84
NORTHBOROUGH,	88
LEOMINSTER,	90
DOUGLAS,	91
NEW BRAINTREE,	93
FITCHBURG,	95
WINCHENDON,	96
TEMPLETON,	96
SUTTON,	97, 144
LANCASTER,	104
HARDWICK,	117
OXFORD,	127
CHARLTON,	136
BROOKFIELD,	150
BARRE,	158
MILFORD,	159
ATHOL,	161
NORTHBRIDGE,	163
ROYALSTON,	164
BERLIN,	164
PAXTON,	164
PRINCETON,	165

EARLY MASSACHUSETTS MARRIAGES.

PREFACE.

The earliest settlements in Massachusetts were along the coast line; and the territory which became the Counties of Essex, Middlesex, Plymouth and Barnstable, all in Eastern Massachusetts, and extending indefinitely westward and inland, plenty large enough for years to meet the needs of a slowly expanding colony. Except the few isolated companies that dared to penetrate the forests, press over the hills and beyond the nearest streams, and there trust themselves to the mercies of impulsive and hostile Indian tribes, a large majority of the inhabitants were content to reach out gradually by mastering their immediate foes and subduing by degrees the neighboring wilds, all the while keeping within easy reach of the sure aid which at any time might even there become necessary.

The territory now embraced in Worcester County was occupied here and there long before its organization in 1731. In the steady march of civilization those sturdy ancestors to whom, through warfare or distant journeyings this region had become familiar, had marked out a number of its most fertile spots for settlement that were later so oft left by will to worthy sons and daughters, who there found for themselves permanent and happy homes. Such localities may now be known by the ancient townships, dating back even as early as 1653, when Lancaster was organized and named.

But the interesting and impressive feature of our early and colonial life in Massachusetts, here so briefly told, is that prior to any thought of an organized township, the Christian church, fulfilling to the letter the Gospel spirit, "where two or three are gathered together," had already planted and erected its church, around and in which might center the best aims and ambitions of the humblest community. It gathered the isolated and scattered households for miles around together in an assembly, holy in its purpose and far reaching in its aim. At home in the wilderness it brought to each lonely fireside comfort, consolation, good cheer. Its all pervading life and light conquered as nothing else could the red savage in his forest den, persuading even him to submit to its precious ordinances. The faithful pastor kept peculiar oversight of all these people from a supreme sense of duty which was not strictly and conscientiously fulfilled if somehow every name was not recorded by him among his baptisms, on his list of membership, or the eligible among those by him joined in the sacred bonds of matrimony.

Now to these old records of the early Church carefully gathered by the clergy, mutilated as they sometimes are by years of usage, genealogists have been greatly indebted. And it seems very strange that town authorities have not seen fit more generally to secure copies of these perishable books and papers, not alone for their better protection, but that the town records might by their aid be made even more complete. Especially evident is this, so well is it known how oft the church records will contain marriages of town people never recorded elsewhere, or the baptism of children whose names at birth never reached the town clerk. It can hardly be said, however, that the Colony or State of Massachusetts itself has ever been indifferent to the importance of this subject, if we may judge from the number of enactments which its Assembly from time to time has passed. Indeed, fortunate is the man who, seeking for his ancestry, is drawn in the search to the old Bay State, since, of all the ancient States, its records as a whole, thanks to an interested people, are the most complete and satisfactory.

For instance we find (and we use as our authority, and to which we are indebted for numerous dates, etc., "Report on the Custody and Condition of the Public Records," by Carroll D. Wright), that as early as September 9, 1639, "It was ordered that records be kept of the days of every marriage, birth and death of every person within this jurisdiction." Mass. Rec., Vol. I, p. 276. June 14, 1642, another step was taken to secure complete and perfect record, when "clerks of the writs in the several towns were hereafter to record all births and deaths and deliver a return of the same yearly to the recorder of the court belonging to the jurisdiction in which they lived. Persons authorized to marry were to return the names of persons married by them, and the date when married, to the recorder of the court nearest their habitation. Such recorders were to faithfully and carefully enroll such births, marriages and deaths as shall thus be committed to their trust." Mass. Rec., Vol. II, p. 15. November 3, 1692. At this time defects in the previous enactment were wisely met when "Every justice and minister was ordered to register all marriages solemnized before any of them and make a return quarterly to the clerk of the Sessions of the Peace, to be by him registered." Prov. Laws, Vol. I, p. 61.

In 1693 town clerks were ordered to register births and marriages. In 1695 justices and ministers were ordered to return within three months the names of all persons married by them, to the clerk of the town, he being ordered to register the same. While on December 1, 1716, " Every town clerk was ordered to give in a list of marriages to the clerk of the Sessions of the Peace annually in April, and every clerk of the court was to record the same." Prov. Laws, Vol. II, p. 60.

These several enactments supplementing each other clearly show how well Massachusetts has sought to do its full duty in the preservation of valuable family data, and explains not only how it is that each town possesses so much of this kind, but also why it is that in the various counties of the state the County Clerk or Clerk of Courts, as called, should have in his possession marriage records as herein found.

Worcester County, organized with this law already in force, began to receive from the various towns within its limits such records as both justices of the peace and ministers possessed. It did not secure the earlier records, which, of course, had gone to the clerk of the county from which Worcester was taken—Middlesex—nor did the law probably secure complete obedience in every case, as it might had some penalty been attached, but it did result in the preservation in compact form of valuable data of ancestors now so earnestly sought for, and which town clerks themselves might not be able from their records to supply.

The period between 1731 and 1785 is covered by two large books filed away in the office of the Clerk of the Courts. The marriages are entered apparently in the order of their reception from the different towns, and not according to any systematic arrangement. The name of the minister or justice of the peace in many cases is recorded, though we have noted herein only such Rev. as occasionally appears. The puzzling handwriting, together with the fact that no index exists, and no order or arrangement in the books, has made the search therein most difficult, and the searcher has, after a fair trial, given up in despair of any reasonable results therefrom.

The following records have been most carefully copied and compared. In a few cases the names could not be determined, and such are marked with an (?). The first and oldest book is contained in this issue. A copy of the second book is on file for reference in hopes of publication at some future day.

FREDERIC W. BAILEY.

NEW HAVEN, CONN., September 7, 1897.

EARLY MASSACHUSETTS MARRIAGES.

WORCESTER COUNTY.

Incorporated 1731. Taken from Middlesex County.

The County records begin with the following marriages. Where and by whom performed is not stated. It is presumed that most of them occurred in Worcester.

Noah Mason & Kezia Mascroft,	Dec. 9, 1736
Thomas Converse & Abigail Fay,	Nov. 3, 1737
Stephen Cary & Mercy Frame,	June 22, 1739
Ebenezer Fay & Thankful Hide,	Sept. 19, 1739
Richard Dresser & Dorothy Marcy,	Nov. 12, 1741
Jeremiah Streeter & Eunice Rice,	April 28, 1742
Samuel Roger & Captivity Peter,	June 29, 1742
Stephen Davis & Esther Haw,	Nov. 9, 1742
Jabez Nichols & Hannah Mirick,	Jan. 4, 1742–3
John Stacy, Jr., & Abigail Allen,	Nov. 1, 1743
Jacob Huntley & Lydia Allen,	April 22, 1744
John Harding & Washts (?) Rice,	Feb. 26, 1744–5
Solomon Pagon & Hannah Chekeys (Indians),	July 10, 1745
Benjamid Hide & Dorcas Dyer,	Nov. 21, 1745
Caleb Harding & Hannah Weld,	Dec. 26, 1745
Edward Simpson & Anna Bond,	May 15, 1746
Joseph Perry & Lois Gilburt,	Jan. 6, 1746
Thomas Moores & Ruth Nichols,	April 24, 1747
Tilly Rue & Mary Buckminster,	Nov. 2, 1748
Oliver Heyward, Esq., & Anna Hinds,	June 8, 1749
Benjamin Wood & Mehitabell Hamilton,	Sept. 13, 1749
John Bell & Susannah Hinds,	Nov. 17, 1749
Oliver Woolcot & Abigail Mills,	Jan. 11, 1749
Thomas Tucker & Hannah Hill,	July 20, 1749
Samuel Leech & Mary Simson,	June 20, 1749
Benjamin Scott & Lydia Johnson,	Sept. 7, 1749
Icchabod Robbins & Zerviah Rice,	Dec. 27, 1749
Elijah Bartlett & Bathsheba Gilburt,	Jan. 11, 1749
Arthur Tucker & Mary Sabins,	May 17, 1750
Jeremiah Woodbury & Jerusha Tucker,	March 22, 1750
Samuel Bascom & Sarah Barns,	Sept. 18, 1750

MARRIAGES.

Benjamin Jennings & Elizabeth Gilburt,	Nov. 8, 1750
William Witt & Abigail Killam,	Nov. 29, 1750
Nathaniel Bartlet & Dorothy Harwood,	July 5, 1750
Joseph Marsh & Abigail Symons,	May 17, 1750
Benjamin Lee & Esther Baker,	June 28, 1750
Beriah Haws & Patience Warner,	Nov. 15, 1750
Thomas Holdin & Ruth Baker,	March 21, 1750
Josiah Bacon & Abigail Holden,	March 21, 1750
Nathan Newton & Experience Stow,	June 5, 1750
Elnathan Newton & Jemima Joslin,	June 19, 1750
Isaac Newton, Jr., & Sarah Collins,	Aug. 17, 1750
Benjamin Morse & Mary James,	Oct. 26, 1750
William Lewis & Mercy Pike,	Dec. 10, 1750
Jonas Woods & Elisabeth Newton,	Dec. 12, 1750
Nathaniel Stacy & Mary Withirbee,	Jan 10, 1750
Timothy Barret & Dinah Witt,	Jan. 24, 1750–51
Nathan Brigham & Martha Gleason,	Feb. 6, 1750–51
Elijah Bellows & Martha Joslin,	Feb. 20, 1750–51
Samuel Adams of Grafton & Elizabeth Gould of Sutton,	Nov. 1, 1750
James Whipple of Grafton & Lydia Powers of Littleton,	Nov. 29, 1750
William Hatfield & Elizabeth Mason,	Nov. 1, 1750
Ralph Wheelock & Experience Denison,	Jan. 24, 1750
William McKinstry & Mary Morse,	—— 31, 1750
Caleb Stacy & Abigail Bond,	June 6, 1751
Samuel Temple & Hannah Gleason,	Nov. 13, 1751
Jonathan Farr & Mary Wells,	June 5, 1751
Timothy Newton & Sarah Mirrick,	July 5, 1751
Simeon Walker & Judith Goss,	Oct. 10, 1751
Seth Lincoln & Lucy Page,	Oct. 10, 1751
John Green & Annah Bradish,	Dec. 7, 1751
Peter Gibbin & Sarah Green,	Dec. 7, 1751
Joseph Powers & Abigail Benjamin,	Dec. 25, 1751
John Auger of Framingham & Bethiah Lyscom of Southborough,	Feb. 22, 1752
Joseph Trumble, Jr., of Leicester & Susanna Richards of Dudley,	April 29, 1752
John Robert & Sarah Abbot,	April 1, 1752

George Page & Priscilla Whitcom, June 4, 1752
Thomas Denny of Leicester & Mrs. Tabitha Cutter
of Grafton, June 25, 1752
Andrew Oliphant of Dedham & Mrs. Elisabeth
Browning of Rutland, Nov. 22, 1752
John Beal (?) & Sarah Rood, March 30, 1752
Ephraim White & Abigail Upham, Dec. 21, 1752
Daniel Mathews and Huldah Putnam, Feb. 20, 1753
Benjamain Green & Mercy Taft, Oct. 2, 1753
Elias Parmenter & Bethial Tyler, March 22, 1753
Joshua Wood & Rachel Hazeltine, May 9, 1754
Jonathan Jones & Mary Wood, May 29, 1754
Paul Hazeltine & Mary Rice, July 25, 1754
Elisha Taft & Experience Taft, July 21, 1754
Jonah Moore of Worcester & Elisabeth Bemis of
Spencer, July 10, 1755
William Thomson, Jr., of Leicester & Jane White
of New Braintree, Jan. 16, 1755
Obed Abbut— & Elizabeth Edmonds of Brookfield,
April 24, 1755
Joseph Barns & Susanna Cannon, Dec. 8, 1755
Dr. Joel Carpenter of Hardwicke & Mrs. Mary
Ruggles, Dec. 9, 1755
James Dudley & Mehitable Woodbury, both of
Concord, Dec. 25, 1755
Jos. Willard of Petersham & Lucretia Ward of
Westboro, Feb. 28, 1757
Noah Harris & Phebee Butler, Feb. 22, 1757
Jonathan Gale & Margaret Crawford, March 10, 1757
Silas Whitney & Jane Porson (?), April 25, 1758
Ezra Bemen (?) & Persis (?) Roys (?), June 1, 1758
Thomas Willard & Elizabeth Davenport, Jan. 10, 1759
Mathew Noble of Westfield & Lydia Eager of
Shrews, May 24, 1758
Anthony Clark & Jane Fairfield, July 31, 1759
Amos Spring & Phebe Porson (?), Oct. 11, 1759
William Goss & Elizabeth Pike, Nov. 8, 1759
David Child & Mehitabell Richardson, Nov. 29, 1759
Edward Newton & Sarah Winch, Feb. 7, 1760

WORCESTER.

Worcester was settled in 1674. October 15, 1684, "It was ordered that the plantation at Quansigamond be called Worcester and that the town brand mark be as illustrated in the record." Mass. Rec., Vol. V, p. 460. Incorporated June 14, 1722. A city, February 29, 1848. First (Congregational) Church organized 1716. Friends, 1735. Clergyman mentioned: Rev. Thaddeus Maccarty.

Josiah Holden & Abigail Bond of Watertown,	Dec. 17, 1747
Nathaniel Tatman & Mary Rice,	Dec. 17, 1747
Jonathan Eaton & Ruth Gleason,	May 12, 1748
John Fisk & Azubah Moore,	June 1, 1748
Joshua Child & Mary Hinds of Shrewsbury,	June 2, 1748
Elisha Hubburd of Hatfield & Lucy Stearns,	June 7, 1748
Solomon Gates & Mary Clark,	Nov. 10, 1748
John Mower & Hannah Moore,	Nov. 23, 1748
Thomas Cowden & Experience Gray,	Nov. 24, 1748
John Osburn, Jr., of Hopkinton & Jane Gray,	Nov. 29, 1748
William Little of Lunenburg & Elizabeth Wallis,	Dec. 1, 1748
James Forbush, Jr., & Margaret McFarland,	Aug. 24, 1749
Robert Blair of Pelham & Margaret MacClewain,	Aug. 24, 1749
Matthias Stone & Susannah Chaddick,	Nov. 16, 1749
John Chaddick & Lydia Gale,	Nov. 16, 1749
William Harris of Holden & Patience Gleason,	Jan. 24, 1749-50
Duncan Campbell of Oxford & Elizabeth Stearns,	Jan. 27, 1749-50
Cornelius Stowell & Livilla Goulding,	March 22, 1749-50
Cyrus Rice & Elizabeth Eaton,	March 27, 1749-50
Samuel Randal & Ruth Bond of Bolton,	Aug. 8, 1750
Asa Flagg & Lois Chaddick,	Nov. 1, 1750
William Browning of Rutland & Rebekah McFarland,	Nov. 22, 1750
Moses Bennet & Joanna Gleason,	Dec. 19, 1750
Elisha Hedge, Jr., & Déliverance Stearns,	Dec. 25, 1750
Henry Potter & Jane Rowlin,	April 25, 1751
Joshua Hide of No. 6 & Rebekah Hubbard,	May 2, 1751

Joseph Gleason & Lydia Whitney,	May 9, 1751
James Smith of Leicester & Zaviah Hubburd,	May 21, 1751
Isaac Stearns & Katherine Crosbey,	Nov. 7, 1751
Daniel Biglo & Mary Bond,	Nov. 21, 1751
Jno. Bond, Jr., & Silence King,	Nov. 21, 1751
Jonas Rice (tertius) & Bathsheba Parmenter,	Dec. 3, 1751
Henry Ward & Lydia Mower,	Jan. 2, 1752
Samuel Lawrence of Pomfret & Hannah Tatman,	Jan. 2, 1752
Moses Peirce of Weston & Mehitabel Rice,	Feb. 10, 1752
Palmer Goulding, Jr., & Abigail Heyward,	Feb. 25, 1752
Phinehas Ward & Eunice Cutting,	April 22, 1752
David Biglo & Sarah Eaton,	May 21, 1752
Phinehas Gleason & Eunice Chaddick,	June 23, 1752
Darius Bugbee of Woodstock & Mary Lovell,	Jan. 10, 1753
Daniel Walker of Brookfield & Mary Lovell,	Nov. 29, 1753
William Biglo of Pequiog & Margaret Gates,	Nov. 29, 1753
Daniel Heyward, Jr., & Anna Wait,	Nov. 29, 1753
John Waters and Kesia Holton,	Dec. 13, 1753
Jabez Paine of Leicester & Elizabeth Hubbard,	Feb. 19, 1754
Mathew Blair of Blanford & Jane Alexander,	Feb. 21, 1754
Jonathan Moore & Sarah Gates,	Feb. 27, 1754
Thaddeus Biglo & Rebeckah Warren,	March 28, 1754
Samuel Wheelock of Shrewsbury & Dorcas Perry,	April 16, 1754
Daniel Greenwood, Jr., of Sutton & Jerusha Eaton,	Nov. 14, 1754
James Carlyle & Mary Mahan,	Dec. 25, 1754
David Peirce of Waltham & Huldah Harrington,	Jan. 22, 1755
Solomon Bixby & Easthar Clark,	April 3, 1755
Charles Davenport, Jr., & Mary Hart of Leicester,	April 16, 1755
Isaac Stearns & Elizabeth Roberts,	April 30, 1755
Seth Russell of Cambridge and Dinah Harrington,	May 8, 1755
John Curtis, Jr., & Elizabeth Hawood,	May 15, 1755
Timothy Green of Leicester & Sarah Cook,	June 10, 1755
Samuel Moore & Grace Rice,	Aug. 13, 1755

MARRIAGES.

David Moore of Leicester & Elenor Rice,	Oct. 16, 1755
James Mcpheson & Sarah Calhoone,	Feb. 15, 1756
George Tracy & Elizabeth Hull,	April 9, 1756
William Ward & Elizabeth Moore,	April 15, 1756
Timothy Whiting of Lancaster & Sarah Osgood,	May 10, 1756
Reuben Hamilton of Brookfield & Lucretia Hubburd,	June 8, 1756
John Kelso & Sarah Crawford,	Sept. 30, 1756
James Trowbridge & Mary Killey,	Jan. 10, 1757
Samuel Bridge & Mary Goodwin,	March 1, 1757
Samuel Curtis & Mary Ward,	March 30, 1757
John Green & Mary Osgood,	April 14, 1757
Joseph Hastings & Mary Stearns,	June 13, 1757
John Crawford & Martha Smith,	July 28, 1757
David Cunningham & Elenor Wallis,	Aug. 10, 1757
John Anderson & Elizabeth McCrackin,	Oct. 25, 1757
Joseph Gray & Mary Thomas,	Nov. 17, 1757
David McClellan & Sarah Stevens,	Nov. 28, 1757
Absalom Cutting & Kesia Rice,	Jan. 10, 1758
Elijah Harrington & Azuba Rice,	Feb. 8, 1758
James Ball & Lydia Rice,	March 2, 1758
Ignatus Goulding & Elizabeth Goodwin,	March 9, 1758
Matthew Barber & Hannah Mcfarland,	March 16, 1758
Jacob Upham of Leicester & Zaviah Smith,	March 22, 1758
Jonathan Chaddick & Hannah Saddler,	April 27, 1758
Joshua Johnson & Lydia Brown,	May 28, 1758
Alexander Calhoon of Leicester & Elenor Mcfarland,	Dec. 28, 1758
Alexander Graham of Rutland & Martha Forbush,	Jan. 18, 1759
Micah Johnson & Phebe Moore,	May 8, 1754
William Taylor & Lois Whitney, both of Leicester,	Aug. 24, 1754
James Putnam & Elizabeth Chandler,	Sept. 20, 1754
Josiah Berry & Mrs. Jane Wright, Al^s Doolittle,	March 16, 1756
Robert Earl of Leicester & Hepzebah Johnson,	March 23, 1756

Abraham, Wheeler & Elizabeth Millet of Mendon,
July 13, 1756
Nathaniel Child & Abigail Adams of Sutton, Oct. 23, 1756
William Oak & Abigail Whitney, Oct. 29, 1763
John Chaddick, Jr., & Sarah Johnson, Nov. 8, 1756
William Bouttell of Leominster & Persis Hubburd,
April 27, 1757
Thomas Lee & Sarah Verry, Nov. 24, 1757
Peter Johnson & Abigail Parks, Oct. 12, 1758
Hezekiah Stowell & Hepzibah Rice, Nov. 24, 1758
Jonas Woodward, Jr., & Rachell Holms, Jan. 16, 1759
John Green & Mrs. Azubah Ward, Dec. 26, 1758
Amariah Parks & Elizabeth Holland, both of Sutton, Feb. 8, 1759
Samuel Wiswall & Sarah Dyar, July 18, 1759
David Richardson & Rebeca Nichols, March 27, 1760
Timothy Bigelow & Mrs. Anna Andrews (in New Hampshire), July 7, 1762
John Moore & Esthar Bigelow, Sept. 11, 1760
Edward Newton & Sarah Winch, both of Shrewsbury, Feb. 5, 1760
Jonathan Phillips of Oxford & Sarah Parker, March 6, 1760
Samuel Bemis, Jr., of Spencer & Mrs. Mehitabel Dannell of Sutton, Aug. 11, 1760
Antipas Earl & Mary Stade, both of Leicester, April 9, 1761
Noah Mendall of New Brantree & Mrs. Mary Low of Rutland, Dec. 22, 1762
John Child, Jr., of Holden & Mary Smith (minor), dau. of Elisha Smith, Jr., Feb. 18, 1762
Jonathan Sawin & Mary Whitney, Feb. 15, 1759
Jonas Hubbard & Mary Stevens, March 7, 1759
Alexander Mills & Mary Millet, March 22, 1759
David Chaddick & Lydia Wait, July 29, 1759
Jonathan Beaman of Shrewsbury & Sarah Seager,
Oct. 3, 1759
Thomas Davenport & Abigail Wilder, Oct. 25, 1759
Jonas Gray of Holden & Susannah Gray, Nov. 22, 1759
George Walcup of Framingham & Jemima Very,
Nov. 29, 1759

MARRIAGES.

Increase Stearns & Deborah Hull,	Jan. 8, 1760
Adam Walker & Rosanna Mcfadden,	Jan. 31, 1760
James Hamilton of Rutland & Mary Knox,	Feb. 13, 1760
John Young of Pelham & Elisabeth Smith	Feb. 21, 1760
James Turner of Pelham & Susannah Thomas,	April 1, 1760
John Elder & Jennet Ross,	April 1, 1760
David McClellan & Elizabeth Harrington,	May 6, 1760
Samuel Sawin & Mary Wesson of Sudbury,	June 19, 1760
Samuel Johnson & Mary Spence,	Aug. 14, 1760
Samuel Smith & Margaret Crawford,	Nov. 19, 1760
Jacob Sanderson & Elizabeth Child,	Dec. 18, 1760
Nathan Patch of Ipswich & Eunice Adams,	Dec. 26, 1760
Jonathan Rice & Euice Whipple of Grafton,	Jan 14, 1761
Silas Moore & Mary Jennison,	Feb. 4, 1761
Ebenezer Millet & Mary Wheeler,	April 6, 1761
Jedediah Tucker of Shrewsbury & Elizabeth Lynds,	April 16, 1761
Eliot Gray of Pelham & Hannah Barber,	June 9, 1761
Samuel Herring of Dedham & Lucy Harthion,	June 25, 1761
Peter Proctor of Littleton & Mary Ball,	June 25, 1761
James Hamilton & Margaret Mahan,	Aug. 20, 1761
Joseph Barber of Westfield & Martha Mcfarland,	Oct. 1, 1761
Jonathan Bullard of Rutland & Mary Barber,	Nov. 16, 1761
Isaac Miller of Westboro & Abigail Gleason,	Dec. 30, 1761
Thomas Lovil of Sutton & Lydia Moore,	Jan. 13, 1762
Daniel Gleason & Patience Stow,	Jan. 27, 1762
Solomon Woodward & Priscilla Holms,	Feb. 3, 1762
John Woodward & Ruth Smith,	April 29, 1762
Samuel Heyden of Marlboro & Mary Harris,	June 1, 1762
Andrew Boyd & Molly Gray,	June 17, 1762
Nathaniel Tatman & Rachel Adams,	Dec. 2, 1762
John Duncan of Londonderry & Hannah Henry,	Dec. 16, 1762
Isaac Mitchel of Petersboro & Jemima Gray,	Feb. 24, 1763
Timothy Sullivan & Eleanor Rice,	June 6, 1763
Simon Oaks & Rhoda Knight,	Aug. 2, 1763
Nathaniel Water of Sutton & Eunice Bancroft,	Oct. 13, 1763

Robert Oliver of Rutland & Mary Walker,   Oct. 13, 1763
James Nichols, Jr., & Jemima (?) Morris,   Oct. 18, 1763
Ephraim Curtis & Sarah Paine,   Dec. 4, 1763
Josiah Harrington, Jr., & Mary Jones,   Jan. 10, 1764
David Biglow & Deborah Heywood of Shrewsbury,   March 8, 1764
Elijah Davenport & Abigail Clark,   April 11, 1764
Asa Moore & Mary Cook,   April 12, 1764
Daniel Boyden, Jr., & Rebecca Barber,   June 7, 1764
Hezekiah Boyden & Elizabeth Green,   Sept. 13, 1764
Edward Knight & Tabitha Hair,   Sept. 21, 1764
William Gates & Joanna Stearns,   Nov. 7, 1764
Ebenezer Hamond of Charlton & Susanna Johnson,   Feb. 6, 1765
John Gambell of Westboro & Elizabeth Elder, Feb. 21, 1765
Robert Henry of Leicester & Susanna Young,   March 14, 1765
William Ward & Sarah Trowbridge,   Nov. 7, 1765
Volentine Harris & Priscilla Gleason,   April 16, 1765
Barzillai Rice & Silence Gould,   April 18, 1765
Edmund Hard & Sarah Willington,   June 20, 1765
Jonathan Stone & Mary Gates,   Oct. 29, 1765
Samuel Brown & Abigail Flagg,   Nov. 25, 1765
Thomas Beard & Mehitable Boyden,   April 10, 1766
Matthew Gray & Margaret Forbush,   May 5, 1766
Duncan Cameron & Mary Smith,   May 8, 1766
George Caldwell of Rutland & Elisabeth Hart, Jan. 22, 1767
Samuel Hutchinson of Lunenburg & Abigail Flagg,   Jan. 29, 1767
Gardiner Earl of Leicester & Rebecca Brown, March 15, 1767
Michael Richmond of Killingly & Margaret Barber,   April 2, 1767
Thomas Baker of Woodstock & Sarah Ward, April 14, 1767
John Smith & Sarah Doolittle,   July 5, 1767
Joseph Brooks & Agnes Walker,   Aug. 31, 1767
Aaron Farnsworth of Groton & Abigail Johnson,   Sept. 21, 1767
Cumberland & Binah (negro servants to Gardiner Chandler, Esq.),   Nov. 29, 1767

MARRIAGES.

Jonathan Gleason & Lucretia Moore,	Dec. 1, 1767
Rufus Flagg & Martha Chapman,	Dec. 3, 1767
Uriah Ward & Jemima Harrington,	Dec. 23, 1767
Samuel Ward of Lancaster & Dolly Chandler,	Dec. 26, 1767
Daniel Beard & Jane Smith,	Jan. 7, 1768
Nathan Hastings of Shrewsbury & Lois Rice,	Feb. 24, 1768
Josiah Ball & Esther Ward,	Feb. 26, 1768
John Moore & Percis Gates,	Aug. 18, 1768
Nathiel Stearns & Mary Rice	Oct. 13, 1768
Isaac Willard & Mary Dudley,	Oct. 27, 1768
John Barber, Jr., & Patience Gleason,	Dec. 1, 1768
Jonas Ward of Shrewsbury & Sarah Draper,	Dec. 1, 1768
Isaac Rice of Hardwick & Mehitable Stearns,	Dec. 1, 1768
Josiah Gale of Sutton & Elizabeth Rice,	Dec. 1, 1768
Stephen Gould & Esther Wilder,	Jan. 5, 1769
James Moore & Rebekah Jones,	Feb. 8, 1769
Samuel Foster & Elizabeth Boyden,	Feb. 23, 1769
Cyprian Stevens & Sarah Prince,	March 2, 1769
Jonathan Grout & Anna Harrington,	March 7, 1769
Thomas Mullens of Leominster & Elizabeth Rickey,	March 16, 1769
Josiah Knight & Anna Willington,	April 6, 1769
Eben Hearns & Martha Holbrook,	April 6, 1769
Jonathan Smith & Sarah Melvin,	June 1, 1769
Jacob Chamberlain & Anna Heywood,	July 4, 1769
John Ball & Lydia Ward,	Aug. 27, 1769
Peter Boyden & Hannah Nichols,	Aug. 31, 1769
Joseph Ball & Esther Mcfadin,	Nov. 16, 1769
Abraham Gale of Shrewsbury & Abigail Rice,	Nov. 28, 1769
Samuel Nichols of Templeton & Jane Wiley,	Dec. 7, 1769
Robert Cook & Elizabeth Parker,	Feb. 7, 1770
Asa Smith of Athol & Lydia Lynds,	March 7, 1770
Jonathan Hunt & Lucy How,	March 7, 1770
Lawrence Kelly & Mary Lovis,	March 12, 1770
Phineas Whitney of Leicester & Sarah Harrington,	May 20, 1770
Joel Wesson & Hannah Bigelow,	May 23, 1770
John Peirce & Lydia Jones,	Aug. 16, 1770

Joseph Howard of Holden & Sarah Chamberlain,
                                        Sept. 13, 1770
Lewis Allen of Shrewsbury & Mary Adams, Sept. 26, 1770
William Barber & Margaret Knox,   Sept. 27, 1770
Joel How & Molly Gates,   Oct. 18, 1770
Nathan Hearsay of Leicester & Mary Brown,
                                        Nov. 11, 1770
Rufus Chandler & Eleanor Putnam,   Nov. 18, 1770
Moses Gray of Templeton & Sarah Miller, Nov. 27, 1771
Jonas Nichols & Hannah Boyden,   Dec. 13, 1770
Josiah Gates & Silence Grout, in Hollis, N. H.,
                                        Feb. 20, 1771
John Phelps of Lancaster & Anna Parker, Feb. 5, 1771
Elijah Harrington & (Mrs.) Mehetable Draper,
                                        April 13, 1768
Asahel Warren & Margaret Spence,   Jan. 21, 1771
Ebenezer Thurston of Fitchburg & Lydia Flagg,
                                        Feb. 13, 1771
Holland Maynard of Bolton & Mary Moore, May 16, 1771
John Chamberlain & Mary Curtis,   June 27, 1771
William Curtis & Sarah Tatman (or Tolman),
                                        Aug. 25, 1771
William Bancroft & Mary Bancroft,   Sept. 5, 1771
Peter Richardson of Shrewsbury & Mary Rice,
                                        Sept. 11, 1771
Asa Ward & Hannah Heywood,   Nov. 7, 1771
Ebenezer Willington, Jr., & Esther Boyden, Nov. 20, 1771
Cato (servant to Adam Walker) & Dido (servant to
    John Chandler, Esq.),   Nov. 24, 1771
Joseph Goodwin & Mary Rice,   Dec. 26, 1771
Phineas Jones & Katherine Gates,   April 21, 1772
Capt. Aaron Jones of Templeton & Meriam Brewer,
                                        April 29, 1772
Simeon Stearns & Elizabeth Clark,   May 6, 1772
Samuel Fullerton & Martha Rice,   May 17, 1772
Nathaniel Stedman of Newfane & Ruth Morse of
    Wor. Gore,   Aug. 24, 1772
Ebenezer Bancroft & Phebe Bancroft,   Sept. 17, 1772
Thomas Henly & Mary Temple,   Sept. 21, 1772

MARRIAGES.

Robert Gray, Jr., & Elizabeth How,	Oct. 8, 1772
Samuel Dunkin & Bettey Stearns,	Oct. 13, 1772
John Patrick of Western & Elizabeth Mcfarland,	Oct. 14, 1772
Ebenezer Bradish of Cambridge & Hannah Paine,	Oct. 22, 1772
Moses Miller & Sarah Gray,	Dec. 1, 1772
Thomas Mower of Leicester & Anna Brown,	Dec. 3, 1772
John Willard & Lucy Davis, both of Wor. Gore,	Jan. 19, 1773
John Woodward & Abigail Gates,	March 31, 1773
Reuben Gray & Lydia Mellet,	June 1, 1773
Matthew Gray, Jr., & Elizabeth Mcfarland,	Aug. 31, 1773
Abel Holbrook & Hannah Chaddick,	Sept. 28, 1773
Charles Stearns & Sarah Town,	Oct. 4, 1773
Edward Knight, Jr., & Elizabeth Flagg,	Nov. 2, 1773
Ezekiel How & Mary Young,	Dec. 21, 1773
Thomas Nichols & Rebecca Crosby,	Jan. 18, 1774
Alexander Graham of Rutland & Margaret Gray,	Nov. 25, 1773
Silas Harrington & Mindwell Wellington,	Nov. 25, 1773
Charles Leonard & Nancy Dillingworth,	Nov. 25, 1773
William Farr, Jr., of Chesterfield, N. H., & Lydia Trowbridge,	Dec. 6, 1773
Darius Borden & Levina Brown,	Dec. 16, 1773
Isaac Clark of Hardwick & Patience Stearns,	Jan. 5, 1774
Elisha Smith, Jr., & Persis Child of Holden,	Jan. 13, 1774
Thaddeus Chambelain & Judith Barnard,	Jan. 27, 1774
Shepard Gates & Hannah Moore,	Feb. 28, 1774
John Shepard of Acton & Naby Eaton,	March 8, 1774
James Kelly of Colchester, Conn., & Anna Hart,	March 17, 1774
Solomon Temple of Charlemont & Abigail Heyden,	May 2, 1774
William Greggs & Kathrine Stearns,	May 23, 1774
Moses Willey of Templeton & Phebe Fitts,	June 14, 1774
John Ward of Westminster & Mindwell Harrington,	July 10, 1774
Benjamin Chapin, Jr., & Dolly Moore,	Sept. 20, 1774

Caleb Lyman & Kathrine Swan, Oct. 25, 1774
Jonathan Gale of Warwick, N. H., & Mary Bancroft,
　　　　　　　　　　　　　　　Feb. 14, (1755?) 1775
Jonathan Gray of Pelham & Elizabeth Willey,
　　　　　　　　　　　　　　　March 8, 1774
Daniel Willington & Rebecca Putnam, Feb. 7, 1775
Thomas Knight & Sarah Hair, March 22, 1775
David Bigelow, Jr., & Hannah Willington, April 10, 1775
William Buxton & Mary Mahan, June 8, 1775
Joshua Harrington, Jr., & Sarah Bigelow, June 22, 1775
Isaac Gleason, Jr., & Prudence Smith, July 27, 1775
Caleb Ellis of Keene & Sarah Griggs, Aug. 11, 1775
William Stearns & Joanna Dunkin, Oct. 3, 1775
John Ephraim of Natick & Hannah Wisor (Indians),
　　　　　　　　　　　　　　　Oct. 16, 1775
Daniel Gates of Fullam & Sarah Moore, Nov. 13, 1775

MENDON.

May 15, 1667, "Ordered that the name of Mendon be given to the Court's grant to Qunstipauge, being the township of Qunshapage as it was laid out according to the grant of the General Court, and that Mendon be settled as a town." Mass. Rec., Vol. IV, Part. 2, p. 341. Town proceedings begin 1662. First church organized 1669 (Unitarian). Friends, 1727, now extinct. Clergyman mentioned: Rev. Joseph Willard.

Silvanus Holbrook of Uxbridge & Thankful Thayer,
　　　　　　　　　　　　　　　Oct. 25, 1748
Aaron Legg & Experience Fish, Nov. 17, 1751
William Sprague & Margaret Cheeney, May —, 1748
Thomas White & Priscilla Bishop, July 27, 1748
John Lesure & Sarah White, March 16, 1749
Elijah Ward & Hannah Read, July 29, 1749
Amasa Frost of Mendon & Abigail Livermore of
　　Framingham, Feb. 1, 1749-50
John Rockwood & Deborah Thayer, March 21, 1750
Thomas Walker of Hopkington & Bethiah Chapin,
　　　　　　　　　　　　　　　April 12, 1750
Joseph Damon & Hopestill Thayer, both of Bellingham, June 7, 1750

MARRIAGES.

Oliver Brown of Hartford & Abigail Sheffield, Oct. 17, 1750
Thomas Albee of Mendon & Jemima Thompson of
    Bellingham,   Nov. 22, 1750
John Rockwood & Elisabeth Daniels,   March 18, 1751
Daniel Hayward of Mendon & Joanna Willson of
    Bellingham,   March 20, 1751
Joshua Chapin & Mary Haywood,   March 20, 1751
John Hayward & Margaret Albee,   April 4, 1751
Richard Poffer of Wrentham & Jemima Albee,
                                                  April 11, 1751
Edward Gay of Wrentham & Margaret Rockwood,
                                                  April 17, 1751
Uriah Thayer & Jemima Thayer,   May 8, 1751
William White & Elisabeth Brumil,   Nov. 16, 1749
Jephtha Chapin & Patience Haywood,   Nov. 5, 1749
—— Pratt of Grafton & Susanna Wood,   Aug. 24, 1749
Thomas Nelson & Sarah Pope, both of Upton, Nov. 28, 1749
Samuel Fisk of Upton & Comfort Thayer,   Nov. 1, 1750
Moses White of Uxbridge & Abigail Holbrook,
                                                  Dec. 12, 1749
Thomas Darling & Rachel White,   Dec. 14, 1749
James Wood & Unity Gause (?),   Feb. 7, 1750
Daniel Hill & Elisabeth Pulcipher,   March 26, 1750
Gershom Whitney of Woodstock & Sarah Wood,
                                                  March 21, 1751
Joseph White & Margery Aldrich,   April 11, 1751
Benjamin Carpenter of Ashford, Conn., & Joanna
    Hayward,   Nov. 7, 1751
Philip White & Rachel Green,   June 5, 1751
Elijah Lyon of Woodstock & Elizabeth Merriam,
                                                    June 9, 1752
Benoni Benson & Abigail Staples,   Jan. 30, 1752
John Crooks & Abigail Burch,   March —, 1751
Seth Taft & Ann Taft,   Feb. 17, 1752
Jesse Wheelock & Mary Taft,   March 20, 1752
Aaron Aldrich & Mary Wheat,   May 1, 1753
Ebenezer Torry & Eunice Sturman (?) (Slueman) (?),
                                                   Jan. 25, 1753
Israel Brown & Experience Thayer,   Feb. 15, 1753

Jesse Holbrook & Abigail Thayer, both of Bellingham, March 28, 1753
Job Warfield & Huldah Thayer, June 12, 1751
Joseph White of Mendon & Ann Colson of Holliston, Sept. 26, 1751
William Rexford of Medway & Hannah Thayer, Nov. 13, 1751
John Fisk & Deborah Ward, May 7, 1752
Isaac Tenny & Susanna Whitney, June 25, 1752
Joseph Torry & Deborah Holbrook, (old style) Sept. 6, 1752
Samuel Wight & Mary Thomson, both of Bellingham, Oct. 18, 1752
Jesse Wheelock & Phebe White, Dec. 4, 1753
Aaron Legg & Mrs. Experience Fish (or Fisk), Nov. 7, 1751
Elisha Wait & Mrs. Susannah Thayer, June 1, 1752
Samuel White of Killingly & Mrs. Sarah Corbett, July 15, 1752
Luke Aldrich & Mrs. Anna French, June 28, 1753
Ebenezer Wheeler of Grafton & Mrs. Priscilla Hayward, Sept. 5, 1753
Noah Aldrich & Mrs. Rachel Thayer, Dec. 19, 1753
Jonathan Cook of Uxbridge & Mrs. Hannah Thayer, March 21, 1754
Henry Penniman & Mrs. Experience Wheelock, April 13, 1769
Ephraim Twitchell & Mrs. Lydia Parkhurst, April 13, 1769
Peter Albee & Mrs. Rhoda Penniman, June 8, 1769
Lieut. Josiah Chapin & widow Mary Corbett, Feb. 7, 1770
Barzillai Albee & Mary Marshall, March 21, 1770
Nathaniel Rawson & Elisabeth Nelson, March 24, 1768
Andrew Peters of Medfield & Beulah Lovitt, April 30, 1768
Phinehas Lovett, Jr., and Abigail Thayer, April 6, 1768
Moses Thayer, Jr., & Rachel Thayer, April 7, 1768
Caleb Boynton & widow Abigail Richardson of Medway, May 24, 1768
Ichabod Robinson & Abigail Smith of Weston, Oct. 6, 1768
Elijah Thayer & Sarah Robinson, Nov. —, 1768
Jacob Aldrich, Jr., & widow Sarah Steel, Nov. 3, 1768
Benjamin Thurston of Grafton & Dorcas Chapin, Nov. 24, 1768

MARRIAGES.

Henry Aldrich & Elisabeth Hunt,	Nov. 24, 1768
Ebenezer Parkhurst & Mercy Hill,	Dec. 22, 1768
Laban Bates & Oliver Wheelock,	Dec. 28, 1768
David Cutler & widow Joanna Atwood,	Dec. 28, 1768
Ralph Haywood & Susanna Thayer,	Dec. 28, 1768
Ichabod Newton & Rhoda Chapin,	Jan. 12, 1769
Jonathan Heywood, Jr., & Mary Vickery,	Jan. 25, 1769
John Gleason of Princetown & Eunice French,	Feb. 2, 1769
Abraham Aldrich & Levina Taft of Uxbridge,	March 31, 1768
Nathaniel Taft & Abigail Holbrook of Uxbridge,	May 31, 1768
Seth Hayward & Marcy Whitman,	June 22, 1768
Obed Rutter & Mary Lesure,	Nov. 10, 1768
Abner Stanford & Jemima Green,	Nov. 24, 1768
William Foster of Upton & Abigail Chapin,	Dec. 1, 1768
Josiah White & Mary Green,	Jan. 26, 1769
Benjamin Benson & Martha McNammar, both of Uxbridge,	Feb. 15, 1769
Thomas Morey of Smithfield & Rhoda Aldrich of Uxbridge,	Sept. 14, 1769
John Clark of Westminster & Hannah Green,	Aug. 29, 1769
Ephraim Taft & Hannah Wheelock,	Nov. 16, 1769
Isaac Kent of Bellingham & Sarah Wheelock,	May 17, 1770
Jesse Rutter & Abigail Lesure,	July 9, 1770
Samuel Scarborough of Pomfret & Mary Amedown,	Oct. 23, 1770
Phillip Amedon & Silva Taft,	Nov. 15, 1770
David Daniel, Jr., & Olive Adams of Bellingham,	Jan. 15, 1771
Ebenezer Auldis of Wrentham & Hannah Penniman,	June 5, 1771
Benoni Smith & Mehetable Staples,	July 25, 1771
Seva Pond and Silva White,	April 4, 1770
John Hunt & Deborah Darling,	Nov. 8, 1770
Benoni Bensan, Jr., & Ruth Holbrook,	Dec. 6, 1770
John Holbrook of Uxbridge & Rhoda (?) Thayer,	Dec. 6, 1770
Turner Ellis & Mary White,	March 16, 1769
Stephan Hilyard & Joanna Darling,	April 13, 1769

Elijah Darling & Sarah Washburn, April 13, 1769
Job Burnham & Mary Obrian, June 25, 1769
Silas Richardson & Silence Daniels, Nov. 14, 1771
Levi Lesuer & Zibiah Rutter, Feb. 26, 1772
David Stearns & Dinah Bullard, May 31, 1770
Josiah Ball, Jr., & Sarah Palmer, July 5, 1770
Simeon Fisher of Holliston & Hepzibah Albee, Dec. 6, 1770
William Cheeney & Hannah Bowher, Dec. 6, 1770
Elijah Ball & Joanna French, Dec. 19, 1770
James Dix & Submit Fairbank of Holliston, March 19, 1771
Levi Thayer & Hannah Parkhust, April 25, 1771
Micah Bates & Urania Thayer, May 22, 1771
Nathaniel Parkhust & Sarah Brown, May 29, 1771
Andrew Adams of Grafton & widow Sarah Torrey,
 May 30, 1771
Noah Keith of Uxbridge & Mary Legg, June 13, 1771
Francis Clark & Anna Gould of Hopkinton, Oct. 10, 1771
Nathaniel Legg of Upton & Abigail White, Nov. 21, 1771
Priseved Baker of Wrentham & Elizabeth Daniels,
 Jan. 30, 1772
Ebenezer Merriam & Margaret Jeppardson, April 22, 1771
Simeon Morey of Charlton & Rachel Taft, May 27, 1772
David Hayward & Abigail Holland, both of North-
 bridge, Nov. 26, 1771
Saul Ramsdell & Mary Balcom, Jan. 8, 1773
William Nichols & Mary Smith, April 1, 1773
Amariah Yeats of Smithfield, R. I., & Margaret
 Thayer, April 1, 1773
Samuel Orel & Susanna Aldrich, both of Uxbridge,
 April 12, 1773
Nicholas Berry & Mary Morgan, both of Upton,
 April 22, 1773
Increase Daniels & Lona Thayer, April 29, 1773
Increase Thayer & Leath Wheelock, Nov. 20, 1771
Timothy Jones & Ann Scammell, Dec. 3, 1771
Aaron Legg & Mrs. Jerusha Holbrook, Jan. 16, 1772
Douglas Marsh & Rachel Merriam, March 12, 1772
Ebenezer Scarbrough of Pomfret & Hannah Ami-
 down, April 2, 1772

MARRIAGES.

Silas Penniman of Bellingham & Huldah Daniels,
April 22, 1772
Sherebiah Baker of Upton & Clotilda Daniels, June 25, 1772
James Sumner, Jr., & Melatiah Jones, Oct. 29 1772
Jotham Taft of Dudley & Mary Wilson, Dec. 2, 1772
John Wharfield & Lydia Taft, Dec. 3, 1772
Joseph Sadler of Upton & Lydia Daniels, Dec. 3, 1772
Samuel Wilbour Heath of Newport & Elizabeth
Thayer, May 26, 1772
Naham Clark of Holliston & Mary Stearns, July 9, 1772
Joseph Fisk & Eunice Lathorne, July 30, 1772
Jacob Hayward & Elizabeth Gibbs, Oct. 29, 1772
Joseph Pasmore & Thankful Barns, Nov. 5, 1772
Silas Wood & Asenath Stewart of Holliston, Dec. 6, 1772
Job Barstow of Holliston & Silence Sumner, Dec. 6, 1772
Barzillai Taft & Abigail Taft, both of Uxbridge, Dec. 17, 1772
Aaron Wood & Sarah Wood, both of Upton, Sept. 2, 1773
Benjamin Ellis & Rosannah Thayer, Sept. 6, 1773
Levi Rawson & Anna Nelson, both of Upton, Nov. 18, 1773
Rufus Chilson & Ruth Hill, both of Uxbridge, Dec. 23, 1773
Paul Lesuer & Susanna Tucker, March 17, 1774

UXBRIDGE.

June 27, 1727, "Part of Mendon established as Uxbridge." Prov. Laws, Vol. II, p. 427. First (Congregational) Church organized 1730. Unitarian, 1731. Friends, 1730.

Josiah Benson of Mendon & Susan Bolster, April 16, 1754
Samuel Thayer, 3d, of Mendon & Sarah Farnum, May 9, 1754
Jonathan Cook of Uxbridge & Jane Dunsmore of
Mendon, Aug. 6, 1754
Elnathan Wight & Mrs. Abigail Blood, both of Bel-
lingham, Aug. 13, 1754
Jonathan Wood of Lunenburg & Rachel Wood, Oct. 10, 1754
Luke Emerson & Ruth Emerson, April 30, 1755
John Burnap of Hopkinton & Anna Whoate (?), May 1, 1755
John Harwood & Margaret De le Marude (?), Dec. 4, 1755
John Prentice of Uxbridge & Mary McClellan of
Sutton, July 29, 1756

Peter Harrwood (?) & Mary Webb, April 22, 1756
Thomas Rawson & Eunice Read, May 6, 1756
Cuff & Dinah (negro servants of Lieut. Draper),
March 6, 1760
Nicholas Baylies, Jr., & Abigail Wood, April 24, 1760
Benjamin Blake & Sarah Kimpton, May 8, 1760
Joseph Jackson of Mendon & Bathsheba Thayer,
May 8, 1760
Benjamin Murdock & Katherine Read, May 20, 1760
Levi Walker of Pomfret & Keziah Thompson,
June 12, 1760
Amariah Preston & Susanna Wood, Sept. 25, 1760
Jonas Prentice & Abigail Comings, Nov. 25, 1760
Dependence Hayward of Mendon & Esther Wood,
Nov. 27, 1760
Jonathan Allen & Ruth Newcomb, Dec. 11, 1760
Lieut. Obadiah Brown & Lucy Hall, March 5, 1761
Edmund Rawson & Mrs. Lydia Daniels of Holiston,
March 5, 1761
Joseph Tyler, Jr., & Ruth Read, April 2, 1761
David Leisure & Sarah Peirce, July 21, 1761
Ichabod Collie & Mary Brown, Oct. 8, 1761
Nathan Rawson & Mary White, Feb. 13, 1762
Stephen Powers & Rachell Winter, April 2, 1762
Benjamin Read & Comfort Taft of Mendon, May 27, 1762
Edward Leisure & Cloe Taft, July 1, 1762
Elijah Ward & Else Holbrook, Sept. 16, 1762
John Taft, Jr., & Mary Harwood, Nov. 25, 1762
Samuel Cumings & Lecia Taft, Dec. 9, 1762
Samul Morse & Deborah Hadlock, Dec. 16, 1762
Joel Rawson & Mary Hall, Feb. 17, 1763
Stephen Taft & Mercy Hazeltine, April 14, 1763
James Bardins & Tryphena White, May 5, 1763
Jesse Taft & Lydia Sibley, May 12, 1763
William Bancroft & Mary Daniels, Sept. 29, 1763
Jonathan Cook & Lydia Aldrich, Oct. 20, 1763
Jesse Penniman of Mendon & Lois Wood, Dec. 8, 1763
Thomas Read & Martha Parks, Dec. 14, 1763
Benjamin Fish & Sarah Wood, Feb. 16, 1764

MARRIAGES.

Gershom Taft & Abigail Read,	May 22, 1764
Nathaniel Rawson & Mary Chase,	May 24, 1764
Jonathan Cook of Douglas & Jerusha Bardins,	June 4, 1764
Reuben Walker & Mary Read,	Nov. 28, 1764
John Hawkins of Providence, R. I., & Sarah Emerson,	Nov. 29, 1764
John Hylard & Mehitable Thompson,	Feb. 14, 1765
Benjamin Pike & Aby Keith,	Feb. 21, 1765
Barnabas Aldrich & Prudence Albee,	April 9, 1766
Benjamin Archer & widow Deborah Hull,	May 8, 1766
Elixander Aldrich & Abigail Clark,	Aug. 21, 1766
James Hull & Rebecca Draper,	Sept. 15, 1766
Stephens Williams & Lydia Hicks of Sutton,	Oct. 16, 1766
Edward Battles of Mendon & Ruth Kimpton,	Nov. 26, 1766
Peter White, Jr., & Cloe Farnum,	Dec. 4, 1766
Nathan Twitchel & Hannah Kimpton,	Dec. 18, 1766
Moses Keith & Mary Cumings,	Jan. 22, 1767
Joseph Rist & Rachal Keith,	Dec. 18, 1766
Ezekiel Powers & Hannah Hall,	Jan. 28, 1767
John Sanger & Eunice Davis of Mendon,	Jan. 28, 1767
Mahun Taft & Rachiel Albee,	Feb. 19, 1767
Asa Taft & Elizabeth Buckman,	March 5, 1767
Peter Taft, Jr., & Mary Arnold of Glocester, R. I.,	June 4, 1767
Eleazer Albee & Dorcas Daniels,	Aug. 27, 1767
Jesse Taft & Hannah Taft,	Sept. 10, 1767
Matthew Darling of Mendon & Hannah Emerson,	Oct. 29, 1767
Elisha Hale & Mary Brown,	Nov. 5, 1767
James Taft & Esther Taft,	Nov. 19, 1767
Samuel Amidown of Douglass & Ruth Wood,	March 3, 1768
Silas Rawson & Sarah Draper,	March 17, 1768
Uriah Thayer of Mendon & Mrs. Abigail White,	June 2, 1768
David Woodard & Molley Farnum,	June 23, 1768
Ebenezer Chase & Mary Friphel,	June 30, 1768
Gersham Ward of Grafton & Prudence Powers,	Sept. 1, 1768
Simeon Fish of Mendon & Tabatha Taft,	Nov. 10, 1768
Thomas Ellison & Dorothy Tampling,	Dec. 6, 1768

Thomas Reed, Jr., & Ruth Carryl of Sutton, Dec. 29, 1768
Roger Thompson of Smithfield, R. I., & Elizabeth
    Fish, Jan. 12, 1769
Nathaniel Fish & widow Mary Farnum, April 13, 1769
Levi Walker & Elizabeth Wallis, May 11, 1769
Aaron Taft, Jr., & Rhoda Rawson, June 1, 1769
Abijah Keyes & Jane Aldrich, June 8, 1769
Samuel Gage & Lydia Fish, June 8, 1769
Thomas Willson & Lydia Butler of Upton, Sept. 27, 1769
David Draper, Jr., & Martha Hull, Feb. 15, 1770
Joseph How of Sutton & Mehatable Darling, April 12, 1770
John Curtis of Dudley & Phebe Keith, April 19, 1770
Amos White & Azuba Taft, May 17, 1770
Joseph Cleaveland & Jermima White, May 24, 1770
Abel Fish & Thankful Brown, Sept. 6, 1770
Israel Salem & Bulah Albee, Sept. 27, 1770
Samuel Penniman of Mendon & widow Deborah
    Taft, Oct. 25, 1770
Daniel Taft & Mary Siblee, Nov. 22, 1770
Samuel Stoddard of Grafton & Eliza Dunn, Dec. 6, 1770
Timothy Taft & Priscilla Taft, Dec. 6, 1770
Robert Taft & Cloe Taft, Jan. 3, 1771
Adam White & Sarah Creighton of Douglass, Jan. 10, 1771
John Thwing of Conway & Ruth Holbrook, Oct. 6, 1771
John Hopkins & widow Sarah Benham, Oct. 13, 1771
Ezra Holbrook of Towsend & Mehitable Tyler, Nov. 18, 1771
Victorius Smith & Susanna Pasmore, Nov. 21, 1771
Paul White & Susanna Parcas, Dec. 5, 1771
Stephen Partridge of Midway & Esther Emerson,
    Feb. 27, 1772
Marvel Taft of Northbridge & Ruth Murdock, April 29, 1784
Josep Mosely of Sutton & Susanny Young, April 19, 1784
Paul Wheelock & Mrs. Deborah Morse, Aug. 30, 1784
John Smith of Sutton & Molly Chilson, Oct. 20, 1784
Col. Joseph Hammon, Esq., of Swanzey & Mrs.
    Mary Fish, Oct. 21, 1784
Daniel Holbrook & Joanna Benson of Mendon, Jan. 9, 1785
Joseph Morse & Olive White, Jan. 13, 1785
Ezekiel Morse of Sutton & Mary Tyler, Feb. 18, 1785

RUTLAND.

February 23, 1713, "Certain common lands," the name in general being "Naquag," "established as Rutland." First (Congregational) Church organized 1727.

Stephen Barret & widow Elizabeth Howe,	May 15, 1750
James Wheeler & Abigail Ball,	May 24, 1750
William Banks & Azubah M. (Mc) Maine,	June 7, 1750
Shears (?) Berry (?) of Rutland & Esther Woodward of Holdin,	June 15, 1750
David Bent & Lucy Moore,	April 3, 1751
Jacob Shaw of Leicester & Anna Fulton,	March 16, 1753
Abraham Black & Mary McIntier (?),	April 18, 1753
Thomas Gill & Margaret Haffron,	April 30, 1753
Daniel Davis, Jr., & Sarah Phelps,	May 3, 1753
Oliver Davis & Mary Read,	May 21, 1753
Phinehas Moore & Anna Rice,	June 14, 1753
Thomas Child & Anna Bullard,	Nov. 23, 1753
William Whitaker & Jane Cunningham,	Nov. 27, 1753
Mathew Caldwell & Mary Browning,	Jan. 31, 1754
George Dun & Rachell Harper,	Jan. 31, 1754
Peter Fletcher & Susanna Rice,	April 12, 1754
Aaron Holden & Anna Clarke,	April 20, 1758
Amos Marsh of Hardwick & Bulah Leonard,	Nov. 3, 1757
James Thompson of Leicester & Mrs. Mary Black,	May 26, 1757
Samuel Hunt of Hardwicke & Sarah Osgood,	Dec. 28, 1758
Edward Rice & Mary Stone,	May 10, 1758
Silas Rice & widow Abigail Stevens,	May 12, 1758
William Ball & Christian McFarland,	Sept. 13, 1759
George Duncan & Mary Slarrow (?),	May 9, 1760
Caleb Benjamin of Hardwick & Elizabeth Rice,	Nov. 18, 1760
John Black & Isabel Moore,	Nov. 27, 1760
Daniel Winch of Framingham & Rebecca Reed,	Feb. 18, 1761
Capt. Thomas Cowdin of Worcester & widow Hannah Craige,	Oct. 2, 1761
Michael Heffron & Mary Stevenson,	Oct. 29, 1761

Eleazor Rice & widow Lydia How,	Dec. 3, 1761
James Ames & Elisabeth Hall,	Dec. 8, 1761
Nathan Davis, Jr., & Mary Nurse,	Dec. 8, 1761
Elisha Mirick of Holden & Pursis Moore,	Jan. 6, 1762
Dr. Solomon Persons of Leicester & Mrs. Elizabeth Sweetser,	Jan. 7, 1762
Robert Clerk of Pelham & Mary Patrick,	March 2, 1762
Samuel Metcalf & Hannah Richardson,	March 11, 1762
Willard Moore & Elizabeth Hubbard,	March 18, 1762
John Stevenson & Sarah Gilbert of Brookfield,	May 18, 1762
Samuel Ball, of Roxbury, Canada (so-called) & Lucy Leonard,	July 9, 1761
David Clark & Sarah Bacon,	Oct. 29, 1761
Oliver Robinson & Elizabeth Hail (Thald),	Oct. 7, 1762
Samson Bixby & Mary Bullard,	Dec. 1, 1761
Theophilus Chandler of Petersham & Elizabeth Frink,	May 26, 1763
John Black & Sarah Work,	May 9, 1763
Adam Wheeler & Marcy Wheeler,	Nov. 17, 1763
Elijah Man & (Mrs.) Susanna Wilder,	June 7, 1764
Ephraim Heyden & Abigail Nurse,	July 11, 1764
Barnabas Sears of Hardwick & Mrs. Rachel Bullard,	Nov. 1, 1764
Aaron Smith & Mrs. Mary Akers (or Acres),	March 8, 1764
Joseph How & Hepzibah How, both of Princetown,	Jan. 24, 1765
John Sweeney & (Mrs.) Abigail Jackson,	Feb. 21, 1765
Samuel Leonard & Silence Ripley,	Nov. 21, 1765
Makepeace Gates & Kathrine Smith,	June 6, 1765
John Haskel of Hardwick & Hannah Rice,	Dec. 9, 1765
Samuel Bullard & Mrs. Sarah Barber,	March 13, 1766
Samuel Smith & (Mrs.) Sarah Fay,	April 22, 1766
Thomas Rice & (Mrs.) Hannah Wright,	May 15, 1766
Asahel Osgood & Mrs. Hannah Wilder,	Jan. 15, 1767
Jonas Permenter & Sarah Butrick,	July 25, 1765
Matthew How & Azubah Davis,	Oct. 8, 1767
Israel Stone & Lydia Barrel of Paxton,	July 12, 1768
John Fesinden & Elizabeth Wyman,	Nov. 23, 1769
Rev. John Strickland & Pattey Stone of Oakham,	Oct. 29, 1767

MARRIAGES.

William Oliver of Athol & Anna Forbes,	Dec. 30, 1767
Solomon Robinson & Abigail Badger,	Dec. 31, 1767
Joel Bent & Mary Mason,	July 13, 1768
Capt. Benjamin Lee & Mehitable Jenkins,	July 28, 1768
Samuel Forbes & Jane Montor,	Nov. 30, 1768
James Berry, Jr., of Pelham & Margaret Smith,	Dec. 1, 1768
Nathaniel Jenison & Isabel Caldwell,	March 28, 1769
Jabez Upham & Hannah Burgess,	May 10, 1768
Ebenezer Johnson & Hannah Chandler,	July 20, 1769
Sheribiah Lee & Esther Miles,	July 20, 1769
John Jones of Princetown & Bettey Hapgood,	Oct. 19, 1769
Joshua Bartlet & Bettey Felton,	Oct. 26, 1769
James Morse & Hannah Smith,	Nov. 26, 1769

DUDLEY.

February 2, 1732, "Part of Oxford and certain common lands established as Dudley." Prov. Laws, Vol. II, p. 626. First (Congregational) Church organized 1732.

David Hall of Killingly & Sarah Robinson,	April 21, 1763
Eleazor Bellows of Oxford & Abigail Putney,	Oct. 27, 1763
Lemuel Corbin of Dudley & Rebecca Davis of Oxford,	Dec. 8, 1763
Jonathan Lyon of Woodstock & Rebecca Corbin,	Dec. 22, 1763
John Jefferds & Mary Sanger,	Feb. 20, 1764
Isiah Putney & Abigail Warrin,	Nov. 24, 1764
Joseph Upham, Jr., & Eunice Kidder,	April 16, 1764
Benjamin Newell & Lucy Dodge,	May 7, 1765
Thomas Taylor & Lucy Dexter,	July 8, 1765
Aaron Jewett of Sheffield & Hannah Curtis,	Jan. 23, 1766
John Hutchins & Olive Rood of Sturbridge,	Oct. 9, 1766
Isaac Lee, Jr., of Killingly & Abigail Jewett,	Dec. 4, 1766
Timothy Barton of Charlton & Amy Allen,	Jan. 20, 1767
Ichabod Chamberlain & Sarah Gale,	March 29, 1767
John Newell & Mary Willard,	Sept. 28, 1767
David Kidder & Susanna Upham,	Feb. 23, 1768

Amos Hooker & Hannah Foster, March 10, 1768
John Edmunds & Silence Emerson, May 19, 1768
Simon Stone of Killingsly & Hannah Robinson, May 19, 1768
Joseph Perrin of Woodstock & Dorothy Corbin, July 13, 1768
Samuel Pagon, Jr., & Sarah Pagon (Indians), July 21, 1768
Daniel Newell & Elisabeth Putnam, Dec. 1, 1768
Ebenezer Taylor & Mary Scott, Oct. 13, 1768
Jonas Fairbank & Mary Carter, Dec. 1, 1768
Isaac Humphrey, Jr., & Susana Libret, Dec. 22, 1768
Samuel Warren & Susanna Farrow, Jan. 4, 1769
John Morss & Eunice Bartholomew, Jan. 12, 1769
Samuel Newell & Rachel Ross, Feb. 23, 1769
Dr. Thomas Sterne & Sarah Gleason, March 5, 1769
Joseph Sabin, Jr., of Dudley & Susanna Adams of
    Killingsly, March 16, 1769
Asa Corbin & Patience Smith, Nov. 16, 1769
Jonathan Shattuck of Oxford & Huldah Curtis,
    Nov. 30, 1769
Elijah Converse of Killingsly & Experience Hibbard,
    Jan. 30, 1770
David Cutten & Dorothy Sabin, March 4, 1770
Ira Green & Elizabeth Dodge, April 5, 1770
John Polley of Charlton & Phebe Chamberlain,
    April 12, 1770
Daniel Bacon of No. Woodstock & Esther Jones,
    March 3, 1770
Henry Huker & Molley Edmund, July 12, 1770
Timothy Gay & Anna Bridges, Sept. 20, 1770
Edward Curtis & Lucy Chamberlain, Oct. 4, 1770
Richard Foster & Lydia Titus, Dec. 6, 1770
Edward Morris & Dorcas Corbin, March 23, 1771
Josiah Brown & Dinah Wetherill, Jan. 14, 1772
Jesse Sabin & Rhoda Waters, April 16, 1772
Jonathan Conant & Lucy Corbin, July 9, 1772
Moses Jewell & Jemima Corbin, July 23, 1772
Jedediah Corbin & Hannah Howe, Oct. 9, 1772
Thomas West & Mary Spear, Nov. 12, 1772
John Bacon & Mary Jewell, Nov. 19, 1772
Ezekial Hovey & Eunice Pease, Nov. 19, 1772

MARRIAGES.

Aaron Barrett of Killingly & Mary Williams,   Dec. 3, 1772
Winthrop Chandler of Killingly & Mary Gleason,
                                              Feb. 16, 1773
Joseph Winter & Azubah Barton of Oxford,   Oct. 6, 1773
William Brewer & Lucy Davis,   Oct. 14, 1773
Josiah Hovey & Hannah May of Pomfret,   Nov. 25, 1773
Samuel May, Jr., & Amy Putnam,   Nov. 25, 1773
Eben White & Lydia Davis,   Dec. 16, 1773
Edward Coburn of Windham & Sarah Wyman, Jan. 20, 1774
Simeon Howard & Abigail Witherell,   April 14, 1774
Samuel Wright of Brookfield & Lois Corbin, May 25, 1774
Dr. William Gleason & Mary Kidder,   May 31, 1774
Seth Perry of Sturbridge & Lois Jennings, June 28, 1774
Leiut. Mark Elwell of Killingsly & Dorothy White,
                                              Aug. 29, 1774
Timothy Corbin & Abigail Vinton,   Oct. 20, 1774
William Brown & Mary Freeman of Killingly,
                                              March 25, 1779
Daniel Arnold & Nancy Brown,   March 25, 1779
Thomas Chafey of Woodstock & Mary May,   April 8, 1779
John White & Lucy Conant,   April 15, 1779
Josiah Barns & Rebecca Kidder,   Nov. 25, 1779
Lemuel Edmunds & Hannah ———,   Dec. 1, 1779
James Brown & Sarah Oaks,   Dec. 9, 1779
Joshua Atwood & Prudence Parker,   Feb. 29, 1780
John Bowers & Sarah Inman,   March 7, 1780
Benjamin Joslin of Killingly & Susannah Robin-
    son,   Nov. 16, 1774
Jacob Chambain, Jr., & Mary Vinton,   Nov. 22, 1774
Capt. Andrew Coburn of New Marlboro & widow
    Phebe Bacon,   Nov. 27, 1774
Daniel Hibberd & Esther Converse,   Jan. 5, 1775
Jacob Warren, Jr., & Lucy Fosket of Charlton, Jan. 17, 1775
Samuel Rogers of Sturbridge & Rachel Hibberd,
                                              Feb. 6, 1775
Elisha Corbin, Jr., & Experience Barns,   Feb. 27, 1775
Samuel Fosket of Charlton & Sarah Hunt,   March 29, 1775
Jacob Barrett of Roxbury School farms & widow
    Hannah Robinson,   April 13, 1775

Jesse Jewel & Zerviah Corbin, June 1, 1775
Zebedee Appleby of Smithfield & Joanna Sly (?),
 June 19, 1775
Joseph Inman & Lucy Sprague, Aug. 17, 1775
Alexander Brown of Killingly & Hannah Kidder,
 Aug. 17, 1775
Benjamin Edmunds & Eunice Parker, Aug. 30, 1775
William Havens & widow Sarah Brock of Wood-
 stock, Sept. 21, 1775
Philip Brown & Louis Upham, Sept. 28, 1775
William Smith & Hannah Albee, Nov. 8, 1775
Benjamin Kidder & Phebe Sabin, Nov. 9, 1775
John Gore & Hannah Carpenter, Nov. 23, 1775
John Bacon & widow Elizabeth Dodge, Jan. 1, 1776
Joseph Edmunds, Jr., & Phebe Andrews of Pom-
 fret, March 28, 1776
Samuel Curtis, Jr., of Charlton & Mary Putney,
 April 3, 1776
Reuben Chamberlain & Rebecca Healey, April 25, 1776
Ebener Edmunds & Molly Gail, May 16, 1776
Jonathan Putney & Tamar Haskell, May 29, 1776
Jonathan Webster & Martha Carpenter, Nov. 17, 1776
John Edmunds & Hanna Graton, Feb. 12, 1777
Jeremiah Haskell & Hannah Newell, April 8, 1777
Jacob Willson of Pomfret & Molly Dodge, April 22, 1777
Moses Dresser of Chesterfield & Abigail Blood of
 Charlton, May 7, 1777
Benoni Adams & Susanna Chamberlain, May 8, 1777
Joseph Keith & Sarah Mayo, May 19, 1777
William Richards, Jr., of Killingly & Rebecca
 Jewell, May 27, 1777
John Bayley of Killingly & Lydia Barstow, Aug. 6, 1777
Daniel Barrett of Killingly & widow Mary Dodge,
 Sept. 18, 1777
Richard Hunt & Elizabeth Warren, Nov. 13, 1777
Amariah Preston of Uxbridge & widow Elizabeth
 Bacon, Nov. 18, 1777
William Carter, Jr., & Hannah Mayo, Dec. 18, 1777
Stephen Edmunds & Sarah Kidder, Jan. 15, 1778

MARRIAGES.

John Albee & Zerviah Sales,	Feb. 26, 1778
Shadrach Smith & Joanna Albee,	Feb. 26, 1778
David Lamb of Charlton & Judith Fitts,	March 12, 1778
Benjamin Dresser & Jemima Scott, both of Charlton,	April 8, 1778
Bezaleel Gould of Douglass & Bathsheba Robinson,	April 9, 1778
John Applebee of Smithfield & Patience Sly,	April 16, 1778
William Abbot of Pomfret & widow Hannah Edmunds,	June 4, 1778
Luther Wakefield of Sutton & Mary Wakefield,	June 10, 1778
Nathan Fletcher & Huldah Clemens,	Aug. 2, 1778
James Town of Charlton & Lucy Bettiss,	Aug. 6, 1778
Elijah Humphrey of Killingly & Esther Brown,	Sept. 13, 1778
Deacon John Davis of Oxford & widow Susanna Kidder,	Oct. 1, 1778
Roger Williams of Glouster & Hannah Howard,	Jan. 7, 1779
Eleazor May & Abigail Prince,	Sept. —, 1779
Amasa Marshall & Tamar Wilder,	March 20, 1780
John Healey & Elizabeth Dalrymple,	April 20, 1780
Moses Hill of Douglass & Dinah Robinson,	Sept. 20, 1780
Bradford Barnes & Sarah Howard,	Oct. 23, 1780
Philemon Parker & Susanna Stone,	Oct. 26, 1780
Elnathan McIntire of Charlton & Martha Thompson,	Dec. 7, 1780
Isaac Dresser of Charlton & Susanna Taft,	Dec. 20, 1780
Samuel Corbin, Jr., of Killingly & Lucy Larned,	Jan. 18, 1781
Wyman Ainsworth & Elizabeth How,	Jan. 31, 1781
Nathan Dennis & widow Rebecca Jewell,	Feb. 6, 1781
William Foster & Mary Brown,	Feb. 8, 1781
John Heath & Eunice Oaks,	Feb. 12, 1781
John Cleveland & Caty May,	March 15, 1781
Dr. John Eliot & widow Beriah Marcy,	April 12, 1781
Dan Warren & Mary Hayden,	May 3, 1781
Oliver Willard & Asenath Newell,	May 3, 1781
John Davisson & Rhoda Putney,	July 26, 1781
Joshua Corbin & Rhoda Wood,	Sept. 6, 1781

Ephraim Willard & Sylvia Albee, Oct. 11, 1781
Thomas McClanathan of Rutland & Dolly Dalrymple, Nov. 22, 1781
Captain Joseph Albee & widow Phebe Turtelot of Killingly, Nov. 29, 1781
John Larned, the 3rd, of Oxford & Martha Wakefield, Dec. 6, 1781
Stephen Wood & Levina Newell, Feb. 11, 1782
Henry Brown & Hannah Brown, March 14, 1782
Jedediah Marcy, Jr., & Ruth Larned, April 4, 1782
Charles Brown of Johnstone & Dinah Fenner, April 15, 1782
Timothy Stow Barton of Whitingham & Phebe Stone, June 20, 1782
John Chamberlain & Mary Lee, Sept. 19, 1782
Edward Pike & Mary Hibberd, Sept. 19, 1782
Stephen Healy & Rhody Marcy, Jan. 23, 1783
Melvin Cotton of Hartford, Vt., & Joanna Dennis, Jan. 30, 1783
Micaiah Robinson & Sarah Ballard of Oxford, May 29, 1783
John Ammidon of Charlton & Olive Sanger, June 19, 1783
Aaron Albee & Martha Willard, Aug. 1, 1783
Benjamin Stone, Jr., & Elizabeth Wilcox, Sept. 11, 1783
Ebenezer Plummer & Hannah Allen, Sept. 25, 1783
Amos Wakefield & Polly Knowland, both of Gore, Oct. 10, 1783
Joshua Wetherell & widow Mary Winter of Killingley, Oct. 23, 1783
Ezra Holbrook & Anna Hedges, Nov. 6, 1783
Jared Curtis of Charlton & Phebe Putney, Dec. 10, 1783
Thomas Davis of Killingley & Rebecca Bracket, Dec. 25, 1783
Jacob Larned of Oxford & Elizabeth Atwood, Jan. 8, 1784
Thomas Upham & Elizabeth Pratt of Oxford, Feb. 19, 1784
Joseph Sheffield of Killingly & Theody Carter, Feb. 19, 1784
John Streeter & Marcy Morse, both of Charlton, March 24, 1784

MARRIAGES.

Thomas Morriss & Margaret Warren,	June 3, 1784
James Hascall & Elizabeth Vinton,	June 3, 1784
James McCallen, Jr., of Sutton & Beulah Bacon,	Nov. 23, 1784
Jabez Vinton & Ruth Putney,	Dec. 22, 1784
Jonathan Bacon & widow Sarah Kidder,	Feb. 3, 1785
Silas Hayden & Rebecca Morriss,	Feb. 10, 1785
Thomas Larned & Hannah Morriss,	May 12, 1785
Simon or Simeon Upham & Miriam Larned,	June 22, 1785
Stephen Haskell & Rachel Larned,	Sept. 15, 1785
William Larned, Jr., & Nancy Amidown,	Oct. 13, 1785
Asa Newell & Jerusha Ward,	Oct. 17, 1785
Nathan Smith, Jr., & Elisheba Atwood,	Feb. 2, 1786
Nathan Waldron & Mary Willard,	Dec. 15, 1785
Ebenezer Fitts, Jr., & Mary Mansfield,	Dec. 15, 1785
Amasa Winter & Rebekah Richard,	Jan. 19, 1786
William Cargill & Lucretia Carter, married in Bennington, Vt.,	March 3, 1786

STURBRIDGE.

June 24, 1738, "The tract of land called New Medfield established as Sturbridge." Prov. Laws., Vol. II, p. 946. First (Congregational) Church organized 1736. Baptist, 1749, at Fiskdale. The following marriages were performed largely by Rev. Joshua Paine.

Eliphalet Allen & Elisabeth Livermore,	Feb. 8, 1753
Eneas Adams & Marcy Rood,	Sept. 26, 1753
Aaron Lyon & Mary Mason,	Dec. 5, 1753
Jabez Harding & Merriam Weld,	June 3, 1754
Elijah Marcy & Sarah Stacy,	Feb. 19, 1754
Eliphalet Allen & Elizabeth Livermore,	Feb. 8, 1755
Eneas Adams & Mercy Rood,	Sept. 26, 1753
Aaron Lyon & Mary Mason,	Dec. 5, 1753
Jabez Harding & Merriam Ward,	Jan. 3, 1754
Elijah Marcy (?) & Sarah Stacy,	Feb. 4, 1754
Jonathan Bond & Lydia Allen,	April 18, 1754
Aaron Elwell & Abigail Wood,	May 23, 1754
Aaron Cromp (?) & Hepzibah Mason,	July 24, 1754
William Plympton & Prudence Marcy,	Nov. 28, 1754

Josiah Partridge & Sarah Martin,	July 30, 1755
David Smith & Mary Smith,	April 8, 1755
Joseph Sollne (?) & Susanna Johnson,	Feb. 12, 1756
Seth Hinds & Elisabeth Hale,	Feb. —, 1755
Methrop (?) Remington & Mary Marcy,	July 9, 1755
Jason Morse & Phebe Stacey,	March 16, 1759
Seth Bond & Martha Blunt,	April 28, 1762
Stephen Fay & Susen Fisk,	July 1, 1762
Joseph Morse & widow Sarah Stacey,	Oct. 20, 1762
Samuel Hamant & Kezia Baker,	Nov. 30, 1762
Adam Martin & Abigail Cheny,	Dec. 19, 1762
Abel Mason & Ruth Hobbs,	Dec. 30, 1762
James Johnson, Jr., & Hannah Harding,	June 13, 1763
Daniel Williams & Rachel Foster,	July 8, 1763
Joseph Lumbird & Lydia Leach,	July 21, 1763
Job Hamant & Jemima Baker,	Sept. 1, 1763
Thomas McKlure & Zilpah Leach,	Nov. 4, 1762
Philip Mahon & widow Ruth Rion,	Feb. 28, 1764
Asahel Corbin & Jerusha Morse,	Dec. 22, 1763
Arriel Blanchard & Abigail Mason,	Jan. 10, 1764
Aaron Allen, Jr., & Abigail Allen,	March 15, 1764
John Cheny, Jr., & Mary Shumway,	May 30, 1764
Moses Weld & Deborah Faulkner,	July 11, 1764
Aaron Clark & Katherine Ingraham,	May 11, 1765
Reuben Alexander & Sarah Foster,	Oct. 3, 1764
Abner Plympton & Esther Man,	Nov. 27, 1764
Asher Rice & Dinah Allen,	Dec. 13, 1764
William White & Mercy Dresser,	April 7, 1763
Josiah Blanchard & Elizabeth Hobbs,	April 7, 1763
Nicholas Harwood & Lucy Alexander,	Sept. 9, 1766
Ebenezer Lovell & Abigail Lyon,	March 14, 1765
Nathan Howard & Sibbel Marsh,	April 10, 1765
Asa Walker & Prudence Bond,	Jan. 10, 1765
John Graham & Mary Child,	April 17, 1765
Israel Ganes & Abigail Fay,	May 1, 1765
Abel Allen & Jerush Tarbill,	May 9, 1765
Zachariah Coburn & Dinah Hobbs,	Aug. 7, 1765
Rowland Taylor & widow Abigail Stacy,	Aug. 8, 1765
Nathan Abbot & Lydia Hatch,	Oct. 10, 1765

MARRIAGES.

Elijah Carpenter & Hannah Corey,	Oct. 10, 1765
Aaron Martin & Olive Harding,	Jan. 9, 1766
Eliphlit Allen & widow Susanna Pollis (?),	July —, 1764
Joseph Smith, Jr., & Sarah Rice,	Dec. 13, 1764
Ebenezer Fay & Mary Mason,	Nov. 19, 1765
Joseph Chamberlain & Susanna Newell,	Jan. 16, 1766
John Streeter & Kezia Morse,	Feb. 12, 1766
Simeon Allen & Sarah Puffer,	June 4, 1766
Benjamin F-umiss (?) & widow Abigail Taylor,	Sept. 1, 1766
Jeremiah Twichell & Rhoda Clark,	Sept. 4. 1766
Samuel Freeman, Jr., & Elizabeth Cheney,	Sept. 25, 1766
John Lace & Mary Guest,	Nov. 6, 1766
Oliver Mason & Lucy Johnson,	Dec. 18, 1766
Silas Corbin & Anna Fisk,	Dec. 30, 1766
Timothy Newell & Miriam Marcy,	Jan. 1, 1767
Abijah Searls & Zilpah Sabin,	July 2, 1767
Silas Hedges & Rachel Freeman,	Sept. 23, 1767
Charles Dugen (?) & Sarah Chubb,	May 14, 1767
Eliphlit Allen & Sabra Lee,	March 12, 1767
Samuel Richardson & Mary Walker,	April 23, 1767
Jonas Pike & Mary Howard,	May 7, 1767
Ephraim Bacon & Hannah Chamberlain,	May 28, 1767
Benjamin Wiser & Abigail Thomas,	June 25, 1767
Daniel Hobbs & Elizabeth Chubb,	July 23, 1767
Samuel Hooker & Mary Pierce,	Oct. 15, 1767
Gideon Sabin & Truelove Serls,	Jan. 21, 1768
Daniel Marcy & Hannah Morris,	March 3, 1768
Nathan Smith & Sarah Pike,	Jan. 13, 1768
David Smith & widow Abigail Stacy,	April 19, 1768
Seth Hamant & Mehitabel Mix,	June 9, 1768
John Blanchard & Mary Stacy,	June 29, 1768
Abner Lyon & Elizabeth Martin,	Aug. 9, 1768
Joseph Morse, Jr., & Mary Martin,	Sept. 14, 1768
Timothy Allen & Mary Moffit,	Dec. 8, 1768
Eleazer Adams & Elizabeth Cory,	Jan. 12, 1769
John Dresser & Anna Clark,	March 23, 1769
Silas Hooker & Francis Tarbill,	April 13, 1769
Elijah Plimpton & Mary Cheny,	July 25, 1769

STURBRIDGE.

Isaac Upham & Hephzibah Shaply,   Oct. 10, 1769
—— Belknap & —— Stacy,   Jan. 25, 1770
Jedidiah Smith & Sarah Blanchard,   Jan. 25, 1770
Thomas Cheny, Jr., & Eunice Gleason,   May 18, 1779
Rufus Robbins & Sabra Whittell,   Dec. 7, 1769
Jonathan Newell & Mehitable Marcy,   May 12, 1771
Joshua Crosman & Sarah Weld,   Nov. 5, 1772
Moses Bliss & Mary Newell,   Nov. 26, 1772
Amos Broughton & Abigail Corbin,   Dec. 3, 1772
Jason Allen & Martha Johnson,   March 4, 1773
John Mason & Sarah Sabin,   April 20, 1773
Luke Harding and Lydia Marsh,   Oct. 19, 1773
Abel Bacon & Sarah McKinstry,   Sept. 19, 1773
Cyral Shumway & Sarah Harding,   Jan. 11, 1774
Jedidiah Ellis & Martha Freeman,   April 28, 1774
Henry Fisk, Jr., & Sarah Fisk,   May 5, 1774
Abel Mackentier & Hannah Mory,   June 9, 1774
Jared Freeman & Martha Marcy,   Dec. 22, 1774
Jacob Mason & Mary Johnson,   Jan. 31, 1775

LUNENBURG.

August 1, 1728, "The south part of Turkey Hills established as Lunenburg." Prov. Laws, Vol. II, p. 520. First (Congregational) Church organized 1835. A Unitarian Church became extinct there in 1860. Date of organization unknown. Officiating clergymen mentioned: Revs. David and Ebenezer Stearns, Rev. Zabdiel Adams.

William Barrow of Ashuelots & Isabella Larrabee,
    Sept. 28, 1752
Bradstreet Spafford of No. 4 & Mary Page,   Oct. 16, 1752
Joseph Hammond of Lower Ashuelots & Esther
    Gould,   Nov. 2, 1752
Joseph Platts of Rowley, Canada, & Deborah Page,
    Nov. 16, 1752
Benjamin Larrabee of Lunenberg & Margaret
    Williams of Groton,   Dec. ?, 1752
Aaron Taylor & Mercy Gould,   Dec. 21, 1752
Gershom Makepeace of Dunstable and Lipha
    Dodge,   Jan. 18, 1753

MARRIAGES.

Joseph Brown of Cambridge & Abigail Foster, Jan. 18, 1753
Timothy Darling of Lunenburg & Joanna Blood
    of Groton, Feb. 8, 1753
David Steel of Londonderry & Jennit Little, Feb. 8, 1753
John White and Mary Whitney, Feb. 22, 1753
Stephen Boynton & Elizabeth Lovejoy, March 6, 1753
Zachariah Tarbell & Mary Gould, March 27, 1753
William Henry, Jr., & Mary Harper, Dec. 6, 1753
Abner Whitney of District of Shirley & Sarah
    Hilton, June 21, 1753
John Smith of Peterborough & Mary Harkness, Oct. 2, 1753
William Mahan, Jr., of Worcester & Mary Kennedy, Dec. 4, 1753
Benjamin Corey, Jr., of Lunenburg & Beulah
    Holden of District of Shirley, Dec. 26, 1753
Benjamin Stearns & Anna Taylor, Jan. 15, 1754
Thomas Putnam of Charlestown, N. H., & Rachel
    Wetherbee, Jan. 24, 1754
Timothy Dorman of Boxford & Eunice Burnam, May 27, 1754
Moses Stearns of Narraganset No. 2 & Ruth
    Houghton, July 29, 1754
Joseph Beman & Hannah Knight, July 23, 1755
Jacob Peabody & Dorothy Foster, both of Leominster, March 4, 1756
Alexander Swan & Lucy Foster, March 7, 1756
Zimri Haywood & Jane Foster, both of Dorchester,
    Canada (so-called), June 5, 1756
William Dodge & Elizabeth Salmon of Harvard, Jan. 28, 1755
John Simonds & Mary Page, March 13, 1755
Henry Hopkins & Mary Dutton, May 8, 1755
Solomon Steward, Jr., & Elizabeth Taylor, May 28, 1755
Benony Wallace & Rebecca Brown of Lyn, July 2, 1755
Jonathan Bennet of Groton & Going (?), Oct. 2, 1755
Levi Stiles & Patience Smith, Dec. 16, 1755
John Fuller & Prudence Gilson, Dec. 18, 1755
Jonas Gilson & Sarah Divoll, Jan. 29, 1756

LUNENBURG.

Phineas Steward & Anne Ireland,	April 22, 1765
Nehemiah Fuller & Mary Conant,	May 4, 1756
Samuel Pool & Mary Potter,	Dec. 4, 1756
Samuel Pool & Sarah Potter,	Dec. 14, 1756
Nathaniel Souchee of Ipswich, Canada, & Eliz. Priest of Stow,	Jan. 13, 1757
William Braybrook of Lancaster & Thankful Dutton,	March 4, 1757
Thomas Dutton & Sarah Fitch,	Sept. 9, 1756
Nathaniel Carlton, Jr., & Olive Farwell,	Nov 1, 1756
Abner Jackman & Elizabeth Bayley,	Feb. 10, 1757
Daniel Steward & Mary Ireland,	March 14, 1757
Benjamin Redington & Ruth Stearns,	March 24, 1757
Jonathan Wood & Sarah Gary,	April 19, 1757
Daniell Austin, Jr., & Pheebee Lovejoy,	April 26, 1757
Elijah Grout & Mary Willard,	July 17, 1757
Samuel Hodgskins & Rebeckah Rice,	Aug. 8, 1757
John Moors, Jr., of Bolton & Unity Willard,	Aug. 3, 1757
Timothy Bancroft & Mary Harriman,	Nov. 1, 1757
Joseph Davis & Elizabeth Forster,	Nov. 8, 1758
Barzillai Willard & Hepsabah Redington,	Nov. 18, 1757
Ephraim Stockwell & Sarah Grout, both of Petersham	Nov. 21, 1757
William Cowdin of Worcester & Mary Henry,	Sept. 7, 1757
James Clark & Anne Freeman, both of Lancaster,	Jan. 5, 1758
Joseph Houghton & Mary Wilson, both of Leominster,	Jan. 31, 1758
Abner Wheelock of Leominster & Mary Brown,	April 12, 1758
John Richards & Elizabeth Mitchel,	Oct 17, 1758
Samuel Russel & Susannah Mitchel,	Nov. 28, 1757
Elisha Bigelow of Narraganset No. 2 & Sarah Goodridge,	Dec. 1, 1757
Moses Child & Sarah Stiles,	March 28, 1758
Thaddeus Harrington of Shirley & Thankful Dodge,	April 6, 1758
Wincal Wright of Dunstable & Sibbil Farewell,	April 7, 1758

MARRIAGES.

Samuel Hart & Mary Fuller,	April 20, 1758
Benjamin Bellows, Esq., of Walpole, N. H., & Mrs. Mary Jenison,	April 21, 1758
Ebenezer Hart & Sarah Poole,	May 4, 1758
Jonathan Stedman of Westminster & Tabitha Hart,	Sept. 8, 1761
Ebenezer Pratt & Lydia Stone of Groton,	Sept. 22, 1761
Josiah Dodges, Jr., & Hannah Conant of Leominster,	Nov. 8, 1761
David Poor of Ipswich, Canada, & Jane Martin,	Dec. 2, 1761
James Carter & Sarah Gilson,	Dec. 3, 1761
Reuben Smith & Prudence Pierce,	Sept. 6, 1762
Henry Hodgkin of Ipswich, Canada, & Jemima Ball of Westminster,	Nov. 7, 1762
Francis Gardiner of Stow & Mrs. Sarah Gibson,	Oct. 5, 1762
Josiah Bailey, Jr., & Sarah Carter,	Oct. 7, 1762
Jacob Wilson & Margaret Freeman, both of Leominster,	Dec. 6, 1762
Samuel McCracken of Worcester & Lettice Corlisle,	Dec. 8, 1762
Asa Carlton & Ruth Bailey,	Feb. 8, 1763
Silas Dutton & Sarah Whitney,	March 3, 1763
John Endicott of Danvers & Martha Putnam,	April 19, 1763
Page Norcross & Elizabeth Bailey,	Feb. 15, 1763
Phinehas Divol & Abigail Stockwell,	June 6, 1763
Rev. Ebenezer Sparhawke of Templeton & Mrs. Abigail Stearns,	Sept. 1, 1763
James Bennet and Elizabeth Fuller,	Sept. 6, 1763
David Stearns & Mary Law,	Oct. 20, 1763
Samuel Hilton & Rebeccah Stickney,	Nov. 17, 1763
Phinehas Hutchins & Abigail Read,	Nov. 24, 1763
Eliphalet Goodridge & Rebeccah Snow,	Dec. 29, 1763
Eleazer Houghton & Susannah Holman	March 8, 1764
Ebenezer Bridge & Mehitabel Wood,	Nov. 3, 1763
Joseph Chaplain & Lois Hastings,	April 5, 1764
Jacob Gates of Harvard & Mrs. Elizabeth Gibson,	May 9, 1764

Benjamin Gould of Rowley, Canada, N. H., &
 Sarah Foster, May 14, 1764
Michal Wood & Lois Willson of Leominster, Aug. 21, 1764
Joseph Bellows & Lois Whitney, Oct. 3, 1764
Samuel Hazon of Stow & Elizabeth Little, Nov. 20, 1764
Joseph Fuller & Rebecca Wyman, Feb. 6, 1763
Thomas Carter, Jr., & Priscilla Reed, or Rud, Feb. 13, 1765
David Carlisle, Jr., & Sarah Cumming, Feb. 11, 1765
Thomas Hartwell & Prudence Carter, May 9, 1765
Timothy Farley of Fitchburg & Sarah Colburn,
 Nov. 19, 1765
Eli Dodge, Jr., & Mary Chaplain, Jan. 21, 1766
Nathaniel Parkhill & Mary Holden, both of Leicester,
 May 30, 1766
William Moffatt of Winchenden & Mary Price (?)
 of Shirley, Sept. 22, 1766
Daniel Goodridge of Winchendon & Mary Low, Oct. 30, 1766
Simeon Burnam & Mary Wanson, both of Shirley,
 May 30, 1765
Amos Davis of Westmoreland, N. H., & Patience
 Griffin, June 11, 1765
Job Colman of Ashburnam & Elisabeth Martin, Feb. 20, 1766
Nathan Plats & Relief Austin, May 27, 1766
Benjamin Darling & Mary Holt, June 26, 1766
John Gibson & Hannah Martin, both of Fitchburg,
 Sept. 16, 1766
John Dunsmore, Jr., & Mary Kimball of Fitch-
 burg, Sept. 30, 1766
Jacob Steward of Fitchburg & Elizabeth Pierce (?),
 Nov. 8, 1766
Moses Whitney of Petersham & Sarah Gray, Nov. 20, 1766
Joshua Peirce of Leominster & Lydia Goodridge,
 Nov. 27, 1766
Nathan Heywood & Mrs. Susanna Divol, Dec. 2, 1766
Joseph Snow & Joanna Jewet, Dec. 4, 1766
John Buss of Fitchburg & Mary Wood, Jan. 1, 1767
Benjamin Page & Susanna Russell, Jan. 8, 1767
John Ireland & Lydia Farwell, Jan. 12, 1767
Isaac Stevens of Hollis, N. H., & Martha Jewett,
 Jan. 15, 1767

MARRIAGES.

Elijah Gould & Eunice Patch, Feb. 26, 1767
Abner Hale of Winchendon & Abigail Goodridge,
    March 12, 1767
Oliver Stickney & Hannah Stiles, May 26, 1767
Barnabas Wood & Sarah Holt, Sept. 10, 1767
Williams Stewart of Petersboro, N. H., & Elisabeth
    White, Nov. 3, 1767
James Grimes of Swansey, N. H., & Elisabeth Gilchrist, Nov. 5, 1767
John Wood & Sarah Thurston of Fitchburg, Nov. 24, 1767
Ebenezer Harrington & Martha Wott (?), both of
    Fitchburg, Nov. 26, 1767
Thomas Dunster & Lydia Pain, both of Westminster, March 23, 1768
Mighill Davis & Mary Johnson, June 30, 1768
James Brophey of Peterboro, N. H., & Martha Holl,
    Aug. 23, 1768
John Rugg of South Hadley & Martha Forbush,
    Aug. 25, 1768
Ezekial Fowler of Fitchburg & Dorcas Bradstreet,
    Oct. 25, 1768
Rev. Aaron Whitney of Petersham & Mrs. Ruth
    Starns, Nov. 9, 1768
Edmund Stone of Templeton & Susanna Whitney,
    Dec. 6, 1768
James Reed, Jr., of Monadnock, No. 4, & Mary
    Dodge, Dec. 11, 1768
Joseph Downe of Fitchburg & Martha Wood, Dec. 22, 1768
Nathan Smith of Weston & Sarah Reed, Dec. 22, 1768
Jonathan Pierce, Jr., & Sarah Chaplin, Jan. 5, 1769
Jonathan Cumming & Hannah Fletcher, Jan. 5, 1769
John Farwell of Fitchburg & Sarah Hovey, March 16, 1769
Thomas Kimball & Sarah Martin, March 30, 1769
William Kendall & Sarah Bradstreet, Aug. 20, 1769
Amos Heald, Jr., of Townsend & Betty Davis, Oct. 2, 1769
Daniel Stearns of Leominster & Hannah Whetherbee, Jr., Oct. 26, 1769
Josiah Flagg of Wor. & Hannah Wetherbee, Nov. 26, 1769
John Wood of Littleton & Lucy Martin, Nov. 16, 1769

Josiah Peirce & Molly Foss, Nov. 23, 1769
John Campbell & Hannah Nickless, Nov. 23, 1769
Elijah Carter of Fitchburg & Jane Goodridge, Jan. 18, 1770
David Beeman of Leominster & Sarah Pierce, Feb. 6, 1770
James Allen & Sarah Charlton, April 22, 1770
Edward Kendall of Monadnock, No. 4, N. H., &
    Prudence Hartwell, Feb. 12, 1769
Josiah Greenwood of Westminster & Martha
    Symonds, March 28, 1769
Stephen Bathrick & Jemima Dodge, Aug. 15, 1769
Isaac Wood & Elizabeth Hartwell, Jan. 11, 1770
Ezekiel Goodale of Templeton, N. H., & Eleoner
    Gill of Westminster, May 29, 1770
John Everett & Elizabeth Gill, both of West-
    minster, May 29, 1770
Josiah Hartwell & Rebecca Walker, Dec. 27, 1770
John Joyner of Westminster & Susanna Rayley or
    Bayley of Hillsburg, June 11, 1771
Samuel Davis & Margaret Down, Nov. 12, 1771
Jacob Walton & Elizabeth Jenkins, both of West-
    minster, Nov. 18, 1771
Silas Holt & Sarah Harrington, Jan. 25, 1772
Aaron Colman of Ashby & Eleanor Boynton, Feb. 20, 1772
Dr. John Taylor & Mrs. Anna Pool, at Dunstable,
    N. H., July 16, 1772
John Steles (?) & Keziah Divol, July 5, 1770
Stephen Boynton & Sarah Stiles, Nov. 9, 1772
Silas Buss & Hannah Pierce, July 23, 1770
Sewell Dodge & Martha Martin, Sept. 5, 1770
Benjamin Wilson of Westminster & Mehitable
    Foster, Sept. 25, 1770
Thomas Harkness & Elizabeth Putnam, Dec. 6, 1770
Jonathan Boynton & Elizabeth Divol, Jan. 1, 1771
Caleb Wilson of Leominster & Phebe Divol, Jan. 1, 1771
Jabez Norcross & Hannah Bayley, March 27, 1771
Thomas Peabody & Hannah Ritter, June 20, 1771
Timothy Gibson & Sarah Foster, July 22, 1771
Benjamin Bayley & Olive Bradstreet, Aug. 22, 1771
Joshua Martin & Phebe Bradstreet, Aug. 22, 1771

MARRIAGES.

Moses Ritter & Mary Goodridge,	Sept. 5, 1771
Stephen Boynton of Winchendon & Tabatha Foster,	Jan. 29, 1772
Jonathan Martin & Susanna Taylor,	Aug. 31, 1772
Ebenezer Allen, Jr., & Mary Henry,	Nov. 10, 1772
Henry Haskel of Shirley & Martha Little,	Dec. 1, 1772
Samuel Whiting & Ruth Goodridge,	Dec. 1, 1772
John Wilmon of Worcester & Mary Chaplin,	Dec. 2, 1772
Ephraim Wetherbee & Keziah Pierce,	Dec. 3, 1772
Thomas Houghton of Leominster & Ruth Kilbourn,	Dec. 9, 1772
Amos Page & Elizabeth Randell,	Dec. 10, 1772
Ephraim Pierce & Huldah Witherbee,	Jan. 12, 1773
Elisha Brown & Elizabeth Dodge,	Jan. 19, 1773
John Witherbee & Susanna Page,	Jan. 21, 1773
Samuel Kendall of Monadnock, No. 4, & Bettey Wetherbee,	Feb. 25, 1773
Samuel Tarbell & Beatrie Carter,	Feb. 25, 1773

BOLTON.

June 24, 1738, "Part of Lancaster established as Bolton. First (Unitarian) Church organized 1740. Friends, 1799. Officiating clergymen mentioned: Rev. Thomas Goss, Rev. John Walley.

Paul Gates & Submit How,	Nov. 18, 1746
Jonas Brooks & Dinah Pike,	Dec. 25, 1746
Nehemiah How of Marlboro & Beulah Wheler,	March 4, 1746-7
Josiah Houghton of Lancaster & Bethesda Brabrook (?),	April 16, 1747
Samuel Moore & Zeresh Houghton,	Aug. 19, 1747
Nathaniel Roberson & Patience Keyes,	Aug. 24, 1747
Jonas More & Dinah Whitcomb,	Nov. 24, 1747
Abraham Rice & Susannah Wild,	Dec. 18, 1747
Philip Goss of Lancaster & Hannah Ball,	May 12, 1748
Samuel Snow & Keziah Hought,	May 12, 1748
Benjamin Edward of Stow & Elizabeth Fairbanks,	Nov. 24, 1748

Peter Joslyn, Jr., of Lancaster & Elizabeth Greenleaf,	Jan. 5, 1748
James Snow, Jr., & Persis Houghton,	Jan. 5, 1748
Eleazer Whitcomb & Mary Putnam,	Oct. 5, 1749
Benjamin Marble & Mary Goss,	Oct. 5, 1749
John French of Shrewsbury & Mary Whitcomb,	Aug. 1, 1749
William Sawyer & Sarah Sawtell,	July 7, 1748
Zachariah Glazier & Martha Snow,	Sept. 1, 1749
Jonas Whitcomb & Hannah Sawtell,	May 17, 1753
Amariah Thought of Bolton & Jane Smith of Marlboro,	May 17, 1753
David Whitcomb & Hannah Priest,	May 31, 1753
Micah Bush of Marlboro & Hepzibah Fairbanks,	Aug. 28, 1753
Peter Mebrow (?) & Dinah Thomas,	Sept. 12, 1754
Abraham Hough & Caroline Houghton,	Nov. 24, 1754
Jonathan Nicholls & Mary McClewean,	Jan. 16, 1755
George Pi——es & Sarah Mcfaden,	Feb. 14, 1755
Nathaniel Longley & Bulah Fairbank,	May 14, 1755
Israel Greenleaf & Prudence Whitcomb,	Nov. 28, 1754
Daniel Nichols & Mary Houghton,	Dec. 5, 1754
Robert Lingley (?) & Anna Whitcomb,	May 17, 1756
Hezikiah Gibbs & Elizabeth Pratt,	May 24, 1745
Ezra Wilder & Betty Welch,	March 9, 1762
Elijah Wilson & Sarah Bruce,	Sept. 22, 1761
Amos Fuller of Marlboro & Mary Coolidge,	March 25, 1762
Thaddeus Hager of Framingham & Lois Sawyer,	Dec. 9, 1762
Thomas Sawyer & Mary Houghton,	March 25, 1762
David Nurse & Rebekah Barratt,	June 3, 1762
John Gregg of Lunenburg & Rosanna Oliver,	Nov. 19, 1761
William Pollard & Hannah Whetcomb,	Oct. 7, 1762
Daniel Priest of Leominster & Lydia Graves,	April 5, 1762
Calvin Greenleaf & Becke Whetcomb,	Nov. 17, 1762
John Wilder & Rebeckah Sawyer,	May 24, 1763
Abner Sawyer of Templeton & Hannah Piper,	May 26, 1763
Samuel Snow & Mrs. Prudence Houghton,	Oct. 11, 1763
Phineas Houghton & Mrs. Eunice Rogers of Harvard,	Nov. 28, 1763

MARRIAGES.

John Bounds Moulton of Brimfield, South District, & Mrs. Eliz. Fosket,	Dec. 7, 1763
James McBride & Lydia Willson,	Dec. 8, 1763
Samuel Harris & Phebe Goodell,	Dec. 13, 1763
Samuel Jones & Dorothy Whetcomb,	Dec. 14, 1763
Abel Moor & Mrs. Betty Whetcomb,	Jan. 11, 1764
William Sawyer, Jr., & Hannah Barret,	Jan. 18, 1764
Andrew McClewain & Rebecca C—— of Lancaster,	Feb. 1, 1764
Silas How of Lancaster & Abigail Moor,	Feb. 2, 1764
Andrew Darby, Jr., & Elizabeth Sawin, both of Westminster,	Dec. 20, 1763
Abraham Knowlton of Narragt. No. 6 & Comfort Holman,	Feb. 13, 1759
Micah Bush of Marlboro & Hannah Wilder,	April 19, 1759
Thomas Osborn & Mary Whitcomb,	April 26, 1759
William Swan of Cambridge & Lucy Rolens,	May 1, 1759
Paul Whitcomb & Rebeckah Whitney of Harvard,	Sept. 19, 1759
Robert Alexander of Cumberland & Mary Alexander,	March 19, 1759
Jonathan Houghton & Susannah Moore,	Nov. 24, 1759
Josiah Moore & Abigail Richardson,	May 10, 1759
David Goodell, Jr., & Elizabeth Hutchinson,	April 10, 1764
Andrew Haskell & Hazediah McClewain,	April 18, 1764
James Flood & Betty Whetcomb,	May 15, 1764
James Townsend & Hannah Merriam,	May 29, 1764
Thaddeus Russell & Elizabeth Pratt,	June 18, 1764
Tille Whitcomb & Rachel Whitcomb,	Feb. 26, 1766
David Stiles & —— Oak,	Dec. 11, 1765
Richard Roberts & Sibil Goodenough of Marlboro,	Feb. 7, 1765
Silas —— & Mary Miriam,	Dec. 20, 1766
John Barrus (?) of Western & Nanney Haskell,	April 4, 1765
Dr. Nathaniel Martyn of Harvard & Mrs. Anna Townsend,	Dec. 23, 1765
Nehemiah Parker of Shrewsbury & Mrs. Mary Richardson,	Dec. 5, 1765

Joshua Atherton of Petersham & Mrs. Abigail
    Goss, Jr., Oct. 27, 1765
Abraham Scott & Mary Kent of Harvard, Oct. 2, 1764
Caleb Church of Templeton & Elizabeth Walker,
    Oct. 2, 1764
David Dickenson & Persis Wheeler, both of Ashburnham, July 16, 1767
Hooker Sawyer & Relief Whetcomb, Oct. 2, 1766
Jacob Holmes, Jr., of Wor. & Elisabeth Gates of
    Harvard, July 2, 1767
Josiah Willson, Jr., & Patience Foskett, Nov. 12, 1766
Phineahas Ward of Marlboro & Dorothy Osgood,
    Sept. 2, 1766
Paul Faulkner & Hepzibah Powers, Aug. 21, 1766
William Wilder, Jr., & Sarah Sawyer, Oct. 16, 1766
John Katherin (?) of —llam (?) & Lois Moor, Sept. 11, 1766
William White & Lydia Goodell, July 3, 1766
Rev. Josiah Winchop of Woolwich & Mrs. Judith
    Goss, July 7, 1766
Robert Holden & Sarah Tuttle, Nov. 25, 1766
Joseph Houghton & Mrs. Susanna Brook, June 23, 1767
James White & Mrs. Hulday Goodale of Danvers,
    Oct. 6, 1768
Jonathan Moor, Jr., & Desire Bayley, July 28, 1768
John Hastings & Submitt Russell, Dec. 31, 1767
Elisha Houghton of Harvard & Mrs. Meriah Peirce,
    Nov. 30, 1768
Benjamin Gould & Mrs. Silence Atherton, July 3, 1767
Eliakim Atherton & Mrs. Elisabeth Sawyer, May 13, 1767
Seth Dean & Mrs. Betty Bruce, Sept. 28, 1768
William Sawyer, 3d, & Kezia Moor, Dec. 22, 1768
Amos Miriam & Mrs. Elisabeth Nurse, July 15, 1767
John Richardson of Templeton & Mrs. Rebecca Moore,
    April 21, 1768
Beriah Oak & Mrs. Tabatha Fosket, Dec. 31, 1767
Jeridiah (Jedediah) Woods of Warwick & Mrs.
    Mary Burt, March 7, 1769
Moses Wooster & Sarah Wott, both of Harvard,
    Jan. 12, 1769

MARRIAGES.

Phinehas Warner & Lydia Whitney,	Feb. 27, 1769
Aholiab Sawyer & Barshebah Barrett,	June 5, 1769
John McClewain & Mrs. Joanna Burge,	Nov. 2, 1769
John Hannah & Hannah Coolidge,	Dec. 18, 1769
Benjamin Bruce & Nanny McBride,	Dec. —, 1768
Jame (?) McWain & Mrs. Rebecca Whitcomb,	Oct. 10, 1769
Abner Moore & Elisabeth Hastings,	Nov. 16, 1769
William Whitcomb & Lucy Meriam,	Dec. 13, 1769
Abraham Crosby of Nobletown, N. Y., & Ruth Digins,	May 15, 1769
Abraham Moor, Jr., & Mrs. Sarah Johnson,	Dec. 7, 1769
Jacob Moor & Elisabeth Baley,	Nov. 30, 1769
Jonas Stratton of Stow & Anna Barnard,	Nov. 15, 1770
Lemuel Burnam & Hannah Peirce,	June 29, 1769
Elijah Foster & Elisabeth Knight,	Dec. 4, 1769
Abel Farwell & Hannah Russell, both of Harvard,	June 14, 1769
Thos. McBride & Sarah Snow,	April 19, 1769
Nathan Jones & Mrs. Mary Bruce,	Nov. —, 1767
Rufus Houghton & Elizabeth Whitcomb,	July 23, 1770
Stephen Wilder (or Wilber) of Lancaster & Betty Sawyer of Harvard,	Sept. 3, 1770
Fradrick Albert of Lancaster & Mary Blood,	Feb. 26, 1770
Aaron Parsons of Swansey & Mrs. Damaras Whitcomb,	Feb. 8, 1770
Able Piper & Sible Sawyer,	Jan. 19, 1769
John Brown of Marlboro & Phebe Fosket,	Dec. 17, 1764
John Bruce & Martha Moors,	Feb. 18, 1768
Moses Cutler (?) of Monadnock No. 5 & Mary Whetcomb,	Dec. 27, 1770
John Sawyer & Mary Moor, 3d,	Nov. 29, 1770
Phinehas Moor & Sarah Nurss,	Nov. 27, 1770
Simon Houghton & Martha Stearns,	Dec. 6, 1770
Thomas Holt & Molley Corey, both of Lancaster,	Dec. 13, 1770
Silas Rice of Northboro & Lois Pollard,	Sept. 20, 1770
Daniel Sabin of Putney & Mary Snow,	Dec. 26, 1770
Joseph Blood of Marlboro & Betty Bruce, Jr.,	June 27, 1770
John Whitney & Sarah Atherton, both of Har——,	Jan. 9, 1771

Josiah Whetcomb of Leominster & Marcy Blood,
    Jan. 29, 1771
Joseph Amsden of Marlboro & Mary Edwards,
    April 12, 1771
Jonathan Puffer & Jemima Taft, both of Westminster,   March 12, 1771
Jeremiah Priest, Jr., of Harvard & Rebecca Houghton,   March 14, 1771
Jonas Richardson & Mary Bailey,   June 6, 1771
John Mahanay of Londonderry & Lydia Kelcey,
    July 9, 1771
William Biglow & Hannah Robbins,   Jan. 1, 1772
Jonathan Horton of Templetown & Ruth Knight,
    Feb. 25, 1772
Calvin Sawyer & Abigail Barrett,   Jan 7, 1772
Oliver Jewet & Bettey Houghton,   Jan. 23, 1772
Oliver Fairbank of Lancaster & Susanne Gates of Littleton,   March 3, 1772
Thomas Osborn & Sarah Whetcomb,   March 10, 1772
Jonathan Whitcomb, Jr., & Achsah Fairbank, March 30, 1772
William McWain & Anna Stun (?),   Nov. 3, 1772
John Sampson & Rachiel Whetcomb,   Dec. 2, 1772
Josiah Sawyer & Bathsheba Moor of Putney,   Aug. 6, 1770
Samuel Stearns & Sarah Witt of Paxton,   March 31, 1773
William Lincoln of Leominster & Release Sawyer,
    April 27, 1773
Silas Houghton & Sarah Wyman of Harvard, May 20, 1773
Jonathan Whetcomb & Releaf Fife (?),   June 1, 1773
Nathaniel Oak, Jr., & Susanna Hastings,   June 2, 1773
Joseph Priest & Tabatha Russell,   July 15, 1773
Daniel Priest & Bettey Dupee,   Aug. 16, 1773
Lemuel Butler & Abigail Houghton,   Dec. 6, 1773
Israel Sawyer & Bulah Willson,   Nov. 25, 1773
Elijah Whitney of Harvard & Sarah Stearns, April 14, 1772
James Wilder, Jr., of Lancaster & Jemima Johnson,
    April 30, 1772
Josiah Cooledge, Jr., & Molley Houghton,   May 22, 1772
Edmund Taylor of Monadnock, No. 7, & Hepzibah French,   July 6, 1773

MARRIAGES.

Stephen Winchet of the Little Nine Partners in
    the province of New York & Relief Glazier, Dec. 24, 1772
Elijah Whitney, Jr., & Lydia McWain,   Jan. 25, 1773
William Burges of Harvard & Elizabeth Richard-
    son, Jr,   March 24, 1774
Nathaniel Burnam, Jr., & Hepzibah Hutchins of
    Harvard,   Sept. 26, 1774
Eli Harrington of Westboro & Susannah Baker,
                                                      Nov. 3, 1774
Aaron Foster & Anna Knight,   March 14, 1775
Hezekiah Gibbs, Jr., & Miriam Powers,   May 4, 1775
John Priest & Anna Houghton,   June 4, 1775
Joseph Jones & Ruth Holden,   Aug. 17, 1775
Stephen Harris & Sarah Butler, both of Templeton,
                                                  Dec. 28, 1775
Robert Fife & Hepzibah Bush of Marlboro, July 11, 1776
Benjamin Edwards & Sarah Stiles,   Nov. 23, 1775
Israel Whetcomb, Jr., & Eunice Willson,   Nov. 28, 1775
John McBride & Phebe Wheeler,   Sept. 17, 1776
Ebenezer Warren, Jr., of Harvard & Deborah Ball,
                                                  Sept. 30, 1776
Ephraim Whetcomb & Sarah Longley,   Jan. 14, 1777
Simeon Whetcomb of Jeffery & Bathsheba Combs,
                                                  June 17, 1777
Ebenezer Blood & Abigail Barnard,   Dec. 13, 1773
Thomas Pollard & Deborah Woods,   Dec. 16, 1773
Holman Priest & Prudence Sawyer,   April 28, 1774
John Priest of Jeffery & Mary Hemenway, March 10, 1774
Josiah Rice, Jr., & Hannah Marble,   March 22, 1774
Josiah Sawyer, Jr., & Judith Ross,   Dec. 7, 1774
Jacob Davis of Harvard & Ruth Atherton, Dec. 15, 1774
Job Priest of Harvard & Martha Butler,   Jan. 3, 1774
Oliver Barret, Jr., & Sarah Whetcomb, March 6, 1775
David Whetcomb, Jr., and Sarah Whetcomb, May 28, 1776
Ephraim Fairbank, Jr., & Prudence Wilder, Nov. 21, 1774
Daniel Laughton & Lucy Dutton, both of Harvard,
                                                  Sept. 2, 1777
Peter Stanhope & Elizabeth Parmenter of Sudbury,
                                                  Nov. 30, 1775

Caleb Gates of Stow & Mindwell Oaks, March 10, 1776
James Stone of Harvard & Susanna Fosgate, Feb. 13, 1777
Simeon Hemenway & Mary Goss, May 4, 1777
Joel Fosgate & Naomi Gilbert, Dec. 11, 1777
Stephen Pratt & Eunice Barnard, March 24, 1778
Benjamin Nurss & Sibel Bailey, Nov. 6, 1777
Micajah Fay of Grafton & Susanna King, Dec. 18, 1777
Abijah Pollard & Hannah Moor, April 30, 1778
William Walker of Sudbury & Elizabeth Stanhope,
 May 29, 1777
Gardner Moore & Abigail Whetcomb, July 23, 1778
Simon Meriam & Phebe Lock of Harvard, April 8, 1779
Philemon Fairbank & Sally Smith, both of Athol,
 June 19, 1779
Nathaniel Southwick & Abigail Moore, Aug. 17, 1778
Abel Wilder & Hannah Green, March 28, 1779
Jesse Jewett & Hannah Johnson, Dec. 10, 1778
William ——— & Mary Houghton, both of Shrews-
 bury, May 19, 1778
Stephen Brooks of Stow & Prudence Whetcomb,
 July 7, 1779
Levi Moor, Jr., & Parnel Parker, both of Lancaster,
 Jan. 24, 1780
Timothy Henry Curtis & Hannah Sawyer, March 20, 1780
David Stearns & Loas Crouch, both of Harvard,
 Dec. 24, 1777
Jabez Fairbank, Jr., & Lucy Bailey, Jr., Jan. 23, 1778
Edward Baker & Hepzibah ———, Jr., Oct. 13, 1778
Barnabas Sawyer & Unity Houghton, Dec. 14, 1778
Ezra Smith of Sudbury & Phebe Walcott, Jan. 12, 1779
Josiah Sawyer, 3d, & Percis Baker, Feb. 10, 1779
Micah Ross & Molly Moor, both of Lancaster, April 4, 1780
Samuel Baker, Jr., & Hannah Bush, Jr., of Marlboro,
 May 25, 1780
Abraham Brigham & Emma Robbins, May 15, 1780
Cyrus Fairbank of Harvard & Marcy Hale of Stow,
 Nov. 10, 1779
Asa Houghton, Jr., & Dorcas Moor, both of Harvard,
 Dec. 9, 1779

Samuel Nichols & Abigail Pierce,   Dec. 26, 1779
John Pitt & Dinah Wood,   April 21, 1780
Abel Whetcomb & Elizabeth Townsend,   May 8, 1780
Samuel Goss & Lucretia How,   March 7, 1780
Oliver Jewett & Keziah Snow,   April 28, 1780
John Whetcomb, Jr., & Azubah Whetcomb,   May 31, 1780
Nathan Priest of Harvard & Mary Bacon of Bedford,
                                                July 5, 1780
Zaccheus Dudley & Mary Conant, both of Harvard,
                                                Aug. 28, 1780
Simon Whetcomb & Hepzibah Houghton,   Sept. 13, 1780
Abraham Holman & Prudence Hills of Leominster,
                                                Oct. 25, 1780
Richard Townsend, Jr., & Susanna Houghton, Jr., Oct. 2, 1780
Silas Whetcomb & Lydia Underwood,   Oct. 12, 1780
Silas How & Silence Moore, Jr.,   Nov. 2, 1780
Samuel Forbush & Mary Warner, both of Harvard,
                                                Jan. 11, 1781
John Warner, Jr., of Harvard & Susanna Barratt of
    Leominster,   Feb. 22, 1781
Nathaniel Longley & Keziah Fairbank, both of
    Harvard,   March 5, 1781
Thaddeus Pollard & Mary Fairbank, both of Harvard,
                                                March 5, 1781
Jonathan Atherton, Jr., & Phebe Nurse,   March 6, 1781
Timothy Bruce & Matilda Wheeler,   April 5, 1781
Jonas Houghton, Jr., & Eunice Houghton,   May 10, 1781
Benjamin Bruce, Jr., & Philadelphia Wheeler,   May 10, 1781

UPTON.

June 14, 1735, "Parts of Hopkinton, Mendon, Sutton and Uxbridge established as Upton." Prov. Laws, Vol. II, p. 764. First (Congregational) Church organized 1735. Clergyman mentioned: Rev. Joseph Door of Mendon.

Thomas Lealand of Grafton & Margaret Wood, July 23, 1747
Henry Walker & Phenwell White,   Dec. 8, 1747
William Green & Hannah Tyler,   Jan. 10, 1744-5
Benjamin Wood & Sybel Perham,   May 4, 1762

UPTON.

Elijah Rice & Prudence Hardy,	Aug. 12, 1762
Phinehas Pratt & Susanna Palmer,	Nov. 25, 1762
Samuel Wright & Deborah Bacon,	Feb. 29, 1764
Alexander Gore & Elizabeth Wood,	June 28, 1764
David White & Mary Woods,	May 24, 1764
Edward Rawson & Sarah Sadler,	July 19, 1764
David Blatcheler & Lois Wood,	Feb. 9, 1764
Jonah Wood & Rachel Wood,	Nov. 29, 1764
Nathan Wood & Levice Morse,	March 14, 1765
Aaron Hayward & Hannah Severy,	April 25, 1765
Peter Hazeltine & Mary Sadler,	Jan. 9, 1766
Abraham Boyd & Hannah Hill,	June 24, 1766
Joshua Jenney & Olive ———,	Oct. 7, 1766
William Batchellor & Lydia Warren,	Oct. 9, 1766
Abner Palmer & Hannah ———,	Nov. 6, 1766
Jonas Butterfield & Jane Hazeltine,	Nov. 11, 1766
Peter Holbrook & Huldah Wood,	Dec. 3, 1766
John Spring & Hannah Crosby,	May 27, 1767
Francis Bowman & Jerusha Wood,	June 9, 1767
Jonathan Nelson & Sarah Warren,	June 30, 1767
Levi Legg & Mary Beels (?),	Dec. 3, 1767
Hezekiah Larnard & Lydia Perham (?),	Dec. 3, 1767
Samuel Fletcher & Mehitable Hazeltine,	April 14, 1768
Jonathan Cutler & Mary Rawson,	April 26, 1768
Thomas Forbush & Submitt Ball,	July 11, 1768
Benjamin How & Hannah Blanchard,	Aug. 19, 1768
Joseph Lesure & Percis Whitney,	Sept. 13, 1768
Robert Fisk & Mary Hall,	Nov. 17, 1768
Isaac Sheffield & Abigail Wood,	Nov. 24, 1768
Nathan Peck & Sarah Tenny,	Feb. 9, 1769
Josiah Ward & Molly Scott Wiswall,	April 12, 1770
Naham Ward & Anna Wood,	May 3, 1770
Benjamin Sadler & Bathsheba Wand,	May 3, 1770
Benjamin Fisk & Jemima Holbrook,	June 14, 1770
Jacob Perham & Susanna Sadler,	Oct. 4, 1770
Matthew Lackey & Mary Rice,	Oct. 11, 1770
James Tony & ——— White,	Jan. 8, 1771
Seth Wood & Lydia Sadler,	April 30, 1771
James Kidder & Deborah Wood,	July 18, 1771

MARRIAGES.

James Morgan & Mary Giles,	Sept. 24, 1771
Caleb Hayward & Elizabeth Taft,	Nov. 7, 1771
Grindel Wood & Mary Nelson,	Dec. 5, 1771
James Fletcher & Margaret Wood,	Dec. 24, 1771
Jonathan Hayward & Lydia Wood,	Jan. 23, 1772
Asa Ober & Susanna Tenney,	Feb. 6, 1772
Timothy Fisher & Levice Wood,	March 30, 1773
Jonathan Wood & Sarah Bradish,	Oct. 26, 1773
Abel Munroe & Rebecca Sadler,	Nov. 23, 1773
Moses Wood, Jr., & Sarah Long of Hopkinton,	Dec. 9, 1773
Farnum White of Mendon & Lois Nelson,	Dec. 16, 1773
John Axtell (a transient person) & Lucy Flagg of Grafton,	Jan. 19, 1774
Daniel Fisher of Townshend, N. Y., & Hannah Sadler,	Feb. 1, 1774
Ebenezer Butler & Thankful Curtis,	Feb. 8, 1774
James Lackey & Charlotte Forbes,	April 6, 1780
Joseph Potter & Elizabeth Childs,	May 9, 1780
William Hall & Sarah Boyce,	May 25, 1780
John Haywood of Mendon & Mary Pease,	Jan. 11, 1781
Elisha Bradish & Hannah Taft,	May 4, 1779
Joseph Wood & Elizabeth Bradish,	Aug. 12, 1779
Timothy Taft of Uxbridge & Abigail Wright,	Oct. 24, 1779
Elijah Harrington of Shrewsbury & Mary Warren,	Jan. 31, 1781
Elisha Warren & Anna Marble,	May 28, 1776
Abiel Sadler & Elizabeth Warren,	May 28, 1776
John Morris of Northbridge & Molly Whitney,	June 27, 1776
Jonathan Wright & Eunice Walker,	July 11, 1776
William Ward of Mendon & Hannah Taft,	Nov. 28, 1776
Peter Forbush & Deborah Flagg,	May 6, 1777
Amos Wood & Sarah Sadler,	July 24, 1777
Thomas Nelson, Jr., & Hannah Brackett,	Sept. 11, 1777
Isaac Nelson & Hannah Fisk,	Jan. 27, 1778
Henderson Walkup & Sarah Drury,	Aug. 26, 1779
Daniel Wood, Jr., & Maribel Hayward,	Sept. 30, 1779
Thomas Ellison & Abigail Goldthwaid, both of Northbridge,	Oct. 28, 1779

Peter Thurston of Grafton & Elizabeth Holbrook,
            Oct. 28, 1779
Artimas Rawson & Dorcas Bachellor of Grafton,
            Nov. 25, 1779
Elijah Warren & Abigail Fish,   April 26, 1781
Grindly Jackson & Elizabeth Peterson, May 24, 1781
Jonathan Nelson & Abiel French of Holliston, Nov. 1, 1781
Capt. Jonathan Wood of Spencer & Mrs. Rebecca
 Warren,   Dec. 19, 1781
Amos Whitney & Eunice Taft,   Feb. 7, 1782
Joel Bolster & Betty Perham,   March 8, 1781
Ezra Wood & Sarah Taft,   May 1, 1781
John Whitney & Sarah Twitchel of Westboro, June 21, 1781
Josiah Torrey & Lydia Fisk,   June 19, 1781
Elias Fisher & Sible Wood,   Jan. 3, 1781
William Bowing, Jr., of Northbridge & Mary Hath-
 away,   March 27, 1783
Nathan Aldridge of Northbridge & Lucy Clark,
            May 28, 1783
Nahum Wheelock & Betty Steel, both of Mendon,
            Dec. 9, 1783
Elias Brown of Alsted & Rebecca Kyes, Feb. 8, 1784
David Chillson of North Providence & Sarah
 Uiall,   Oct. 3, 1784
Ceasor Tonney, Jr., & Susanna Harry, Dec. 16, 1784
Henderson Walkup & Susanna Condon or Coudon,
            Dec. 30, 1784
James Huzza & Susanna Tobe,   Jan. 20, 1785
Elisha Wood & Mary Warren,   May 26, 1778
Jonathan Warren & Elizabeth Woodward, May 27, 1778
Enoch Batchelor & Jemima Fisk, June 4, 1778
William Putnam & Submit Fisk,   June 25, 1778
Thomas Hayden & Molley Fobes, Sept. 7, 1778
Ichabod Fisher & Rhoda Wood,   Sept. 24, 1778
Nathaniel Paige of Hardwick & Martha Fish, Sept. 4, 1783
Ebenr. Walker, Jr., & Molley Wood, Nov. 6, 1783
Josiah Fisk & Elizabeth Gore,   Nov. 16, 1783
Samuel Fisk, Jr., of Sheburn & Rebecca Fisk, Jan. 23, 1784
Stephen Temple, Jr., & Susannah Wood, Feb. 5, 1784

MARRIAGES.

Ezra Whitney & Mary Forbush, April 29, 1784
Asa Child & Rebecca Taft, Oct. 29, 1784
David Forbush of Grafton & Sarah Temple, Sept. 6, 1785
Samuel Hills of Sterlington (so called) & Abigail
    Child, March 2, 1786
Abner Lazell & Lucretia Temple, April 16, 1786
Elazar Flagg & Patty Parks, April 20, 1786

HARVARD.

June 29, 1732, "Parts of Groton, Lancaster and Stow established as Harvard." Prov. Laws, Vol. II, p. 644. First (Congregational) Church organized 1733. Unitarian, 1733. Baptist, 1776. Officiating clergymen mentioned: Rev. John Seecomb, Rev. Joseph Wheeler, Rev. Daniel Johnson.

Timothy Whitney of Lancaster & Alice Whitney,
    May 20, 1752
Robert Powers of Littleton & Anna Wetherbee,
    May 26, 1752
Aretas Houghton & Anna Rand, June 24, 1752
John Davis, Jr., & Hannah Johnson, Nov. 28, 1752
Oliver Whitney & Abigail Hutchins, Nov. 16, 1752
Joseph Atherton & Sarah Hutchins, Dec. 19, 1752
Stephen Gates & Dinah Meeds, Feb. 5, 1753
Joseph Willard, Jr., & Elisabeth Hapgood, Feb. 14, ——
Jonathan Symonds & Judith Cole, June 14, 1753
Joseph Moffet of Ipswich, Canada, & Dorothy
    Preist of Stow, Aug. 2, 1753
James Read & Ann Conn (?), Aug. 8, 1754
James Burt & Bulah Mead, Dec. 3, 1754
John Pratt & Mary Hall, Oct. 24, 1754
Amos Stone & Adna Hale, Feb. 27, 1754
David Whitney of Harvard & Sarah Hill of Lan-
    caster, Nov. 25, 1753
Samuel Harper & Mary Wheeler, Dec. 16, 1755
Manassah Sawyer & Lydia Fairbank, Feb. 18, 1756
Nathaniel Marble of Stow & Abigail Houghton,
    March 31, 1756
Clark Brown & Lucy Davis of Westford, March 9, 1757
Aaron Rand & Elizabeth Randall of Stow, March 31, 1757

Benjamin Hutchins & Lucy Davis, April 5, 1757
Ephraim Read & Elizabeth Pierce of Groton, May 26, 1756
Peter Atherton, Jr., & Betty Atherton of Bolton,
May 26, 1756
George Pierce of Lincoln & Deborah Tarball, Jan. 17, 1757
Peter Edes of Charlestown & Mrs. Anna Haskell,
Nov. 26, 1762
Tilly White of Lancaster & Ketura Somes, Dec. 15, 1761
Jeremiah Bridge of Lexington & Sarah Buttrick,
March 31, 1761
Ephraim Houghton & Lois Rogers of Boxford, Dec. 31, 1761
John Farwell & Eunice Snow, Jan. 18, 1762
Oliver Wetherbee & Rachel Willard, March 11, 1762
Jonathan Oak & Abigail Read (?), April 26, 1762
Silas Parkhurst of Pepperel & Sarah Atherton, April 29, 1762
Silas Rand & Sarah Farwell of Groton, Feb. 22, 1763
Samuel Fellows, Jr., & Mary Blodget, March 24, 1763
Ephraim Davis & Sarah Farnsworth, Sept. 26, 1763
Joseph Kneeland of Harvard & Abigail Bigelow of
  Stow, Oct. 26, 1763
Abel Farnsworth & Elizabeth Mcfarland, Dec. 6, 1763
Josiah Haskell & Mary Gates, Dec. 15, 1763
Joshua Whitney of Stow & Mrs. Rebecca Whitney,
Jan. 25, 1764
Isaac Gates & Submit Lawrence, Feb. 16, 1764
Paul Fletcher of Groton & Abigail Willard, March 1, 1764
Charles Taylor & Mercy Sterns of Littleton, March 29, 1764
Ephraim Farr of Westminster & Elizabeth Cob-
  leigh of New Braintree, Sept. 8, 1762
Thomas Sawyer of Templeton & Prudence Carter
  of Bolton, Sept. 13, 1762
Oliver Stone & Lucy Willard, Dec. 30, 1762
Elisha Jaickson & Bulah Taylor, both of Westmins-
  ter, Dec. 20, 1763
Josiah Houghton & Abigail Goodfrey, both of Lan-
  caster, Dec. 21, 1763
Samuel Hunt & Lydia Willard, Jan. 19, 1764
Joseph Hurd of Oxford & Mary Livermore of
  Framingham, Dec. 15, 1763

MARRIAGES.

Samuel Cleland of Greenwich & Hannah Hale,
                                            Sept. 17, 1767
Lemuel Farnsworth & Hannah Daby,   Jan. 12, 1768
Jonathan Priest Houghton of Bolton & Sarah Priest,
                                            March 23, 1768
Thomas Parks of Groton & Rosanna Conn,   May 3, 1768
Thomas Willard, Jr., & Sarah Farwell,   May 3, 1768
Joseph Russell of Hatfield & Sarah Russell, July 25, 1768
Moses Richards of Lunenburg & Ruth Willard,
                                            Feb. 18, 1768
Ambrose Hale & Mary Daby,   July 25, 1768
Simon Whitney & Patience Hazeltine,   May 5, 1768
Thomas Gould of Lunenburg & Elisabeth Willard,
                                            April 5, 1768
Timothy Phelps & Sarah Farnsworth,   June 28, 1768
Nahum Daby, Jr., & Susanna Worster,   Oct. 18, 1768
Richard Harris, Jr., & Lydia Atherton,   Dec. 1, 1768
Jonathan Page of Fitchburg & Esther Willard, Feb. 2, 1769
Ebenezer Burges, Jr., & Anna Fairbank,   April 11, 1769
William Miles & Sarah Sanderson,   Aug. 14, 1769
Josiah Wetherbee & Lucy Haskell,   Sept. 27, 1769
Josiah Willard & Eunice Farnsworth,   Nov. 16, 1769
Nathaniel Whittimore & Martha Farnsworth, Nov. 16, 1769
William Farmer & Hannah Holt,   Feb. 22, 1770
Leonard Proctor of Westford & Mary Keep,   Dec. 23, 1769
Abel Whitcomb & Sarah Whitney of Stow,   Dec. 23, 1769
Joshua Holden & Huldah Sampson,   Jan. 23, 1770
Thomas Holt of Lancaster & Dinah Cory,   March 8, 1770
Ezra Atherton & Ann Willard,   March 8, 1770
Nathaniel Hastings & Jemima Bennett,   April 23, 1770
Abram Carlton of Lunenburg & Eunice Willard,
                                            April 30, 1770
Shadrach Hapgood, Jr., & Elizabeth Keep,   July 23, 1770
Samuel Worster & Nancy Wizel,   July 26, 1770
Simon Daby & Judith Lymonds,   July 29, 1770
John Keley, Jr., of Shirley & Molly Park,   Sept. 11, 1770
Oliver Sanderson & Elizabeth Wentworth,   Sept. 11, 1770
Nathan Knight of Stoneham & Susanna Putnam,
                                            Sept. 13, 1770

Jonathan Couch, Jr., & Derothy Law, Oct. 11, 1770
Ephraim Barnard & Hannah Fairbank, Oct. 25, 1770
Gibson Willard & Mary Hall, Oct 25, 1770
John Farwell & Lydia Taylor of Townsend, Dec. 4, 1770
Daniel Zwear (?), Jr., of Lancaster & Abigail (?) Willard, Dec. 6, 1771
Samuel Haskell & Ruth Safford, Dec. 6, 1770
Reuben Wetherbee of Stow & Hannah Burges, Jan. 31, 1771
Phinehas Sawyer & Hannah Whitcombe, Feb 14, 1771
George Leason of Bolton & Bettey Sanderson, Feb. 20, 1771
Joshua Kendal of Lancaster & Dorothy Warner, April 16, 1771
William Henry, Jr., of Lunenburgh & Mary Conn, Dec. 4, 1770
*John Farwell & Lydia Taylor of Townshend, Dec. 4, 1770
Daniel Levear (?), Jr., of Lancaster & Abigail Willard, Dec. 6, 1770
Samuel Haskell & Ruth Saffor, Dec. 6, 1770
Reubin Wetherbe of Stow & Hannah Burges, Jan. 31, 1770
Phinehas Sawyer & Hannah Whitcomb, Feb. 14, 1770
George Leason of Bolton & Betty Sanderson, Feb. 20, 1771
*John Kendall of Lancaster & Dorothy Warner, April 16, 1771
John Mead & Sarah Whitney, Aug. 26, 1771
Samuel Willard & Molley Stearns, Aug. 26, 1771
Jonathan Pierce & Anna Hyle, Sept. 10, 1771
Timothy Coburn of Campdon & Pegg Whittemore, Nov. 12, 1771
Joseph Atherton, Jr., & Hannah Farnsworth, Nov. 24, 1771
Colman Sanderson & Submit Adams, Dec. 5, 1771
Elijah Wiles, Jr., of Shirley & Eunice Saffor, Dec. 26, 1771
Amos Lawrence & Sarah Wetherbe of Littleton, Jan. 22, 1772
John Priest, the 3rd, & Hannah Stow, March 19, 1772
Samuel Garfield & Sarah Cole, March 30, 1772
Israel Whitney & Hannah Mead, May 14, 1772
John Park & Rhode Cooper, May 14, 1772
Jacob Whitney & Lois Hapgood, May 25, 1772
Levi Whitney of Concord & Sarah Lawrence, Sept. 17, 1772

* Record evidently repeated, but with slight alterations not explained.—ED.

MARRIAGES.

Abner Sampson & Lucy Farnsworth, Oct. 20, 1772
Richard Whitney, Jr., & Marcy Willard, Dec. 15, 1772
Francis Wright of Middleton & Anna Harper, Oct. 15, 1771
Nathan Agar of Lancaster & Dinah Sawyer, Sept. 17, 1772
Isaac Holden & Sarah Hale, June 7, 1773
Jonathan Puffer, Jr., & Abigail Fairbanks, May 5, 1774
Hezikiah Whitney & Lucy Pollard, May 5, 1774
Elisha Fullam & Mary Willard, July 27, 1774
John Overlook & Molly Bigelow, both of Ashburnham, Dec. 19, 1774
John Farnworth & Hannah White, March 9, 1773
Samuel Finney & Sibel Wright, March 15, 1773
Isaac Gibson of Fitchburg & Lois Sampson, March 16, 1773
Edmund Farwell of Groton & Mary Russel, July 15, 1773
Aaron Hodgkins of Fitchburg & Phebe Wintworth, July 19, 1773
John Knight & Elizabeth Davis, Aug. 26, 1773
John Richards of Lunenburg & Margaret Conn, Oct. 20, 1773
David Farwell & Hannah Taylor, Nov. 25, 1773
Capt. Josiah Whitney & Sarah Dwelly (?), Feb. 3, 1774
Aaron Whitney & Sally Pollard, April 21, 1774
Solomon Haskell & Betty Davis, April 21, 1774
Ward Safford & Priscilla Randal of Stow, April 26, 1774
Abel Whitcombe & Jemima Keepe, April 28, 1774
Daniel Wetherbee of Stow & Mary Stone, April 28, 1774
Michael Sawtel & Sarah Foster, May 3, 1774
Isaac Whitney of Stow & Lucy Meads, May 12, 1774
Samuel Cooper & Sarah Willard, May 17, 1774
John Hall of Lunenburg & Sarah Willard, July 5, 1774
Wetherbe Whitney & Abigail Warner, July 7, 1774
James Willis & Molly Willard, July 13, 1774
Zachariah Whitney of Fitchburg & Eliza. Wetherbe, Aug. 18, 1774
Simeon Turner & Anna Bridge, Oct. 6, 1774
Benjamin Robbins & Lydia Hale, Oct. 13, 1774
Thomas Atherton of Bolton & Betty Whitney, Dec. 15, 1774
Francis Dickerson of Shelburn & Mary Fairbank, March 13, 1776

James Willis & Alice Adams,	March 14, 1776
Reuben Willard & Catherine Parkhurst,	Jan. 3, 1775
John Burges & Betty Wetherbee of Stow,	March 22, 1775
Elijah Willard & Mary Atherton,	March 30, 1775
Abraham Munroe & Lydia Hapgood,	April 4, 1775
Oliver Gates, Jr., of Stow & Patience Meriam,	Oct. 25, 1775
Joseph Chandler & Elizabeth Dopson,	Nov. 19, 1775
Prince Turner & Rebecca Keep,	Dec. 5, 1775
Thomas Chamberlain & Anna Brown,	Dec. 19, 1775
Josiah Whitney, Jr., & Anna Scollay,	Jan. 10, 1776
Matthias Farnsworth of Groton & Azuba Farnsworth,	Feb. 21, 1776
Philimon Priest & Lois Hartwell,	March 21, 1776
Moses Hale & Molly Hale of Groton,	April 10, 1776
Reuben Grafield & Lydia Symonds,	April 23, 1776
Aaron Warner & Mary Stow,	April 30, 1776
Samuel Barrett, Jr., of Lancaster & Abigail Houghton,	Aug. 7, 1776
Jonathan Adams & Ruth Whitney,	Feb. 19, 1776
Jonathan Davis & Alice Whitney,	Aug. 10, 1777
Francis Farr & Abigail Haskell,	Sept. 14, 1777
Joshua Bowers & Mary Whitney,	Sept. 14, 1777
James Farmer & Deborah Stone,	Nov. 20, 1777
Lemuel Stone & Martha Fullom,	Nov. 20, 1777
Marlbroa Kingman & Sybil Haskell,	Sept. 23, 1777
Gideon Sanderson & Hannah Dodge,	Jan. 11, 1778
Jonathan Symonds & Hannah Clark,	Jan. 23, 1778
Harbour Farnsworth of Groton & Lucy Haild,	March 12, 1778
Phineas Taylor, Jr., of Stow & Sarah Haseltine,	March 19, 1778
Barzillia Willard & Silva Kingman,	March 31, 1778

MARRIAGES.

LEICESTER.

Feb. 15, 1713. Resolve. The petition of those who purchased lands at a place called Towtaid, near Worcester, confirmed, "the town to be named Leicester." First (Congregational) Church organized 1718. Baptist, 1737, at Greenville. Officiating clergymen mentioned: Rev. Benjamin Forster, Rev. Benjamin Conklin.

Joseph Wilson of Leicester & Grace Harrington of Brookfield,	Oct. 8, 1745
Ebenezer Tolman & Ann Wilson,	April 24, 1746
William Breckendridge of Kingston & Agnes Tinkler,	Dec. 11, 1746
Benjamin Willson & Mary Stowers,	July 17, 1748
Benjamin Baldwin & Winified Green,	April 6, 1749
James Graton & Hannah Baldwin,	April 27, 1749
Arther Forbus of Rutland & Ruth Lamon,	June 30, 1749
Oliver Seagur & Lydia Clark,	July 12, 1749
Asa Baldwin & Abigail White,	March 7, 1749
Pliny Lawton & Lucretia Sargent,	June 18, 1750
William Bemis & Rebecah White,	July 5, 1750
Samuel Lynde & Dorcas Smith,	July 5, 1750
Samuel Garfield, Jr., & Phebe Worster,	Aug. 9, 1750
Nathaniel Garfield & Tobitha Newhall,	Aug. 9, 1750
Abell Woodward & Mary Worster,	Dec. 20, 1750
Jonathan Sargeant, Jr., & Mary Earl,	Jan. 24, 1750
Nathan Rice & Mehitabel Baldwin,	April 23, 1751
David Allen & Sarah Barton,	June 6, 1751
Daniel Lynd & Sara Bemus,	June 10, 1751
Benjamin Ellis & Dorcas Smith,	Aug. 1, 1751
John Lamb & Abigail Smith,	April 15, 1752
Daniel Gray of Pelham & Elisabeth Lammond,	Aug. 18, 1752
Benjamin Garfield & Eunice Cooley,	April 2, 1752
John Taylor & Susanna Parsons,	May 28, 1752
George Smith of Rutland & Jane McClewain,	June 9, 1752
Solomon Parsons & Elisabeth Taylor,	Sept. 5, 1752
William Campbell of Volentown & Sarah Barns,	Oct. 1, 1752

LEICESTER. 59

Robert Paul of Union & Elisabeth Watson, Nov. 23, 175–
John Cumings & Rachell Snow, Dec. 14, 1752
Nathaniel Bemis of Leicester & Ruth Harrington
    of Brookfield, Jan. 10, 1753
Nathaniel Sergeant & Ann Garfield, Nov. 15, 1753
Joseph Merrit & Mary Farnsworth, June 25, 1754
Francis Dodge & Deborah Sylvester, Oct. 16, 1754
Oldham Gates & Patience Bartlet, both of Spencer,
    Nov. 20, 1754
Benjamin Green of Leicester & Lucy Marston, of
    Spencer, Dec. 10, 1754
Ephraim Brown of Spencer & Hannah Edmunds
    of Oxford, Feb. 21, 1755
John Lynde & Rebecca Denny, Feb. 4, 1755
Richard Paley of Sudbury & Grace Rice (?), April 16, 1755
Daniel Newell of Leicester & Elizabeth Stebbins
    of Spencer, April 7, 1755
James Harrod & Martha Barney, May 21, 1755
Alexander Kathan & Margaret Beard, Dec. 4, 1755
James Browning of Rutland & Rebecca Scott, Jan. 15, 1756
James Baldwin & Tamah Vinten, Jan. 22, 1756
Thomas Newell, Jr., & Deborah Sargent, July 1, 1756
Nathaniel Wait & Pheebee Read, March 18, 1756
Joseph Bigelow of Framingham & Sarah Stebins,
    April 30, 1756
William Tucker & Anna Thompson, both of Gore,
    Sept. 1, 1756
John Thomas & Susanna Farnsworth, Sept. 16, 1756
Thomas Snow & Thankful Bellows, Oct. 19, 1756
Thomas Parker of Gore & Susanna Thompson of
    Maldin, Dec. 2, 1756
James Call & Hannah Masters, March 8, 1757
Abiather Vinton & Rhoda Wheelock of Gore, April 14, 1757
William Thompson of Holden & Anna Thompson,
    June 23, 1757
John Brown, Jr., & Rebecca Baldwin, July 21, 1757
Elias Bowker & Sarah Harwood, Sept. 13, 1757
William Gillhay (?) & Elisabeth Barns, Sept. 15, 1757
James Carlile of Worcester & Lydia Jackson, Sept. 27, 1757

MARRIAGES.

Samuel Denny & Elizabeth Henshaw (?),	Sept. 29, 1757
Jonathan Stoddard of Spencer & Mary May,	Oct. 25, 1757
Thomas Denny & Mary Storer of Pomfret,	Oct. 21, 1755
Elisha Pratt & Lucy Fletcher,	Feb. 10, 1757
Caleb Dodge & Merriaim Gilbert,	April 4, 1757
Ephraim Rice & Thankful Walker,	April 14, 1757
Jabez Crosby & Mary Hamilton,	June 16, 1757
Israel Richardson & Susanna Forbush,	Nov. 10, 1757
Benjamin Griffen & Hannah Wedge,	Nov. 29, 1757
John Pike & Mehitabel Heyward,	Dec. 11, 1757
Daniel Rolf & Mary Adams,	Nov. 3, 1757
John Hayward & Elizabeth Brooks,	Dec. 29, 1757
Jonas Bemis & Dorothy Wood,	Jan. 5, 1758
Charles Rice & Leah Jenings,	Jan. 6, 1758
Timothy Brooks & Mary Gilbert,	Jan. 12, 1758
Benjamin Merrit & Sarah Blanchard,	Jan. 28, 1758
Joseph Trumble & Lydia Hayward,	June 14, 1758
David Wicker & Ann Davis,	May 1, 1761
Jonas Livermore & Sarah Ward,	Nov. 10, 1761
Benjamin Sanderson, Jr., & Rachell Merritt,	Nov. 12, 1761
Samuel Babbitt of Killingsley & Abigail Goodspeed,	Dec. 3, 1761
James Whitemore & Dorothy Green,	Dec. 31, 1761
Abijah Stowers & Tabitha Hasey,	Jan. 14, 1762
William Hinshaw & Ruth Sergeant,	Feb. 4, 1762
Israel Spraige & Pheebee Hasey,	March 25, 1762
Perley Brow & Elizabeth Wilson,	April 20, 1761
Matthew Watson & Mary Taylor,	April 27, 1762
David Newton of Rutland & Meriam Smith,	May 13, 1762
Amos Wheeler of Worcester & Mary Belcher Henshaw,	May 20, 1762
Robert Converse & Sarah Newton,	May 24, 1762
Richard Southgate, Jr., & Sarah Sprague of Spencer,	June 2, 1762
Joktan Green & Esther Newhall,	May 27, 1762
William Drewry & Mary Shaw, both of Spencer,	June 22, 1762
Benjamin Parsons of Palmer & Elizabeth Stone,	Oct. 26, 1762

Benjamin Baldwin, Jr., & Mary Whitemore, Nov. 10, 1762
Jabez Lewis of Spencer & Rachel Wallis of
    Oxford, Jan. 29, 1763
Daniel Hill & Mary Clark, Sept. 28, 1769
Asa Waite & Zerviah Smith, Oct. 10, 1771
Phinehas Sargeant & Abigail Dunbar, March 20, 1772
William Frink & Sarah Eaton, May 3, 1772
Nathaniel Stearns & Phebe Upham, May 3, 1772
James Blair & Molley Watson, June 2, 1772
Ashbael Johnson & Jael Porter, Oct. 15, 1772
Daniel Lynds & Sarah Newhall, Dec. 3, 1772
Ebenezer Kent, Jr., & Esther Stone, Oct. 29, 1772
Gad Chapin & Sarah Brown, Dec. 31, 1772
Thomas Sawin & Hannah Merritt, Jan. 7, 1773
Ephraim Seager & Katey Sprowl, March 10, 1773
Asa Sprague & Martha Wilson, March 11, 1773
—— Gilbert & Abigail Nickols, both of Brookfield,
    Nov. 10, 1772
Ezra Parker & Mary Cook, both of Worcester,
    Jan. 30, 1768
Thomas Jones & Mary Bemus (?), both of Paxton,
    Nov. 2, 1769
Samuel Mower, Jr., & Nancy Leach, both of
    Worcester, Dec. 30, 1770
Benjamin Dix of Sturbridge & Hannah Sanderson,
    March 11, 1772
John Goodwin & Martha Mower, both of Worcester,
    Feb. 11, 1773
Demon Sheffield & Esther How, both of Worcester,
    March 5, 1773
David Henshaw & Mary Sargeant, Feb. 17, 1774
Frederich Balies & Hannah Brown, April 29, 1773
Richard Gleason & Bulah Swan, Sept. 23, 1773
Jonas Gleason & Lucy Harwood, July 8, 1773
Michael Hatch & Martha Rice, Oct. 13, 1773
David Dunbar & Hannah Hammond, Nov. 16, 1773
Ebenezer Baldwin & Phebe Baldwin, Nov. 26, 1773
Daniel Tenny & Mrs. Molly Bond, March 28, 1781
Francis Choat & Mrs. Betsy Lyon, July 29, 1781

MARRIAGES.

Josiah Blake & Mrs. Judith Lyon,	Sept. 27, 1781
Thomas Waite & Mrs. Hannah Allen,	Oct. 8, 1782
John Green and Mrs. Phebe Brown,	Dec. 15, 1782
George Rogers & Dolle Livermore,	May 23, 1780
Hezikiah Sanderson & Elizabeth Pain,	Aug. 24, 1780
Andrew Scott & Sarah Hinshaw,	Nov. 23, 1780
Nathan Kingsly & Sarah Watson,	March 1, 1781
Livy Chilson & Hannah Warrin,	April 5, 1781
Samuel Sargent & Mary Washburn,	Oct. 11, 1781
Matthew Jackson & Elizabeth Work,	May 3, 1781
Peter Gun & Clove Rod. Revera,	Oct. 24, 1781
Daniel Newell & Esther Warrin,	Jan. 17, 1782
Ebenezer Hastings & Marriah Porter,	Jan. 24, 1782
John Alden & Elizabeth Gleason,	Feb. 27, 1782
James Greaton & Lydia Brown,	Nov. 21, 1782
Thomas Walker Ward & Elizabeth Denny,	Nov. 28, 1782
Thomas Warters & Rachall Commins,	May 28, 1782
Francis Pike & Keziah Morse,	May 30, 1782
Jacob March & Eleanor Moore,	July 4, 1781
Joel Earll & Percis Witt—,	Nov. 28, 1782
James Snow & Lydia Moore,	Jan. 2, 1783
Barnabas Aldrich & Betty Newhall,	March 6, 1783

SPENCER.

April 12, 1753, part of Leicester established as the district of Spencer. Prov. Laws, Vol. III, p. 653. First (Congregational) Church organized 1744. Baptist, 1819, which became extinct 1877.

Joshua Bemis & Sarah White,	Sept. 18, 1755
Samuel Garfield & Abigail Peine of Holden,	May 27, 1756
James Blanchard & Hannah Tucker, both of County Gore,	Dec. 28, 1756
Thomas White & Abigail Muzzy,	Dec. 30, 1756
Jonathan Stoddard & Elizabeth Baldwin of Leicester,	April 10, 1760
Israel Ball & Percis Stone,	April 17, 1760
John Worster, Jr., & Mary Muzzy,	Nov. 20, 1760
David Lamb & Mary How of Rutland,	Dec. 25, 1760

Adam Prouty & Dorothy How of Rutland, Jan. 19, 1761
George Lovell of Sutton & Hannah Roberts, Jan. 21, 1761
Jonathan Lamb & Rebecca Warrin, March 23, 1761
Reuben Morey & Sarah Eustice, both of Charlton,
April 14, 1761
Phineas Slayton of Brookfield & Eleanor Morey of
Charlton, May 14, 1761
Josiah White & Sarah McClure of Brookfield, June 4, 1761
Isaac Bridges & Mary Mixer, Nov. 5, 1761
David Prouty, Jr., & Hannah Ball, Nov. 24, 1761
John Muzzy, Jr., & Mary Ball, Nov. 26, 1761
Richard Bears, Jr., & Hannah Sloper, Feb. 4, 1762
Joseph Gibbs of Brookfield & Anna Clark, June 3, 1762
David Barnes of Leicester & Rebecca Clark, Dec. 23, 1762
James Capen & Sarah Sawen, Dec. 30, 1762
Nathan Hamilton, Jr., of Brookfield & Mary Bemis,
April 21, 1763
John Worster, Jr., & Rebecca White, April 28, 1763
Peter Hawood of Brookfield & Phebe Prouty, May 25, 1763
David Baldwin, Jr., & Sibilah White, June 9, 1763
Obediah Man & Marcy Fisher, July 14, 1763
Robert Morgan, Jr., & Mary Woodard, July 14, 1763
William Patterson of Litchfield & Lydia Thompson
of Leicester, Aug. 30, 1773
Isaac Morgan & Abigail Tucker of Leicester, Sept. 29, 1763
Benjamin Clemens of Charlton & Deborah Woodard,
Jan. 5, 1764
David May & Mary Stoddard of Leicester, April 5, 1764
John Bisco & Deborah Prouty, May 10, 1764
John Stebbins & Olive Muzzy, Oct. 11, 1764
Caleb Bridges, Jr., & Lucy Tucker of Leicester,
Nov. 14, 1764
John Ball & Bulah Whitney, April 14, 1765
David Hammond of Charlton & Rebecca Ormes,
April 23, 1765
Silas Stevens of Brookfield & Lydia Prouty, June 20, 1765
James Prouty & Mary Dunsmore, June 25, 1765
Allen Newhall & Rebecca Bemis. July 2, 1765
Amos Adams & Mary Lynds of Leicester, Feb. 25, 1766

MARRIAGES.

Daniel Henderson of Rutland & Sarah McIntyer,
            Aug. 25, 1766
Robert Nickols of Berkle & Grissel Nickols of Paxton,
            Oct. 23, 1766
Johnson Lynds & Abigail White, May 21, 1767
David Lamb, Jr., & Sarah Clark, Sept. 9, 1767
Ebenezer Smith of Leicester & Anna Rice, Dec. 2, 1767
William Watson & Phebe Garfield, Jan. 14, 1768
Jason Right & Elizabeth Muzzy, Jan. 21, 1768
Thomas Bridge, Jr., & Elizabeth Jones, April 21, 1768
William White & Esther Lynds, May 12, 1768
Benjamin Bemis, Jr., & Rebecca Draper, Nov. 17, 1768
Jeduthen Green & Ruth Slayton of Brookfield,
            Dec. 1, 1768
James Draper, Jr., & Mary Prouty, May 31, 1769
Rev. Benjamin Conklin & Lucretia Lawton, July 26, 1769
Asa Thayer & Martha Morgan, Aug. 28, 1769
James Ormes, Jr., & Sarah Harrington of Brookfield,
            Aug. 31, 1769
Shadrach Pierce & Anna Bridges, Oct. 19, 1769
Jonathan Monrow & Ruth Prouty, Oct. 19, 1769
Ebenezer White, Jr., of Charlton & Christian Adams,
            Feb. 22, 1770
Eleazer Coller & Bulah Smith, March 19, 1770
Israel Morgan & Sarah Jackson, May 24, 1770
David Cranson & Bathsheba Brigs, Dec. 20, 1770
John Draper & Rebecca Muzzy, Dec. 24, 1770
Isaac Rice, Jr., of Sudbury & Sarah Lamb, Jan. 14, 1771
Jonas Muzzy & Sarah Draper, May 2, 1771
Ezekiel Willis & Lucy Woodard, June 17, 1771
Jude Adams of Brookfield & Jemima Adams, Aug. 29, 1771
Zebedee Edminster of Oakham & Mary Bemis,
            Sept. 12, 1771
John Prouty, Jr., & Lucy Gleason, Oct. 13, 1771
Moses Bowen of Sturbridge & Martha Ball, Nov. 21, 1771
Simeon Woods & Mary Muzzy, Dec. 24, 1771
Isaac Prouty, Jr., & Anna Dunnell, Jan. 20, 1772
Daniel Ball, Jr., of Brookfield & Elizabeth Prouty,
            Feb. 6, 1772

Samuel Watson, Jr., of Leicester & Ruth Baldwin,
                                        Jan. 28, 1773
Ephraim Eddy of Brookfield & Esther Smith, Oct. 19, 1773
Thomas Dunbar of Leicester & Lucretia Smith,
                                        Oct. 24, 1773
N. David Lamb & Jemima Rice,   Nov. 6, 1773
John Knap & Asenath Green of Leicester, Nov. 25, 1773
John Prouty & Anna Livermore,   April 5, 1774
Thomas Sprague & Thankful Hatch,   May 3, 1774
William Knight & Beulah Prouty,   July 7, 1774
Timothy Green & Ruth Bemis,   Aug. 25, 1774
Ezra Wilson & Lucy Wilson,   Aug. 30, 1774
Jabez Lamb of Leicester & Sarah Wilson, Aug. 30, 1774
David Baldwin of Leicester & Sarah Tucker, Sept. 22, 1774
Jacob Prouty, Jr., & Rachel Eddy,   Sept. 29, 1774
Samuel Garfield, Jr., & Phebe Rice,   Oct. 4, 1774
John Dunn of Northbridge & Elizabeth Sinclair,
                                        Oct. 6, 1774
Benjamin Hayward of Holden & Sarah Prouty,
                                        Dec. 29, 1774
Jonathan Warren of Leicester & Martha Bemis, Jan. 3, 1775
Benjamin Prouty & Sarah Green,   Jan. 10, 1775
Asa Whittemore & Lucy Muzzy,   March 2, 1775
David Bent of Rutland & Phebe Whittemore of
    Paxton,   April 26, 1775
James Lamb & Sarah Knap,   May 4, 1775
Ephraim Morey of Charlton & Katharine Munye,
                                        Feb. 1, 1776
Nathaniel Thomas Loving & Sarah Watson of
    Leicester,   Aug. 8, 1776
John Southgate & Eleanor Sargent, both of Leicester,
                                        Oct. 10, 1776
Reuben Bemis & Abigail Smith of Charlton, Dec. 26, 1776
Abel Wheeler & Lydia Wilson,   Jan. 2, 1777
Elijah Blood & Eunice Haman,   Jan. 3, 1777
Amasa Bemis & Persis Bemis,   Aug. 19, 1777
Luther Rich of Brookfield & Mary Jones, Nov. 9, 1777
Ebenezer Sanderson of Leicester & Abigal Upham,
                                        Dec. 4, 1777

MARRIAGES.

Samuel Newton of Winchendon & Martha Davidson of Charlton, Dec. 22, 1777
Jonathan Curtis of Charlton & Dolly Wilson, Jan. 15, 1778
Charles Morey & Phebe Blanchard, both of Charlton, Jan. 29, 1778
Saul & Dinah, (negro servants belonging to John Sumner, Esq.), Feb. 19, 1778
Deacon John Muzzy & Eleaner Snow, May 15, 1778
Edmund Bridges & Ruth Parks, May 15, 1778
Jones Muzzy & Abigail Lamb, June 9, 1778
Samuel Ryan & Mary Stoddard, June 18, 1778
Reuben Bemis & Sibbilah Bemis, Aug. 27, 1778
Jabez Hamilton of Brookfield & Abigail Willson, Oct. 1, 1778
Barnard Bemis & Sarah Whittemore, Nov. 10, 1778
Peter Rice & Olive Baldwin, Nov. 12, 1778
Isaac Prouty, 3d, & Molly Watson of Leicester, Dec. 10, 1778
Reuben Whittemore & Abigail Watson, March 2, 1779
Abial Hatch of Hanover & Deborah Parker, April 1, 1779
James Sprague & Chloe Baldwin, May 4, 1779
Jethro Kinney of Murryfield & Ruth Jackson, May 26, 1779
Joseph Wheet & Anna Mercy, Oct. 21, 1779
Nathan Wright & Mary Whittemore, Oct. 26, 1779
Noah Furbush of Brookfield & Mehitabel Draper, Nov. 9, 1779
Noah Woodward & Betty Jackson, Dec. 9, 1779
Ebenezer Warran of Leicester & Pheba Garfield, March 30, 1780
John Graham & Olive Prouty, May 30, 1780
Jesse Smith of Charlton & Sarah Bemis, June 8, 1780
Sylvanus Gats & Elizabeth Graham, April 4, 1780
Elisha Whitney & Esther Clark, Feb. 20, 1783
Isaac Morgan, Jr., & Sarah Cowel, Feb. 27, 1783
Simeon Perry of Fitzwilliam & Hannah Barns, April 20, 1783
Isaac Cutler of Brookfield & Susanna Watson, June 17, 1783
Eli Whittemore & Lucy Prouty, July 24, 1783
David Corey of Sturbridge & Abigail Adams, Nov, 20, 1783
Nathaniel Lamb & Rebecca Prouty, Nov. 20, 1783.

James Biglow & Mary Graham, Dec. 18, 1783
Nathan Esterbrooks of Putney & Mary Upham,
Dec. 25, 1783
John Smith of Paxton & Persis Hunt, Jan. 8, 1784
Kerly How & Abiah Howland. Jan. 15, 1784
William Hiscock of Westfield & Susanna Whitney,
Feb. 5, 1784
Alexander Dean of Oakham & Sage Prouty, March 18, 1784
Buckminster White & Mercy Prouty, April 8, 1784
David Stow & Sarah Prouty, both of Ward, April 12, 1784
John Woodard, 3d, & Sarah Drury, May 5, 1784
John Lamb, Jr., & Abigail Prouty, July 1, 1784
Nathan Prouty & Patience Convers, Sept. 30, 1784
Isaac Coman & Dinah Rice, Nov. 22, 1784
Abner Snow of Leicester & Hannah Watson of
Brookfield, Nov. 25, 1784
Benjamin Gleason & Sarah Underwood, Feb. 24, 1785
Jesse Graham & Anna Parker, May 12, 1785
Hezekiah Saunderson of Westminster & Lucy
Upham, May 26, 1785
Ephraim Adams of Brookfield & Sibillah Bemiss.
June 26, 1785
Silvester Bemiss of Brookfield & Molly Bemiss,
June 26, 1785
Benja. Green & Martha Watson, June 26, 1785
Asa Draper & Routh Whittemore, July 7, 1785
Joseph Chadwick of Oakham & Elizabeth Willson
of Berri, July 19, 1785
John Pike & Ruth Bemiss, both of Paxton, April 7, 1785
James Capen & Susannah Drury of Brookfield, May 5, 1785

HOLDEN.

Jan. 9, 1741, part of Worcester, called North Worcester, established as Holden. Prov. Laws, Vol. II, p. 1043. First (Congregational) Church organized 1742. Baptist, 1806. Officiating clergyman mentioned: Rev. Joseph Avery.

Nathan Whitney of Stow & Tabitha Bennet of Holden,	Jan. 22, 1752
Thomas Stevens & Martha Rogers,	March 24, 1753
Samuel Nichols & Anne Stevens,	Feb. 5, 1755
David Lynde of Leicester & Jerusha Peirce,	Feb. 6, 1755
Jonathan Lovell of Holden & Mrs. Rachel How of Worcester,	May 18, 1756
Thomas Dryden & Lydia Ward,	June 17, 1756
Jonathan Wheeler, Jr., & Lydia Fletcher,	April 13, 1763
John Willington of Worcester & Priscilla Heard,	June 2, 1763
Elijah Demons of Brookfield & Lucy How of Rutland,	Sept. 8, 1763
Thomas Perkins of Middleboro & Esther Thompson,	Jan. 17, 1764
Isaac Cutting & Abigail Flagg,	Sept. 1, 1764
Ebenezer Belknap & Silence Winch of Shrewsbury,	Oct. 27, 1764
Samuel Bigelo & Elizabeth Hubburd,	Jan. 1, 1765
Ephraim Smith of Worcester & Ruth How,	Jan. 17, 1765
Wm. Hartwell of Rutland & Mary Lovell,	July 4, 1765
Josiah Stratton of Brookfield & Mary Davis,	Oct. 31, 1765
Israel Davis, Jr., & Rebecca Hubbard,	Jan. 16, 1766
John Stone, Esq., of Rutland & Mrs. Mary Brown,	Dec. 4, 1766
Bartholomew Sterns of Worcester & Mary Raymond,	Feb. 25, 1767
Nathaniel Felch & Hannah How of Northboro,	June 24, 1767
William Boyd of Grafton & Dinah Marshall,	April 26, 1770
Elisha Hubbard & Mercy Hubbard,	Dec. 3, 1767
William Dods & Annah Child,	April 10, 1768
William Raymond, Jr., & Eunice Glazier of Shrewsbury,	April 19, 1768

Jonathan Lovell, Jr., & Marcy Raymond, Aug. 25, 1768
Dr. Isaac Chenery & Mrs. Susannah Peirce of Worcester, Sept. 15, 1768
Joseph Morss & Lucy Whittemore, Sept. 27, 1768
James Winch & Sarah Greenwood, Oct. 10, 1769
John Black & Hannah Davis, Dec. 21, 1769
Ephraim Miller of Worcester & Mary Flagg, Feb. 20, 1770
Paul Goodale & Eunice Lovell, March 20, 1770
John Wheaton of Leicester & Phebe Hubbard, June 14, 1770
Jotham How of Worcester & Dorothy Smith, July 2, 1770
Willoughby Prescott of Concord & Elizabeth Haywood, Oct. 11, 1770
Isaiah Brown & Phebe How of Princetown, Nov. 8, 1770
David Livermore of Leicester & Anna Howard, March 14, 1771
Micah Sprout & Lydia Warner, Oct. 10, 1771
Martin Holt & Abigail Wheeler. Feb. 13, 1772
Moses Wheeler, Jr., & Anna Fisk, Jan. 31, 1775
Josiah Cheney, Jr., & Lydia Gleason, April 4, 1775
Dr. David Fisk & Elizabeth Chickering, May 11, 1775
Hezekiah Walker & Lucy Raymond, May 16, 1775
Jacob Black & Mrs. (?) Abigail Flagg, Sept. 22, 1776
Joshua Gale & Mrs. (?) Molly Hubbard, Oct. 10, 1776
Paul Davis & Lydia Black, Nov. 14, 1776
Simeon Stickney & Zerviah Rice, Dec. 12, 1776
John Dodds & Hannah Morse, Feb. 6, 1777
John McMullen & Mary Smith, March 5, 1777
James Davis & Eunice Newton of Paxton, April 25, 1777
Aaron Glazier & Orpha Cutting, both of Lancaster, Dec. 25, 1776
Simeon Snow & Esther Smith of Lexington, Jan. 8, 1777
Moses Ball & Vasliti Oaks, March 6, 1777
Valentine Harris & Sarah Heywood, Sept. 17, 1777
Joseph Fletcher & Mary Crosby, Jan. 15, 1778
Nathan Wheeler & Rachel Flagg, March 10, 1778
Ebenezer Barber & Mary Fletcher, April 9, 1778
Edmund Davis & Eunice Hubbard, June 2, 1778
Hosia Brigham & Cate Davis, Sept. 17, 1778
Jabez Metcalf & Hannah Marshal, Feb. 4, 1779

MARRIAGES.

John Foster & Lydia Harrington,	March 11, 1779
James Lamb & Hannah Heywood,	June 13, 1779
Robert Earll & Abigail Harr—ton,	June 22, 1779
Thomas Craige & Katharine Bennett,	July 13, 1779
Abiel Buttrick & Mrs. Eunice Heywood,	Aug. 19, 1779
Jonathan Fisk & Mrs. Zerviah How,	March 12, 1778
Ephraim Bayley & Mrs. Sopha Glazier,	May 6, 1778
John Bennet of Shrewsbury & Mrs. Lucretia Rice of Lancaster,	May 7, 1778
Zedikiah Belknap of Worcester & Elizabeth Wait of Ward,	Sept. 8, 1778
Abel Biglow & Martha Biglow, both of Shrewsbury,	Oct. 1, 1778
Oliver Hale of Marlboro & Dorcas Bennet of Shrewsbury,	Oct. 1, 1778
Silas Cutting & Lucy Cutting, both of Shrewsbury,	May 20, 1779
Ebenezer Glazier & Martha Potter,	June 2, 1779
Zachriah Partridge & Marcy Whitney,	Aug. 4, 1779
Luke Reed & Martha Floyd, both of Shrewsbury,	Aug. 11, 1779
John Mellen & Lucy Kendal, both of Lancaster,	July 13, 1780
Benjamin Rice & Abigail Smith, both of Barre,	Aug. 31, 1780
Gardner Godard of Oakham & Sophia Rice of Rutland,	Dec. 11, 1782
Solomon Davis & Dorcas Glezen,	Nov. 24, 1779
Samuel Chaffin, Jr., & Abigail Hemmenway,	Dec. 9, 1779
Daniel Sergeant & Mary Lycett,	Feb. 10, 1780
Daniel Black, Jr., & Esther Davis,	Feb. 24, 1780
William Parker of Winchendon & Mary Gale,	June 1, 1780
Judah Mayo & Sarah Fuller,	Aug. 3, 1780
Jacob Gray of Pelham & Jennet Smith,	Sept. 26, 1780
Paul Raymond, Jr., & Sarah Gale,	Nov. 21, 1780
John Perry, Jr., & Tabitha Raymond,	Jan. 16, 1781
John Blair of Rutland & Eunie Harrington,	Nov. 30, 1780
John Forbes of Rutland & Elizabeth Heywood,	Jan 28, 1781
Artemas Dryden & Susannah Perry,	April 5, 1781

Gershom Stow of Northboro & Levinah Bartlett,
                                        Sept. 24, 1781
Jonathan Moore & Patty Goulding,   Oct. 2, 1781
Joshua Hemenway & Miliscent Eaton,   Dec. 7, 1781
William McMullen of Pelham & Hannah Smith,
                                        May 15, 1782
Jude Williams & Dorothy Davis,   Aug. 14, 1782
Lemuel Heywood & Lucy Heywood,   March 7, 1782
William Flagg, Jr., & Abigail Black,   May 2, 1782
Timothy Marshal & Lucy Robinson,   May 9, 1782
John How of Paxton & Lucy Hubbard,   June 13, 1782
Thomas Davis & Lettice Rice,   July 18, 1782
David Fisk, Jr., & Naomi Winch,   July 11, 1782
John Williams & Sarah Davis,   Sept. 2, 1782
Abner Rogers & Dorothy Nichols,   Sept. 29, 1782
Jonathan Lovel & Hopestill Taft of Mendon, Jan. 1, 1783
William Heard & Betsey Dix,   Jan. 16, 1783
Samuel Rowe & Submit Rice,   Feb. 13, 1783
David Gray of White Creek & Sarah Smith, Feb. 27, 1783
Israel Johnstone Mills of Groton & Mary Frost of
    Rutland,   March 27, 1783
Charles Rozer of Rutland & Mary Smith,   April 7, 1783
Sol. Clark Chany & Molly Estabrooks,   May 6, 1783
Abel Marshal & Lydia Driden,   May 15, 1783
Isaac Smith of Westmoreland, N. H., & Prudence Cut-
    ting of Shrewsbury,   Nov. 20, 1783
Samuel Herring and Ruth Stratton,   Jan. 18, 1784
James Young & Mary Moore,   April 21, 1785
Phinehas Bartlett & Rosinah Harris, both of Worces-
    ter,   Nov. 22, 1785
Reuben Knight & Hannah Allen, both of Worcester,
                                        Nov. 24, 1785
Jonathan Flagg & Mitty Gay,   May 29, 1783
Rufus Forbush of Westboro & Mary Brown, June 12, 1783
Ezra Rice & Rebecca Gardener,   July 24, 1783
Robert Blair of Worcester & Betsey Harrington,
                                        Dec. 11, 1783
Jonas Reed of Rutland & Elizabeth Wilson, Jan. 8, 1784
Nathan Turner of Walpole & Lucy Johnstone, Jan. 14, 1784

MARRIAGES.

Tilla Hubbard & Anna Joslyn,	Jan. 15, 1784
Simon Davis of Princetown & Lucretia Davis,	March 25, 1784
Samuel Heyward, Jr., & Ruth Melvin,	April 22, 1784
Noah Harrington, Jr., & Elizabeth Davis,	April 29, 1784
John Rice Goulding & Ruth Webb,	June 10, 1784
Samuel Hubbard, Jr., & Lucy Wheeler,	Aug. 5, 1784
Thomas White, Jr., of Spencer & Hannah Estabrook,	Sept. 2, 1784
Ebenezer Glazier of Sterling & Lois Edgel,	Sept. 2, 1784
Abel Hubbard & Lucy Tainter of Hubbardston,	Dec. 28, 1784
Benjamin Andrews & Sarah Blair, both of Worcester,	Feb. 10, 1785
Jonathan Rogers & Phebe Sheppard,	May 12, 1785
Nahum Fisk & Sally Gay,	July 7, 1784
Thomas Wheeler & Hannah Grant,	Nov. 24, 1784
John Rice & Elizabeth Flagg,	Dec. 13, 1784
Jason Glezen & Elizabeth Goulding,	Dec. 15, 1784
Tilla Chaffin & Hannah Mirick,	Dec. 15, 1784
Moses Smith & Dorcas Gould, both of Worcester,	June 2, 1784
James Blake & Rebecca Cunningham, both of Worcester,	July 14, 1784
Joel Flagg & Betta Smith, both of Worcester,	Nov. 17, 1784
Aaron Smith of Worcester & Huldah Webb,	Nov. 25, 1784
Nicholas Powers & Sarah Knight,	Feb. 11, 1787
Stephen Cree & Mrs. Hannah Smith,	Feb. 27, 1787

SOUTHBOROUGH.

July 6, 1727, part of Marlborough established as Southborough. Prov. Laws, Vol. II, p. 428. First (Baptist) Church organized at Fayville 1825. Congregational, 1831. An old Unitarian church extinct. Officiating clergyman mentioned: Rev. Nathan Stone.

Joel Mathews & Abigail ———,	Nov. 22, 1752
Joseph Morse & Joannah Newton,	Jan. 3, 1753
Abraham Bond & Submitt Joslin,	April 5, 1753
Benoni Shertliff & Submit Pike,	July 23, 1753
Thomas Whitney & Ann Gould,	April 3, 1753

Ebenezer Dunton & Lydia Bellows,	Aug. 6, 1753
Ebenezer Walker & Sarah Fisk,	Dec. 17, 1754
Francis Nelson & Hannah Tyler,	Feb. 4, 1755
Daniel Wood & Rachel Aldrich,	April 1, 1755
Nathan Bridges & Sarah Parker,	Feb. 4, 1755
Timothy Peine & Abigail Knap,	March 27, 1755
Benjamin Parker & Thankful Fay,	May 27, 1755
John Hyscom (?) & Rachell Hudson,	Nov. 27, 1755
Robert Spaulding & Hasadiak Johnson,	June 4, 1755
Edward Newton & Silence (?) Bartlet,	June 5, 1755
Benjamin Mixer & Dinah Newton,	July 8, 1755
David Newton & Abigail Lawrence,	July 30, 1755
Aaron Fay & Eunice Farr,	Oct. 8, 1755
Jona Clemens & Hannah More,	Oct. 13, 1755
Hannaniah Parker & Abigail Ward,	Dec. 2, 1755
Edward Bingham & Sarah Lyscom,	Nov. 2, 1757
Nehemiah Newton & Elizabeth Morse,	Feb. 2, 1758
Josiah Fay & Mary Bent,	March 22, 1758
Reuben Cumings & Elizabeth Butler,	Nov. 30, 1756
Ebenezer Chamberlain & Joana Morse,	Dec. 23, 1756
Amos Newton & Phebee Johnson,	Dec. 29, 1756
Joseph Newton & Experience Drury,	Dec. 29, 1756
Nathan Newton & Lydia Hagor,	Jan. 13, 1757
William Richards & Sarah Bixby,	Feb. 16, 1757
Nathan Bridge & Tamar Hutson (?),	March 23, 1757
Thomas Witherbee & Anna Berry,	April 14, 1757
Edmund Brigham & Sarah Lyscom,	Nov. 2, 1757
Nehemiah Newton & Mary Morss,	Feb. 2, 1758
Joshua Fay & Mary Bent,	March 22, 1758
Daniel Newhall & Sarah Mixor,	Feb. 3, 1761
Joshua Newton & Mary Bellows,	March 11, 1761
Henry Balcom & Kezia Stow,	April 29, 1761
Elisha Bruce & Easther Buck,	May 4, 1762
Robert Fay & Anna Harrington,	May 19, 1761
Joel (?) Newton & Lydia Beary,	June 3, 1762
Charles Newton and Eunice Bellows,	July 22, 1762
Jonas Bali & Molle Taylor,	Dec. 6, 1762
Daniel Gregory & Pierces Newton,	Jan. 6, 1763
Peter Joslyn & Thankfull Mathew,	April 18, 1763

MARRIAGES.

Aaron Hardy & Lydia Ward,	May 4, 1763
Jonathan Cliford & Mary Bridges,	Nov. 26, 1778
Bezaleel Walker & Huldah Newton,	Dec. 3, 1778
John Phillips & Huldah Amsden,	April 6, 1778
Ezek'l Newton & Sarah Whiteing,	May 19, 1779
David Newton, Jr., & Elizabeth Newton,	Dec. 7, 1779
Timothy Chase & Sarah Newton,	March 2, 1780
Jona. Nurse & Thankful Newton,	July 6, 1780
Jotham Bellows & Abigail Bellows,	July 27, 1780
Peter Fay & Eunice Matthews,	Oct. 31, 1780
Timothy Bellows & Hannah Bellows,	Nov. 15, 1780
Silas Ball & Katharine Newton,	Feb. 1, 1781
William Onthank, Jr., & Mitle (?) Newton,	Feb. 14, 1781
Andrew Adams & Molly Morse,	Jan. 4, 1780
Francis Fay & Lovisa Ball,	Feb. 22, 1781
Daniel Graves & Rhoda Fay,	May 31, 1781
Isaac Newton & Molly Bruce,	Sept. 20, 1781
James Onthank & Elizabeth Newton,	Oct. 18, 1781
Sylvanus Reed & Caroline Taylor,	Oct. 31, 1781
James Onthank & Elizabeth Newton,	Oct. 18, 1781
Sylvanus Reed & Caroline Taylor,	Oct. 31, 1781
Hezekiah Johnson & Rebecca Newton,	March 19, 1782
Joel Lee & Molly Newton,	March 21, 1782
Peter Stone & Batsee Eastabrook,	May 26, 1782
David Gardner & Lovina Wetherbee,	May 1, 1782
Joseph Graves & Zerviah Williams,	June 7, 1782
Silas Newton & Lovina Newton,	Aug. 15, 1782
Luke Newton & Sally Hayden,	Nov. 21, 1782
Benjamin Collins & Rebecca More,	Nov. 28, 1782
Elijah Snow & Abigail Hopping,	Dec. 17, 1782
Erasmus Ward & Hannah Chamberlain,	Dec. 24, 1782
Seth Newton & Patience Hervey,	Feb. 6, 1783

GRAFTON.

April 18, 1735, the plantation of Hassanamisco established as Grafton. Prov. Laws, Vol II, p. 743. First (Congregational) Church organized 1731. Baptist, 1830. An old Baptist church extinct. Officiating clergyman mentioned: Rev. Aaron Hutchinson.

Joshua Winchester & Mary Whipple, Dec. 6, 1750
Moses Haven of Framingham & Anna Stow, May 23, 1751
Samuel Chase, Jr., of Sutton & Silence Stow, May 29, 1751
Eliphalet Wood of Littleton & Abigail Child, Nov. 7, 1751
Peter Brooks & Rebekah Ball, Jan. 8, 1752
Jacob Steven & Martha Sherman, Feb. 16, 1752
Phinehas Leland & Sarah Warren, May 12, 1750
Thomas Deny (?) of Leicester & Tabitha Cuttler,
June 25, 1752
William Anthony (negro) & Abigail Abraham (Indian), Nov. 14, 1752
William Gibson of Pelham & Martha Ware, Dec. 19, 1752
Joshua Biglow of Sutton & Elis Stimpson (?), June 28, 1753
Jonathan Marble & Anna Sheapcott, Oct. 4, 1753
Daniel Axtell of Hopkinton & Elisabeth Whitmore,
Nov. 12, 1754
Sampson Abram & Elisabeth Abram, May 30, 1756
Fortune Barun (?) (negro) & Abigail Anthony (Indian), Jan. 27, 1757
Benjamin Wheelock of Mendon & Hannah Chapin,
June 4, 1752
John Gould & Lucy Brooks, Feb. 22, 1753
Aaron Kimball & Mary Brooks, April 5, 1753
William Holbrook & Sarah Batchellor, May 15, 1753
Nathan Whitney of Spencer & Abigail Marstass (?),
Feb. 20, 1754
David Haron of Framingham & Jerusha Whiple,
Nov. 28, 1754
Deacon Joseph Meriam & Hannah Wadsworth,
Dec. 26, 1754
Josiah Child & Elisabeth Ball, April 24, 1755

MARRIAGES.

John Stow & Hannah Ball,	May 22, 1755
Joseph Arnold & Abigail Newton,	Oct. 9, 1755
Joseph Winchester & Lucy Harrington,	April 15, 1756
Mark Collins of Southboro & Hepzibah Hardy,	July 6, 1756
Joseph Temple (?) & Mary Whitmore,	Oct. 28, 1756
Daniel Godard of Shrewsbury & Mary Willard,	Nov. 17, 1756
Elisha Brigham & Sarah Roberts,	Dec. 30, 1756
John Wesson & Rebona Davis,	Aug. 24, 1757
Isaac Harrington, Jr., & Hannah Whiple,	Aug. 25, 1757
Jonathan Hall & Mary Stow,	Jan. 19, 1758
James McClallan of Sutton & Sarah Axtell,	Feb. 2, 1758
Ebenezer Maynard of Westboro & Sarah Brigham,	March 19, 1776
Samuel Abbee of Catham, Conn., & Sarah Leland,	April 4, 1776
Thomas Griggs of Sutton & Mary Goddard,	July 4, 1776
Daniel Whipple & Martha Adams,	August 7, 1776
William Collens & Lydia David, both of New Braintree,	Oct. 27, 1776
Simon Willard & Hannah Willard,	Nov. 29, 1776
Livi Leland & Anna How,	March 13, 1777
Elijah Stanton & Hannah Leland,	March 13, 1777
Jonah Goulding & Grace Knowlton of Shrewsbury,	April, 1777
Thomas Axtell, Jr., & Deborah Jones,	June 10, 1777
Eleazer Leland of Croyden & Elizabeth Sherman,	June 30, 1777
William Town of Royalston & Sarah Sherman,	Oct. 13, 1777
Jonathan Melven of Conway & Beulah Leland,	Nov. 12, 1777
Joseph Wood, Jr., & Martha Willard,	Dec. 25, 1777
Jonathan Robinson & Sarah Taylor,	Jan 29, 1778
Elijah Bruce & Eunice Rice,	Jan. 30, 1778
Jonathan Wheeler & Marcy Rawson,	Feb. 12, 1778
James Wheeler & Vashti Biglow,	Feb. 26, 1778
David Forbush, Jr., & Deliverance Goodell,	March 20, 1778
Philemon Stacey & Mary Fairbanks,	June 2, 1778

William Walker & Lucy Sadler, June 8, 1778
Ebenezer Leland & Molly Lyon, June 25, 1778
Abner Stow, Jr., & Eunice Gooldsbury of Warwick,
July 2, 1778
Forten Burnee (negro man) & Phillis (a negro woman) of Mendon, July 31, 1778
Thomas Leland of Sutton & Anna Bachellor Rawson,
Aug. 21, 1778
Ephraim Whitney, Jr., of Upton & Jemima Whipple,
Oct. 1, 1778
Nathaniel Batchelor & Betty Wait, Oct. 8, 1778
Gershom Chapin of Uxbridge & Mary Sherman,
Nov. 5, 1778
David W. Leland & Mary Rawson, Jan. 21, 1779
Ebenezer Lyon & Matilda Boon, March 30, 1779
Reuben Hoit of New Braintree & Lucy Stow, June 20, 1779
Daniel Prentice & Abigail Stanley of Medford, July 18, 1779
Rev. Joseph Farrer & Mrs. Mary Brooks, July 20, 1779
Joel Brooks & widow Mary Hall, Aug. 23, 1779
John Carlyl & Eunice Willard, Oct. 3, 1779
Daniel Robbins of Westboro & Martha Miller, Nov. 25, 1779
Samuel Richards of Watertown & Phebe Willard,
March 9, 1780
Thaddeus Reed of Uxbridge & Hannah Taylor,
May 24, 1780
John Robert & Tabitha Leland, July 6, 1780
Enoch Forbush of Upton & Mary Batchelor, Sept. 14, 1780
Cyrus French & Susannah Harrington, Oct. 4, 1780
Thomas Leland & Lydia Sherman, Oct. 11, 1780
Jonathan Hall & Mary Kimball, Oct. 12, 1780
Levi Leland & Sarah Wooddy of Sutton, Oct. 12, 1780
Simon Wait & Marcy Flagg, Nov. 28, 1780
Paul Warfield & Elizabeth Taylor, Dec 11, 1780
James Putnam & Elizabeth Willard, Dec. 28, 1780
Benjamin White & Hadassah Esther Prentice,
March 5, 1781
Daniel Rand & Abigail Rockwood, June 21, 1781
Eliphalet Smith & Beriah Leland, June 28, 1781
Nathaniel Balch Dexter & Lucy Willard, July 26, 1781

MARRIAGES.

Joshua Turner & Lydia Drury,	Aug. 22, 1781
Comfort Chaffee & Lucy Hoit,	Sept. 25, 1781
Benjamin Perham of Upton & Azubah Sadler,	Oct. 4, 1781
Truman Clark & Anna Braman,	Oct. 8, 1781
Aaron Kimball, Jr., & Molly Goulding,	Oct. 18, 1781
Christian Ehlich & Meriam Flagg,	Oct. 22, 1781
Forten Burnee & Sarah Hector of Sutton (negroes),	Nov. 8, 1781
David Temple of Marlboro & Rebecca Brooks,	March 14, 1782
Thomas Fay of Westboro & Mime Garfield,	March 29, 1782
Zebulon Daniels & Sarah Brigham,	April 18, 1782
Moses Harrington, Jr., & Hannah Prentice,	May 7, 1782
Isaiah Fairbanks & Molly Goodell,	Nov. 28, 1782
Eliphalet Smith & Betty Brown,	April 14, 1783
Elijah Brooks & Mary Hall,	Dec. 25, 1783
Robert Taft of Upton & Rhoda Rockwood,	Jan. 8, 1784
Ezekiel Brigham, Jr., & Patience Gowing,	Feb. 5, 1784
Nathaniel Adams & Mary Harrington,	Feb. 8, 1784
Josiah Holbrook & Mary Sherman,	Feb. 26, 1784
Jonathan Furbush & Betty Hayden,	Nov. 5, 1782
Noah B. Kimball & Molly Chase,	Dec. 12, 1782
Moses Marsh & Betty Lyon,	Dec. 12, 1783

SHREWSBURY.

Dec. 6, 1720. Resolve. A committee is paid for "running the lines of Whitehall Farm and Shrewsbury," which service they performed in July, 1717. First (Congregational) Church organized 1723. An old Baptist church extinct. Officiating clergymen mentioned: Rev. Ebenezer Morse, Rev. Job Cushing, Rev. Joseph Sumner.

Jonathan Keyes, Jr., & Sarah Taylor,	Jan. 23, 1752
Micah Pratt & Dinah Cutting,	May 18, 1752
Samuel Stearns of Grafton & Jemima Hoyt,	Aug. 19, 1752
Ephraim Pratt, Jr., & Abiel Leland,	Oct. 10, 1752
Jotham How & Priscilla Rice,	Jan. 3, 1753
Abiel Bragg & Abigail Wilson,	Jan. 29, 1753
Samuel Hibbert & Mary Collar,	Feb. 6, 1753
Asa Bouker & Hannah Crosby,	Jan. 3, 1753

Jason Parmenter of Neshawagg & Abigail Frissell,
                                            March 7, 1753
Daniel Hastings, Jr., & Priscilla Keyes,   Aug. 16, 1753
Jonathan Wheelock & Anna Drury,   June 20, 1753
Nathaniel Whittemore & Sarah Rice,   Aug. 17, 1753
Stephen Choat & Bathsheba Newton,   March 27, 1754
John Baker, Jr., & Persis Wheeler,   June 11, 1754
Bezaleel Maynard & Elizabeth Keyes,   Feb. 28, 1754
William Chestnut & Huldah Maynard,   Nov. 4, 1754
Benjamin Wilson of Gardiners Farm & Sarah Sawyer,
                                            July 4, 1754
Isaac Drury & Lois Muzzy,   Dec. 25, 1754
Jasper Stone & Grace Goddard,   April 17, 1755
Aaron Smith & Dinah Wheeler,   Aug. 4, 1757
Stephen Hastings & Martha Walker,   June 16, 1757
Ephraim Allen of Rutland & Huldah Chestnuts,
                                            July 12, 1757
Samuel Hastings & Anna Biglo,   Oct. 26, 1757
William Crawford of S. & Mary Dunsmore of Lan-
    caster,   Feb. 26, 1758
Ep. Temple & Mary (?) Frarrow (?),   March 7, 1758
Ebenezer Pike of S. & Lydia Glaris (?) of Lancaster,
                                            March 21, 1758
Cyprian Roys (?), Jr., & Martha Bush,   Jan. 27, 1756
Jonas Temple & Olive Keyes,   March 22, 1756
Jacob Hind & Triphena Roys (?),   Nov. 24, 1756
Josiah Wood of Upton & Ziporah Wheelock of Mendon,
                                            Feb. 3, 1757
Solomon Biglo & Sarah Newton,   March 4, 1762
Levi Goodanow & Melicent Keyes,   June 8, 1762
Seth Heyward and Martha Temple,   Aug. 24, 1762
Joseph Arnold & Lydia Fay,   Dec. 10, 1762
Eli Keyes, Jr., & Hannah How,   April 1, 1762
John Britain & Esthar Newton,   April 14, 1762
Solomon Newton & Hannah Hastings,   May 18, 1762
John Hastings & Betty How,   May 25, 1762
Artemas Maynard & Miriam Keyes,   May 27, 1762
Asaph Sherman & Lucy Whitney,   July 14, 1762
Constantine Hardy & Jemima Brigham,   Jan. 25, 1763

MARRIAGES.

Timothy Newton & Huldah Wheelock,	Feb. 10, 1763
Silas Cook of Norton & Elizabeth Nixon,	April 1, 1763
Elisha Ward & Mary Baldwin,	April 7, 1763
Ezra Baker & Hannah Warrin, both of Westboro,	June 23, 1763
James Goodnough & Elizabeth Crosset,	July 4, 1763
Asa Rice & Miriam Wheeler,	July 25, 1763
Lemuel Rice & Abigail Lynds,	Sept. 15, 1763
Paul Johnson & Hannah Olds, both of Westboro,	Dec. 7, 1763
Jedidiah Tucker & Lucy Mixer,	Oct. 4, 1763
Charles Adams, Jr., of Worcester & Abigail Drury,	Feb. 8, 1764
Amos Rice of Northboro and Sarah Graves,	May 8, 1766
Benjamin Hinds & Tabatha Holland,	July 1, 1766
Abiel Stone of Lancaster & Mary Bradstreat,	Dec. 25, 1766
Jonas Goodenough of Princetown & Mary Davenport,	Jan. 29, 1767
Thaddeus Pollard & Submit Maynard,	March 24, 1767
Joshua Randall & Patte Wright of Rutland,	April 17, 1767
Ephraim Smith of Grafton & Sarah Bigelow,	June 8, 1767
James Goddard of Athol & Betty Goddard,	June 24, 1767
Thomas Miles & Rachel Keyes,	Oct. 29, 1767
William Brittan of Rutland & Lydia Whitney,	Nov. 3, 1767
David Cutting & Mary Keyes,	Nov. 10, 1767
Thomas Baker & Mary Newton,	Feb. 22, 1768
William Drury & Elizabeth Drury,	March 10, 1768
John Keyes Wetherbee & Levinah Rand,	May 3, 1768
Jonathan Peirce & Jemima Miles,	May 3, 1768
Israel Allen & Thankful Greenwood,	July 26, 1768
Isaac Moor of Bolton & Mary Bigelow,	June 2, 1768
Samuel Brittan of Rutland & Ruth Parker,	Oct. 4, 1768
John Bellows of Southboro' & Susanna Whitney,	Oct. 4, 1768
Daniel Hemenway & Mrs. Elisabeth Johnson,	Dec. 1, 1768
Seth Swan of Paxton & Dorcas Biglo,	Dec. 1, 1768
Ebenezer Drury of Temple, N. H., & Meriam Goodale,	Dec. 2, 1768
Timothy Whitney & Katharine Davenport,	Dec. 8, 1768

Jotham Flagg & Rebecca Kimball, Aug. 15, 1765
David Brigham & Mercy Maynard, March 21, 1765
Thomas Keyes of Westminster & Mary Temple,
April 14, 1765
Zebulon Throop & Lucy Wheeler, May 27, 1765
John Glazier & Sarah Temple, Oct. 21, 1765
Abel Holt & Eunice Keyes, Oct. 21, 1765.
John Wright & Jane Crosett of Templeton, April 30, 1765
Isaac Stone & Rachel Fisk, May 3, 1765
Archelus Anderson of Chesterfield & Meriam Biglo,
May 30, 1765
Aaron Temple & Elizabeth Smith, June 4, 1765
Simeon Keyes & Lucy Temple, Dec. 5, 1765
Rev. Asaph Rice of Westminster & Mary Morse,
Dec. 26, 1765
Abel Osgood of Rutland & Eunice Holland, Feb. 13, 1766
James Mahoney & Jemima Temple, Feb. 20, 1766
Samuel Lee of Rutland & Bulah Child, Feb. 27, 1766
Josiah Boyden & Lydia Whitney, both of Worcester,
April, 1766
Francis Temple & Elizabeth Holland, Dec. 18, 1766
Jonathan Wheeler of Grafton & Anna Rand, April 2, 1765
Elijah Stone of Framingham & Elizabeth Lynd,
April 4, 1765
Nathaniel Watt of Leicester & Joanna Tucker,
April 25, 1765
Josiah Bowker, Jr., of Westboro' & Sarah Muzzy,
May 23, 1765
Daniel Drury, Jr., & Sarah Knowlton, May 28, 1765
Jacob Hapgood & Abigail Stone, June 20, 1765
Rev. William Goddard of Westmoreland & Mrs.
  Rachel Goddard, Aug. 14, 1765
Jonathan Newton & Sibbilah Harrington of Grafton,
Sept. 25, 1765
Phinehas Byam of Templeton & Mary Miles, Oct. 7, 1765
Rev. Nathan Stone of Yarmoth and Mrs. Mary
  Cushing, Oct. 17, 1765
Asa Mixer & Mary Newton, Nov. 26, 1765
Joseph Sherman, Jr., & Abigail Muzzy, Feb. 4, 1766

MARRIAGES.

James Simonds of Templeton & Sarah Knowlton,
                                            Feb. 19, 1766
Daniel Holden of Leicester & Jemima Tucker, Aug. 20, 1766
Daniel Knight, Jr., of Worcester & Mehitable Bancroft,   Dec. 4, 1766
William Johnson of Southboro' & Zerviah Bragg,
                                            Jan. 1, 1767
Ebenezer Hatshorn of Athol & Eunice Hapgood,
                                            April 20, 1767
Michael Martyn & Zilpah Eager, both of Northboro',
                                            May 11, 1767
Simon Phelps of Rutland & Tabitha Maynard, June 24, 1767
Robert Smith of Worcester & Elizabeth Goodale,
                                            Dec. 16, 1767
—— Brown & Lydia Robertson,   Nov. 24, 1768
Jacob Ellis & Relief Bennett,   Feb. 10, 1769
Ephraim Wheeler & widow Elisabeth Temple,
                                            March 22, 1769
Edward Goodenow of Westminster & Lois Rice,
                                            June 17, 1770
Solomon Biglo, Jr., & Mary Damon,   April 6, 1769
Nathan Pike & Abigail Holland,   May 10, 1769
John Morse & Elisabeth Andrews,   May 11, 1769
Joseph Bixbee & Miriam Briant of Lancaster, July 13, 1769
Nathan Banister of Brookfield & Sarah Whitney,
                                            Dec. 17, 1769
Joshua Blanchard of Wilton & Elisabeth Keys, Feb. 6, 1770
Nathaniel Whitney of New Marlboro & Molly
    Houghton of Lancaster,   Jan. 21, 1771
Oliver Barns of Northboro & Dinah Bennitt, Dec. 24, 1770
Richard Barns, Jr., & Anna Bathrick, both of Westboro,   Jan. 1, 1772
Amsden Gale of Westboro & Elizabeth Henderson,
                                            March 17, 1772
Simeon Allen & Candice How,   July 20, 1772
Phinehas Heywood, Jr., & Kezia Snow of Westboro,
                                            Nov. 19, 1772
Peter Hubbard & Phebe Brigham, both of Holden,
                                            Aug. 12, 1773

Jonas Bennett & Mary Williams, Jan. 10, 1773
David Bennett & Persis Cutting of Lancaster, Feb. 14, 1773
Joshua Morse & Levinah Holland, April 29, 1773
Caleb Kendel & Priscilla Townsend, Dec. 8, 1773
Samuel Richardson of N. Fain & widow Sarah
  Holland, Feb. 6, 1774
Jonathan Stone, Jr., & Hannah Gates of Worcester,
  July 7, 1769
Thomas Drury of Temple & Martha Knowlton,
  Sept. 11, 1769
Rev. Edward Goddard of Swansey & Miss Lois How,
  Nov. 1, 1769
Samuel Biglo & Abigail Hastings, May 7, 1770
James Curtis of Worcester & Sarah Eager, May 24, 1770
Joseph Jeseph of Worcester and Jemima Bozworth,
  July 10, 1770
Daniel Hemingway, Jr., & Mary Carryl, Aug. 1, 1770
Abijah Kendal of Templeton & Millesent Miles,
  March 26, 1771
Edward Goddard, Jr., & Margaret How, May 23, 1771
Jonah How & Prudence Bouker, July 4, 1771
Solomon Wheeler & Zipporah Harrington of Grafton,
  Aug. 26, 1771
Joseph Ballard of Andover & Molly Smith, Sept. 10, 1771
Thomas Johnson & Elizabeth Smith, Sept. 24, 1771
Jonathan Heywood, Jr., of Concord & Zerviah Baldwin,
  Nov. 7, 1771
Jonas Wyman of Lancaster & Hannah Smith, May 27, 1772
Joseph Stone & Lydia Rice, Nov. 18, 1772
Ebenezer Kint of Leicester & Sarah Stone, Nov. 19, 1772
Joseph Holland & Elizabeth Gleason of Worcester,
  Dec. 29, 1772
Thaddeus Easterbrook of Rutland & Sarah Wyman,
  Dec. 31, 1772
Jonas Whitney & Tamar Houghton of Lancaster,
  Jan. 11, 1773
Jonathan Thurstin & Lois Wheeler, May 5, 1773
Nathan Wait of Leicester & Hannah Pierks, May 20, 1773
Jacob Kent of Leicester & Mary Tucker, May 23, 1773

MARRIAGES.

Abner Miles & Deborah Underwood of Westford,
June 24, 1773
Rev. Isaac Stone of Douglass & Susan Goddard,
Oct. 27, 1773
Elnathan Allen, Jr., & Lydia Pratt,   Nov. 24, 1773
Stephen Wheelock & Lucretia Newton,   Jan. 18, 1774
Joseph Hastings, Jr., & Katherine Joslin,   Nov. 15, 1770
Elijah Southgate of Leicester & Patty Hastings,
Jan. 19, 1774
Joseph Curtis of Worcester & Eleaner Flint,   Aug. 1, 1774
Jotham Bush & Mary Taylor of Northboro,   June 23, 1781
John Wright & Deliverance Houghton,   Sept. 26, 1781
William Raa of Greenwich & Patience Wyman,   Nov. 5, 1782
Asa Fay of Grafton & Mary Robins of Westboro,
April 13, 1780
Samuel Andrews & Judith Flagg,   July 10, 1777
John Keyes of Wilton & Lucy Hale,   Sept. 11, 1777
Jacob Wheelor of Petersham & Huldah Maynard,
March 5, 1778
Daniel Ball & Lydia Smith,   Sept. 8, 1778
Francis Biglow of Boston & Levinah Beaman,   Oct. 29, 1778
Jonas Rice of Ashburnham & Zilphar Townsend,
May 10, 1779
Ebenezer Ingolsbee, Jr., & Phebe Easterbrooks,   Nov. 20, 1779
Charles Henny & Happy Tompson (negroes),   March 3, 1780
Joseph Morse & Sophia Biglow,   May 4, 1780
John Parker & Olive Temple,   May 25, 1780

WESTMINSTER.

Oct. 20, 1759, the plantation called Narragansett Number Two established as the district of Westminster. Prov. Laws, Vol. IV, p. 265. Made a town April 26, 1770. Prov. Laws, Vol. V, p. 50. First (Congregational) Church organized 1742. Clergymen mentioned: Rev. Asaph Rice, Rev. Elisha Fish.

Nathan Peirce & Mary Cottingham,   Oct. 31, 1765
Daniel Munjoy & Katey Randall of Stow,   Feb., 1766
Abel Lawrence & Deborah Gordan,   March 26, 1767
Josiah Wilder & Luce Graves,   May 24, 1767

Silas Kendall & Eunice Conant,	Dec. 24, 1767
Joseph Miller, Jr., & Luce Walker,	Jan. 12, 1768
Solomon Harvey & Mary Woodward,	Feb. 5, 1768
John Matthews & Patience Graves,	April 14, 1768
Peter Graves and Susanah Hagar,	Feb. 10, 1768
Moses Thurston & Easter Bigelow,	April 21, 1768
Thomas Newhall & Sarah Dwight,	March 1, 1770
Charles Richardson & Susannah Taylor,	March 21, 1770
Christopher Wheaton & Abigail Brewer,	July 26, 1770
Ezekiel Fosgate & Hannah Harrington,	Sept. 30, 1770
Edward Goddard & Ruth Shaw,	Jan. 17, 1770
Jonathan Evens & Lydia Clemons,	March 28, 1769
Jonathan Batchelor & Thankful Whitney,	April 6, 1769
Eleazer Ball & Mary Bradish,	April 7, 1769
James Watkins & Sarah Whitney,	Nov. 16, 1769
Jonas Warren, the 3d, & Mary Ober,	Feb. 1, 1770
Phillip Ardenay & Anna Brown,	May 15, 1768
Ephraim Miller & Bulah Wheeler,	Nov. 6, 1768
Asa Taylor & Sarah Williams,	Jan. 5, 1769
James How & Mary Sherman,	June 19, 1769
Hubbard Dunster & Ruth Bayley,	Aug. 31, 1769
Elijah Gibbs & Mary Whitney,	Nov. 9, 1769
David Merium & Martha Conont,	Nov. 30, 1769
Francis Wheeler & Huldah Stedman,	Dec. 26, 1769
Joshua Mostman & Sarah Barnard,	April 10, 1770
Abner Whitney & Elizabeth Glazier,	May 14, 1770
Ephraim Weatherbee & Hannah Woodward,	Dec. 11, 1770
Dorcas Sawyer & Sarah Garey,	March 26, 1771
Jeremiah Gayer & Ruth Walker,	May 29, 1771
Samuel Sawine & Martha Miller,	Nov. 6, 1771
Paul Walker & Rebecca Haines,	Nov. 6, 1771
Thomas Wheeler & Mary Child,	Jan. 2, 1772
Nathan Kezer & Hannah Morse,	May 27, 1772
Dudley Bayley & Reuhamah Dunster,	Oct. 26, 1772
William Bemis & Abigail Annis,	Nov. 12, 1772
Elijah Simons & Abigail Roff,	April 20, 1773
Edmund Bernard & Elizabeth Holden,	Nov. 25, 1773
Silas Whitney & Sarah Withinton,	Jan. 27, 1774
Jonas Baker & Elizabeth Adams,	Feb. 27, 1774

MARRIAGES.

Jonathan Kezer & Abigail Snow,	Feb. 24, 1774
Samuel Warren & Anne Merium,	March 3, 1774
Joshua Fletcher & Ruth Holden,	June 30, 1772
William Wicker of Hardwicke & Susanna Parker of Paxton,	June 4, 1772
John Whitney & Polly Jones,	Feb., 1781
James Bowers & Abigail Herrington,	May 14, 1782
Elisha Whitney & Eunice Sever,	Dec. 27, 1781
Thomas Amory & Polly Sawin,	Nov. 15, 1—
Livi Brooks & Bettsa Flint,	Feb. 20, 1784
James Fosgate & Sarah Emmorson,	Dec. 18, 1783
Samuel Wood & Anna Calef,	June 8, 1784
Samuel Jones & Marthy Willard,	Jan. 22, 1783
Abner Holden, Jr., & Elizabeth Howard,	Feb. 9, 1785
Stephen Hoar & Hannah Wood,	June 22, 1780
Barth Senior & Mary Stebings,	1780
Aaron Saunders & Sarah Hosley,	April 12, 1774
Aaron Bolton & Dorcas Winship,	April 12, 1774
Isaac Williams & Hannah Walker,	Nov. 3, 1774
Jonathan Brooks & Mary Winship,	Dec. 13, 1774
Joseph Cummins & Hannah Bride,	Aug. 15, 1775
Samuel Miller & Lydia Cutting,	Oct. 23, 1775
Jonathan Goodale & Mary Hadley,	Jan. 26, 1776
John White & Ruth Fletcher,	April 10, 1776
Thomas Farnsworth & Relief Holden,	April 29, 1776
Elias Stearns & Sarah Keyes,	Dec. 21, 1776
John Bemas & Abigail Stevens,	Dec. 30, 1776
Joseph Flint & Mary Hartwell,	Feb. 20, 1777
Joseph Hapgood & Ruth Jackson,	June 4, 1778
Zachariah Rand & Jerusha Sawyer,	June 23, 1778
Nehemiah Bowers & Sarah Sawin,	June, 1777
Sibes Jackson & Elizabeth Watten,	March 16, 1778
Abner Bemis & Catherine Deering,	July 6, 1778
Thomas Farnsworth & Anna Estherbrooks,	Nov. 26, 1778
Jude Sawyer & Phebe Keyes,	Nov. 26, 1778
Joseph Holden & Rebeckah Hoar,	March 18, 1779
Abner Whitney & Levinah Ward,	April 22, 1779
George Taylor & Abigail Sever,	July 13, 1779
Edmon Bemas & Phebe Spring,	July 22, 1779

Nathan Heward & Rebeckah Wood,	Oct. 27, 1779
Abijah Wood & Dorothy Wheeler,	Dec. 9, 1779
Isaac Miller & Sarah Bennett,	Dec. 9, 1779
Thomas Noe & Anna Miles,	Feb., 1780
Zeeb. Green & Sarah Cowee,	May 9, 1780
John Woodward & Rebeckah Stowell,	May 18, 1780
Stephen Holden & Elizabeth Miller,	June 8, 1780
Jonathan Phillips & Elizabeth Bemas,	Nov., 1780
Abel Wood & Phebe Holden,	Nov. 21, 1780
Eli Smith & Sarah Holden,	Dec. 21, 1780
Joel Miles & Mary Ester Brooks,	Dec. 26, 1780
Levi Graves & Rebeccah Wood,	Dec. 26, 1780
Amos Shed & Tripheny Hadley,	Jan. 4, 1781
Stephen Miles & Sarah Hoar,	
William Pennyman & Sarah Bigelow,	Dec. 18, 1782
Ezra Pennyman & Lovisa Eagur,	Nov., 1782
Peter Prescott & Mary Wilson,	Feb., 1783
James Cowee & Susannah Baldwin,	Feb., 1783
Joseph Hadley & Naomi Perse,	Jan., 1784
Elias Holden & Olive Smith,	Jan., 1784
John Chandler & Mary Jackson,	1782
Samuel Taylor & Prudence Winship,	1782
David Weld & Abigail Osgood,	Feb., 1783
David Wiman & Sarah Stedman,	Feb., 1784
Shadrach Newton & Mary Dike,	April, 1784
James (or Jaines) Richardson & Sarah Jackson,	June, 1784
Nicholas Dike & Joanna Baker,	Jan., 1785
Samuel Miriam & Elizabeth Fessenden,	Jan., 1785
Pelatiah Everett & Mary Cutting,	Jan., 1785
William Mills & Sarah Bowman,	Jan., 1785
Nathan Wood & Mehitabel Cohe,	March, 1781
Oliver Jackson & Mary Pierce,	1780
Jonas Winship & Mary Jackson,	Sept., 1781
Samuel Brown & Abigail Darby,	Nov., 1782
Josiah Conant & Annes Darby,	Nov., 1784
Thomas Conant, Jr., & Ruth Rice,	Dec. 21, 1784
Joel Hail & Jana Ramor,	April 26, 1785

NORTHBOROUGH.

June 24, 1766, part of Westborough established as the district of Northborough. Prov. Laws, Vol. IV, p. 839. District of Northborough made a town August 23, 1775. Prov. Laws, Vol. V, p. 419. First (Unitarian) Church organized 1746. Clergyman mentioned: Rev. Peter Whitney.

Joseph Eager & Elizabeth Green,	March 28, 1768
Joseph Sawyer & Sarah Townsend,	April 28, 1768
Nathan Green & Abigail Williams,	July 26, 1768
Aaron Davis of Harvard & Ruth Rice,	Dec. 1, 1768
Zackeus Cutler of Amherst & Hasadiah Eager,	Oct. 6, 1771
Silvanus Oak & Abigail Ball,	Nov. 21, 1771
Jonathan Hastings of Lancaster & Mary Fay,	Feb. 21, 1771
Nathaniel Bragg of Shrewsbury & Sarah Wilson,	March 14, 1771
Zephaniah Briggs & Margaret Lambert,	June 25, 1772
Jonas Badcock & Miriam Hudson,	Nov. 30, 1772
William Kelley of Shrewsbury & Lucy Carruth,	Oct. 14, 1772
Jonathan Bruce, Jr., & Anna Barnes,	June 13, 1775
William Winslow & Martha Hayward,	June 17, 1775
Timothy Hall of Wilton, N. H., & Sarah Keyes,	Aug. 15, 1775
Daniel Allen of Shrewsbury & Martha Maynard,	Sept. 20, 1775
Dr. Jonathan Livermore & Jane Dunlap,	Nov. 16, 1775
Adam Fay & Lydia Badcock, Jr.,	Jan. 18, 1776
Abel Tenney & Anna Rice,	Feb. 12, 1776
Isaac Stow (or How?) & Hannah Fay,	May 16, 1776
Breek Parkman of Westboro' & Susannah Brigham,	Jan. 9, 1777
Silas Hastings & Hannah Reed,	April 23, 1777
Asa Rice & Betty Taylor,	May 20, 1777
Reuben Gaschet & Cate Witt,	June 19, 1777
Robert Baylies & Patience Haiden,	Aug. 16, 1777
Daniel Gaschet & Hannah Wilson,	Aug. 21, 1777

Major Joseph Mixtor of Shrewsbury & Elizabeth
    Ball, Sept. 3, 1777
William Parmenter, Jr., of Sudbury & Submit
    Fairbanks, May 25, 1780
Zadock Bartlett & Hannah Severs, 1780
Edward Johnson, Jr., & Relief Johnson, both of
    Bolton, Feb. 14, 1781
John Hosmer of Marlboro & Anna Fosgate of Bolton,
    June 21, 1781
Nathan Johnson of Bolton & Beulah Wood, Dec. 13, 1781
Eliab Wheelock & Mary Gaschet, Jan. 2, 1782
Elisha Rice of Westboro & Ruth Rice, April 4, 1782
Gershom Brigham of Marlboro & Sarah Allen,
    May 23, 1782
Lemuel Munroe & Anna Toozer, June 13, 1782
Eliphalet Wood of Harvard & Mary Badcock, Sept. 1, 1782
Jesse Brigham, Jr., & Elizabeth Henderson, Dec. 15, 1782
Daniel Harris of Bolton & Abigail Reed, Jan. 1, 1783
Daniel Brigham of Westboro (physician) & Anna
    Munroe, Nov. 9, 1783
Dean Wyman & Betty Rice, Nov. 30, 1783
James Longley of Shrewsbury & Molly Bartlett,
    Jan. 15, 1784
Ephraim Wilson & Persis Daschet, Jan. 18, 1784
Samuel Mahan & Grace Harrington of Shrews-
    bury, Feb. 18, 1784
Caleb Seager & Hannah Goodenow, Feb. 23, 1784
Jonathan Gage & Mary Brigham, March 28, 1784
Jonathan Conn & Mary Wilder, Sept. 19, 1784
John Ward of Westminster & Copia Rice, Oct. 14, 1784
Israel Saunderson of Putney, Vt., & Relief Rice,
    Nov. 9, 1784
Levi Bush of Sterling & Patty Ball, Nov. 23, 1784
Silas Rice & Mehitable Goodenow, Dec. 3, 1784

MARRIAGES.

LEOMINSTER.

June 23, 1740, part of Lancaster established as Leominster. Prov. Laws, Vol. II, p. 1023. First (Unitarian) Church records begin 1743. Clergyman mentioned: Rev. John Rogers.

Elisha Coolidge & Sarah Boutell,	June 4, 1754
Jonathan Harris & Abigail Phillips,	Dec. 31, 1759
Thomas Wilder & Abigail Carter,	Feb. 12, 1760
Nathaniel Carter, Jr., & Dorothy Joslin,	June 26, 1760
Joseph Daby & Elizabeth Wheelock,	May 11, 1761
William Warner & Mary Wilder,	Jan. 4, 1762
Caleb Sawyer, Jr., & Sarah Rogers,	Aug. 1, 1762
Philip Sweetser & Mary Parmenter,	Nov. 5, 1762
Abel Wilder of Winchendon & Anna Butler (?),	June 27, 1764
Thomas Gowing & Esther Richardson,	Jan. 17, 1763
Henry Sweetser & Lucy Johnson,	Oct. 5, 1763
Joseph Joslin & Sarah Tarbell,	Oct. 20, 1763
Josiah White, Jr., & Tabitha Carter,	May 15, 1764
Gideon Ellis of Keen & Lucy Osgood,	June 6, 1764
Jonathan Priest Whitcomb of Swansey & Dorothy Carter,	Sept. 5, 1764
Thomas Mears & Mary Stewart,	Sept. 19, 1764
Elisha Whitcomb of Swansey & Joanna Whitcomb,	Oct. 7, 1764
Benjamin Rogers and Susanna Battles,	Jan. 17, 1764
Abraham Houghton of Bolton & Sarah Divol,	Oct. 8, 1764
Daniel Peirce & Marcy Gates,	Dec. 11, 1766
Josiah Swan, Jr., & Elizabeth White,	Dec. 11, 1766
James Joslin & Mary Daby,	Jan. 8, 1767
William Lincoln & Prudence Buss,	May 27, 1767
John Beaman & Mary Fuller,	Aug. 6, 1767
Enos Jones of Ashburnham & Mary Whitimore,	Jan. 20, 1768
David Wilder & Lucy Joslin,	Jan. 24, 1768
Joseph Witherbe of Stow & Sarah Gates,	Jan. 27, 1768
Ephraim Hale & Hannah Spofford of Lancaster,	May 22, 1768

Jeramiah Wilson of Bolton & Eunice Whetcomb, Dec. 1, 1768
Elisha Davis & Rebecca Wyman, Jan. 31, 1770
Samuel Wilson of Swansey, N. H., & Susanna Divoll,
    April 17, 1770
David Wilson & Dorcas Osgood of Lancaster, Dec. 6, 1770
James Gray & Rebecca How, both of Lancaster, Dec. 20, 1770
Reuben Pierce & Mary Wood, Jan. 1, 1771
James White of Charlemont & Ruth Ballard of Lan-
    caster, Feb. 4, 1771
Amos Brown & Marcy Gates, May 30, 1771
Nathan Colburn & Betty Fuller, May 10, 1769
Nathaniel —— & Elizabeth Symonds, Feb. 8, 1770
Elias Gates of Westmoreland & Mary Beamon, Feb. 26, 1770
Ephraim Carter & Joanna Wheelock, April 2, 1770
Nathaniel Beamon of Lancaster & Thankful Farns-
    worth, April 10, 1770
Josiah Carter & Elizabeth Graves, April 22, 1770
Jonathan Thayer of Charlemont & widow Dinah
    Stearns, Nov. 1, 1770
John Woods & Elizabeth Nickols, Dec. 4, 1770
David Kendall & Annise Johnson, Jan. 17, 1771
Josiah Richardson & Rebecca Beaman, Feb. 17, 1771
Elijah Garfield of Petersham & Jenny Nickols, May 29, 1771
Nathaniel Brown & Priscilla Robins, Dec. 25, 1771
Samuel Buss & Lydia Lincoln, June 18, 1772
Reuben Kendall & Priscilla Beaman, Dec. 25, 1771

DOUGLAS.

June 5, 1746, the district or precinct of New Sherburn to be called by the name of Douglas. August 23, 1775, district of Douglas made a town. Prov. Laws, Vol. V, p. 419. First (Congregational) Church organized 1747. Clergymen mentioned: Rev. William Phips, Rev. Isaac Stone.

Caleb Whitney & Hannah Southwath of Sutton,
    March 20, 1760
Ward Nye of Rochester & Mary Chase, by Rev. David
    Hall, Jan. 28, 1768
Elisha Smith & Luce Balkom, April 21, 1772

MARRIAGES.

Joseph Titas, Jr., & Mary Biglow,	June 11, 1772
Nathan Lackey of Sutton & Susanna Nye,	Sept. 3, 1772
Seth Fish & Louis (Louise?) Cummings, both of Uxbridge,	Dec. 10, 1772
Abel Aldrich & Olive Lovell,	Jan. 7, 1773
William Robins & Mellison Hill,	April 8, 1772
Peter Reed & Olive Marsh,	Dec. 3, 1772
Caleb Hill, Jr., & Elizabeth Whitney,	Dec. 3, 1772
Jesse Aldrich of New Salem & Rachel Brown of Uxbridge,	Dec. 3, 1772
Jonathan Mansfield of Waltham & Martha Hayward,	Dec. 3, 1772
Aaron Herendeen & Bulah Cook,	Dec. 3, 1772
Thomas Biglow & Hannah Chase,	March 3, 1774
James Hayword of Upton & Rebecca Aldrich,	March 27, 1774
David Parker & Susanna Atcenson (?) of Sutton,	Sept. 14, 1775
Aaron Hill & Mary Whitney,	May 5, 1775
Lu^t Samuel Jonesen & Neomi Enirdon,	Dec. 7, 1775
Nathaniel Davidson & Sarah Reed,	Sept. 29, 1774
David Elixander & Sarah Whitney,	Oct. 23, 1774
George Linton of Uxbridge & Deliverance Nye,	March 13, 1775
Amiriah Holbrook of Uxbridge & Keziah Nye,	Nov. 20, 1777
Jacob Perun of Woodstock & Abigail Woodward,	Feb. 10, 1778
Amos Marsh & Elizabeth Jeperson,	April 22, 1778
Bezeliel Balcom & Jemima Morse,	May 13, 1778
Benjamin Duelley & Mercy Walles,	Aug. 18, 1778
Elijah Crosman of Sutton & Rebecce Mersh,	May 22, 1757
Stephen Streeter of Oxford & Sarah Chamberlin,	Sept. 10, 1778
Asa Blake of Uxbridge & Jonna Nye,	Dec. 10, 1778
Aaron Benson & Lydia Fairbanks,	Dec. 30, 1778
Samuel Davidson (?) & Hannah Rich of Sutton,	April 22, 1778
James Wallis & Chloe Humes,	March 15, 1781

David White & Huldah Marsh, April 19, 1781
Samuel Whitney & Azubah Hill, Dec. 13, 1781
Daniel Whitney of Chesterfield & Eunice Marsh, Jan. 3, 1782
Solomon Stockwell & Mary Howell, Feb. 20, 1782
Richard Lee & Bethiah Gould, Feb. 21, 1782
Josiah Reed, A. M., of Uxbridge & Elizabeth Taylor,
April 21, 1782
Edward Corbitt & Mary Rutter, May 22, 1782
Alexander Wilson of Mendon & Patience Nye, Nov. 7, 1782
Jacob Staples of Pomfret & Molly Sears, Nov. 17, 1782
Eli Stockwell & Eunice Hill, Nov. 20, 1782
Gideon Gould & Hannah Marsh, both of Sutton, Dec. 5, 1782
Denies Darling of Mendon & Deborah Bolkcom,
Dec. 24, 1782
Peter Sherman & Hannah Ross, June 30, 1783

NEW BRAINTREE.

Jan. 31, 1751. Resolve. "The precinct consisting of the lands called New Braintree and part of the town of Hardwick is erected into a district." Aug. 23, 1775, the above district made a town. Prov. Laws, Vol. V, p. 419. First (Congregational) Church organized 1754.

Beriah Haws & Mrs. Dorothy Joslyn, Nov. 10, 1762
Lott Whitcomb of Hardwick & Lydia Nye, Dec. 9, 1762
John Cannon & Abigail Messer, Jan. 13, 1763
George Nye & Mrs. Jane Timton, April 26, 1764
Dr. Percival Hall & Margaret Ware, May 10, 1764
Joseph Little & Elizabeth Willson, May 29, 1764
Jonathan Force (?) & Mary Woods, June 28, 1764
Moses Gilbert of Brookfield & Merriam Bains, Jan. 24, 1765
Silas Mathews of Brookfield & Priscilla Woods,
Sept. 10, 1765
Joseph Parker, Jr., & Zerviah Lincoln, Feb. 6, 1766
John Steal & Sarah Culveson (?), May 8, 1766
Alevander Woolson & Huldah Gilbert, June 5, 1766
John Woods & Lydia Woods, Feb. 5, 1767
Daniel Eldridge of Hardwick & Prudence Warner,
Feb. 10, 1767

MARRIAGES.

James Barr & Deborah Nye,	April 16, 1767
Bille Hancock & Percis Woods,	May 9, 1767
Reuben Fay of Hardwick & Elizabeth Perkins,	June 11, 1767
Joseph Johnson & Sarah Hunter,	Feb. 4, 1768
David Ayres & Mary Perkins,	March 17, 1768
Ebenezer Nye & Thankfull Dean,	July 7, 1768
Nathaniel Weeks & Marcy Richmond,	Feb. 16, 1769
Joseph Finton & Sarah Steel,	Feb. 23, 1769
Samuel Warren & Unity Ware,	April 11, 1769
James Hunter & Sarah Hall,	April 13, 1769
James Washburn & Ruth Rice,	Sept. 7, 1769
George Barr & Eunice Woods,	Sept. 21, 1769
Thomas Rainger of Brookfield & Marcy Woods,	Jan. 9, 1770
Benjamin Woods & Sarah Adams,	March 8, 1770
Jonathan Ware & Sarah Woods,	April 26, 1770
James Blair & Sarah Joslin,	April 26, 1770
John Cunningham, Jr., of Spencer & Anna Thomson,	May 31, 1770
Isaac Patrick of Western & Jane Anderson,	Nov. 1, 1770
Nathan Thomson & Mary Haws,	Nov. 15, 1770
Samuel Ruggles & Elizabeth Fisher,	Dec. 11, 1770
Isaiah Butler of Hardwick & Abigail Thrasher,	Feb. 7, 1771
George Caswell & Wealthy Richmond,	March 28, 1771
Elias Hall & Judith Walker,	May 26, 1771
Henry Chase of Petersham & Rachel Lincoln,	July 11, 1771
Silvester Richmond & Lucy Weston,	Aug. 8, 1771
Jonathan Cunningham of Oakham & Bethyah Thrasher,	Sept. 13, 1770
Jonathan Witherby & Mehitable Fisher,	Oct. 21, 1771
Nathan Upham of Brookfield & Eleaner Gilbert,	Feb. 27, 1772
Dr. Gershom Gilbert & Mary Hall,	April 2, 1772
James Steal & Sarah Willson,	April 21, 1772
William Gilcrest & Agnis Thomson,	Sept. 8, 1772
John Fenton & Joanna Torrence,	Nov. 19, 1772
Simeon Cannon & Mary Nickols,	Jan. 21, 1773
John Hunter & Elizabeth Matthews,	Jan. 28, 1773
George Cannon & Abigail Craigue,	Feb. 28, 1773
Stephen Thrasher & Anna Cutter (or Cutler),	March 11, 1773
Thomas Steal & Anna Downing of Ware,	April 1, 1773

FITCHBURG.

Feb. 3, 1764, part of Lunenburg established as Fitchburg. Prov. Laws, Vol. IV, p. 685. First (Congregational) Church organized 1763. Unitarian, 1768. Clergyman mentioned: Rev. John Payson.

Jonathan Dix (?) of New Ipswich & Anna Kimball,
              Oct. 20, 1767
James Litch and Rebecca Upton,   Feb. 9, 1768
Mordacai Moors & Lucy Buncraft (?), April 6, 1769
Jonathan Ware & Hannah Battles of Leominster,
              April 11, 1769
Joseph Gibson of Lunenburg & Esther Pierce,
              July 3, 1769
Matthew Brooks & Dolley Kimball,   June 19, 1770
Samuel Downes & Eunice Wentworth, Jan. 1, 1771
Daniel Melven of Holliston & Mrs. Susannah Farwell,
              Jan. 21, 1771
Jacob Gibson & Mary Polley,   Feb. 20, 1772
William Small & Miriam Thurston,   May 10, 1772
Joshua Billings of Ashburnham & Lois Gibson,
              June 13, 1772
Benjamin Frost & Rachael Kimball, Dec. 3, 1772
Silas Gibson of Lunenburg & Damaras Bennett,
              Feb. 20, 1772
Joseph Baldwine & Elisabeth Danforth, May 2, 1782
John Thurston & Esther Wood,   Aug. 20, 1782
John Polley & Abigel Kimball,   Nov. 4, 1782
Elijah Phelps & Keziah Gibson,   Feb. 10, 1783
Thomas Gibson & Relefe Hartwell,   April 1, 1783
Benjamin Hawks of Leominster & Mrs. Mary Boutell,
              April 22, 1783
Thomas Gibson & Lucy Marten of Westminster,
              May 7, 1783
John Upton & Abigel Low,   Oct. 20, 1783
Dr. Samuel Lock & Hannah Cowdin, Dec. 30, 1783

MARRIAGES.

WINCHENDON.

June 24, 1764, the plantation called Ipswich-Canada established as Winchendon. Prov. Laws, Vol. IV, p. 721. First (Congregational) Church organized 1762. Methodist Episcopal, 1796. Advent Baptist, 1798. Clergyman mentioned: Rev. Daniel Stimpson.

Thomas Sweetland & Abigail Puslia (?), both of Ipswich-Canada, N. H.,	Jan. 4, 1763
Bartholomew Pearsons of Ipswich-Canada & Lydia Kendall of Lunenburg,	Nov. 3, 1763
Aaron Hodgkins & Eunice Bixby, both of Ipswich-Canada,	Jan. 24, 1764
Henry Poor of Royalshire & Kezia Foster,	Sept. 11, 1764
James Mansfield & Lois Darling,	March 4, 1766
Isaac Stimson & Elizabeth Bixby,	March 26, 1767
Richard Pearsons & Kezia Bixby,	July 6, 1767
Daniel Gould & Mary Porter,	Feb. 15, 1770
John Torner & Jerusha Bixby,	July 5, 1770
John Day & Elizabeth Joslin,	Jan. 10, 1771
David Goodridge & Silence Joslin,	Aug. 20, 1772
Abijah Stimson & Lois Bixby,	Sept. 28, 1772
Ephraim Sawyer & Peggy Fisher,	Dec. 3, 1772
Job Boynton & Mary Joslin,	March 18, 1773
Samuel Steel & Rachel Putnam,	Nov. 4, 1773
Nathan Green & Lucy Gardner,	March 20, 1774

TEMPLETON.

March 6, 1762, the plantation called Narragansett Number Six established as Templeton. Prov. Laws, Vol. IV, p. 533. First (Unitarian) Church organized 1733. Baptist, 1782. Clergyman mentioned: Rev. Ebenezer Sparhawk.

Joel Fletcher & Ruth Church,	May 31, 1764
Ezra Hudson of Petersham & Relief Atherton,	July 23, 1764
Uriah Witherbee & Mary Nichols,	Oct. 9, 1764
Richard Stewart & Eunice Stewart,	Oct. 11, 1764
Joshua Wright & Olive Church,	Nov. 29, 1764

TEMPLETON.

Jonathan Holman & Olive Farce,	June 3, 1765
Israel Lamb & Lucy Wheeler,	Oct. 31, 1765
David Thurston & Eunice Whitney,	April 16, 1766
Samuel Treadwell & Sarah Nickless,	June 18, 1766
Hezekiah Sprague & Rachel Byam,	Aug. 13, 1767
William Crosiel & Susanna Jackson,	Jan. 7, 1768
Henry Sawtell, Jr., & Joshua Hudson,	April 4, 1768
Oliver Holman & Olive Reed,	Nov. 30, 1768
George Nickless, Jr., & Betty Sawyer,	Feb. 9, 1769
Aaron Whitney & Hannah Wait of Petersham,	July 20, 1769
James Caruth & Lucy Gary of Lancaster,	Oct. 5, 1769
Josiah Willis Seaver (?) & Sarah Whitcomb,	Dec. 28, 1769
Simon Stone & Hannah Whittemore,	Feb. 27, 1770

SUTTON.

Oct. 28, 1714. Resolve. "Voted a concurrence with the Representatives approving and confirming a survey and plat of the laying out of the township of Sutton." First (Congregational) Church organized 1720. First Baptist, 1785. Officiating clergymen mentioned: Rev. David Hall, Rev. James Wellman, Rev. Ebenezer Chaplain, Rev. Jeremiah Barstow.

Benjamin Fitts & Sarah Rich,	Oct. 31, 1749
Follensbee Chase & Hannah Marsh,	Jan. 2, 1749-50
Jonathan Marsh, Jr., & Hannah Holt,	July 20, 1749
Thomas Fuller of Uxbridge & Sarah Wheeler,	Feb. 6, 1749-50
Enoch Marble & Abigail Holland,	Jan. 9, 1749-50
John Severy & Hannah Holman,	March 8, 1749
Nathaniel Fairfield & Priscilla Wilkins,	March 13, 1749-50
William Ellis of Medway & Mary Walker,	May 10, 1750
Joshua Carter & Elizabeth Lovell,	July 25, 1750
Rev. Ezekiel Dodge of Abington & Mrs. Mary Goddard,	Sept. 27, 1750
Joseph Moseley & Sybella Dudley,	Oct. 18, 1750
Robert Dunklee of Brimfield & Martha Singlebury (or Singletury),	Oct. 22, 1750
Samuel Clark of Chester, N. H., & Mary Town,	Nov. 30, 1750
Amos Gould & Desire King,	Oct. 31, 1749

MARRIAGES.

Arthur Dagget & Mehetabell Marsh,	Jan. 28, 1750–51
Caleb Gould & Sarah Adams,	Dec. 13, 1750
Timothy Claflin & Mary Gould,	Jan. 16, 1750–51
Jonathan Dunil, Jr., & Mary Gould,	Dec. 13, 1750
Amos Mullicken of Bradford & Mehetibell Dodge,	Feb. 28, 1750–51
Samuel Bixby & Lydia Bond,	March 13, 1750–51
Benjamin Davis & Mary Whitemore,	April 29, 1751
Rev. James Wellman & Mrs. Sarah Barnard,	Nov. 8, 1750
Daniel Kinny, Jr., of Sutton & Abigail Davis of Western,	April 29, 1751
Henry Harbach & Rebeckah Stockwell,	Sept. 5, 1751
Dr. Thomas Chase & Mrs. Mary Whipple,	Sept. 26, 1751
Josiah White, Jr., & Lucy Whipple,	Nov. 28, 1751
James Richardson of Leicester & Elizabeth Chase,	Nov. 7, 1751
Elijah Sibly & Mary Carril,	Dec. 12, 1751
Jeremiah Stockwell & Mary Cutler,	Nov. 27, 1751
Stephen Holman & Ruth Putnam,	Nov. 5, 1751
Samuel How & Rebekah Gould,	Dec. 3, 1751
David Bates & Lydia Gale,	March 4, 1752
Moses Chase & Hannah Brown,	April 15, 1752
Daniel Day & Susannah Hutchinson,	May 14, 1752
Ichabod Town & Jemima Stockwell,	Dec. 5, 1751
Eliphalet Rowell & Sarah King,	Dec. 26, 1751
Timothy Bacon & Lydia Rice,	Aug. 6, 1752
David Harwood, ye 3d, of Sutton & Rebekah Twist of Oxford,	April 30, 1752
Joshua Woodbury & Dorcas Park,	July 6, 1752
William Kinny & Sarah Stockwell,	Aug. 13, 1752
Richard Bartlet, Jr., & Hannah Bucknam,	Oct. 19, 1752
Nathaniel Carril & Jane Dwight,	Oct. 10, 1752
Daniel Gleason of Oxford & Martha Bartlet,	April 26, 1753
Jonathan Stockwell, Jr., & Mary Kinny,	May 10, 1753
Eleazer Hawes & Ruth Comings,	May 1, 1753
Daniel Allen & Mary Holman,	May 30, 1753
Fuller Putnam & Mary Comings,	Dec. 4, 1752
Ebenezer Whitney & Lydia Goodale,	Feb. 6, 1753
Cornelius Putnam, Jr., & Elisabeth Perkins,	Aug. 2, 1753

SUTTON.

Stephen Southworth & Hannah Sibley, Sept. 27, 1753
Timothy Sibley & Ann Wait, Oct. 16, 1753
Rogers Chase & Sarah Walker, Feb. 6, 1754
John Harbach & Hannah Greenwood, Dec. 4, 1753
Benjamin Sibley & Lucy Park, Feb. 6, 1754
Dr. Benjamin Morss & Mrs. Abigail Dudley, May 25, 1735
Jonathan Dudley & Hannah Putnam, Aug. 18, 1736
Ebenezer Whiple & Prudence Dudley, March 25, 1736
Abell Chase & Judith Gale, Jan. 3, 1754
John Feling (?) of Pomfret & Mary Keyes, March 20, 1754
Edward Holman of Sutton & Rebekah Gale of Oxford, May 7, 1754
Jona Wheeler, Jr., of Sutton & Ann Davenport of Douglas, May 2, 1754
James Caldwell & Elisabeth Hicks, Aug. 15, 1754
Stephen Bartlett & Elisabeth Whitney, Feb. 27, 1754
Dr. John Hale of Hollis & Mrs. Elisabeth Hale, Sept. 5, 1754
Joshua Barnard & Abigail Hazeltine, Sept. 5, 1744
Samuel Buck, Jr., & Sarah Fisk (or Fish), Sept. 18, 1754
Thomas Hall & Mrs. Huldah Park, June 24, 1758
Asa Kenney & Mehetabel Stockwell, July 24, 1762
Moses Tyler Dodge & Lydia Gibbs, Feb. 11, 1762
Jonathan Sibley, Jr., & Eunis Perkins, April 26, 1762
Benjamin Rich & Rebeccah Dagget, July 15, 1762
John Daniels of Mendon & Lydia Putnam, May 26, 1762
Ralph Richardson & Sarah Bartlett, March 5, 1762
Comfort Streater & Bethiah Rich, June 24, 1762
Jonathan Bartlett & Mahetabel Hull of Worcester, Oct. 6, 1762
Joseph Aldrich of Bellingham & Experience Stockwell of Oxford, Dec. 9, 1764
Daniel Gould & Mary Putnam, Dec. 9, 1762
Josiah Bond & Sarah Mellady, Jan. 28, 1762
Israel Richardson of Woburn & Elisabeth Hutchinson, Aug. 13, 1762
Jonas Gale & Tamer Marsh, Dec. 23, 1762
Richard Mower & Margaret Burnham, Feb. 10, 1763
David Lillie, Jr., & Elizabeth Gibbs, Sept. 23, 1762

MARRIAGES.

Deacon Jonathan Newell of Dudley & Mrs. Eliz.
    Putnam, Nov. 17, 1762
Ephraim Fletcher of Grafton & Sarah Davenport,
    Dec. 7, 1762
Thomas Nichols & Kezia Fitts, Dec. 9, 1762
Archibald Campbell of Oxford & Mrs. Hannah
    Barnard, Nov. 15, 1762
Stephan Stockwell and Mehitable Holman, Dec. 14, 1762
Jonathan Dudley, Jr., & Mary Garfield, Feb. 1, 1763
Bartholomew Woodbury & Ruth Greenwood, May 5, 1763
Bradford Chase & Abigale Sibley, June 21, 1763
Elisha Sibley & Lydia Carriel (?), July 14, 1763
Joseph Buxton, Jr., & Lydia Rice, July 28, 1763
Nathaniel Stockwell & Abigail Dodge, March 31, 1763
Francis Kidder, Jr., & Mary Chase, April 21, 1763
Bartholmew Hutchinson & Ruth Haven, Aug. 4, 1763
Moses Chase & Susanna Lillie, Oct. 6, 1763
Theophilus Kenney & Abigail Gibbs, Oct. 13, 1763
Nathaniel Whitemore & Elizabeth Marsh, Feb. 9, 1764
Francis Temple of Shrewsbury & Anna March,
    Nov. 16, 1763
Jonathan Pierce & Mary Goodell, Feb. 2, 1764
John Eliot & Hannah Dudley, Jan. 19, 1764
David Harwood, 3d, & Mary Streeter, Feb. 6, 1764
Abraham Fitts & Mary Holman, April 14, 1767
Reuben Town & Sarah Dodge, July 7, 1767
Nathaniel Gibbs & Sarah Holton, July 9, 1767
Nathaniel Stone & Abigail Town, Aug. 2, 1767
Jacob Leland & Anne Taylor, Aug. 2, 1767
Aaron Eliot & Lydia Taylor, Oct. 13, 1767
John Burdon, Jr., & Lucy Sibley, Oct. 19, 1767
Willis Hall, Jr., & Rebecca Parsons, Dec. 3, 1767
Ebenezer Waters & Mary Adams of Grafton, Dec. 10, 1767
Asa Curtis of Dudley & Hannah Carriel (?), Dec. 25, 1767
James Giles & Martha Gould, Feb. 11, 1768
Jonathan Sibley & Hannah Burnap, Dec. 3, 1739
Jonathan Waters, Jr., & Hannah Trask, Nov. 27, 1766
Caleb White and Rebecca Marsh, Feb. 26, 1767
Elisha Gale & Mary Singletary, April 8, 1767

Andrew Eliot & Anne Carter, May 7, 1767
Robert Fitts & Lydia Town, June 2, 1767
David Bacon & Tabitha Wakefield, Dec. 17, 1767
Joseph Harwood, Jr., & Mary Pratt, Jan. 7, 1768
Reuben Swan of Leicester & Rachel Butnam, Feb. 25, 1768
Edward Holman & Sarah Kenney, March 22, 1763
Richard Bartlet, Jr., & Ruth Holman, July 7, 1763
Daniel Knap & Hannah Lyon, April 22, 1763
Solomon Holman, 3d, & Sarah Goold, Dec. 22, 1763
Andrew Putnam of Winchester & Lucy Park, Jan. 10, 1764
Thomas Gleason of Oxford & Hannah Walker,
    March 29, 1764
Timothy Child & Lydia Kidder, Jan. 17, 1764
Asa Roberts & Ruhamah Brown, March 22, 1764
Simeon Gleason of Petersham & Martha Dudley,
    June 2, 1764
Thomas McKnight of Oxford & Abigail Goold,
    March 1, 1764
Asa Waters & Sarah Goodale, June 14, 1764
Lot Hutchinson & Hannah Morss, Sept. 25, 1764
Solomon Lealand & Lois Haven, Nov. 27, 1764
Asa Walker of Hopkinston & Sarah Burbank, Dec. 13, 1764
Capt. Caleb Hill of Douglas & Ruth Hicks, Jan. 10, 1765
John Corban of Dudley & Abigail Harback, Jan. 30, 1765
Reuben Sibley & Ruth Sibley, Jan. 30, 1765
Benjamin Garfield of Grafton & Lucy Case, Nov. 15, 1764
William Foster of Oxford & Hannah Richards, Dec. 3, 1764
William Sibley & Hannah Stockwell, Jan. 24, 1765
Elisha Putnam & Abigail Chamberlain, April 2, 1763
John Harwood, Jr., & Lydia Holman, Aug. 13, 1763
Joseph Pearse & Abigail Carriel, Oct. 10, 176–
Joel Stevens of Charlton & Rebeckah Marble, Nov. 19, 1765
Joel Wheeler of Petersham & Mary Dudley, Dec. 19, 1765
John Blanchard & Sarah Carriel, Dec. 19, 1765
Dr. Ephraim Woolson of Weston & Mrs. Mary Richardson, July 30, 1765
Samuel Bouttell, Jr., & Hannah Barton, Oct. 29, 1765
John Hicks & Margaret Burbank, April 10, 1765
Benjamin Marsh, ye 4th, & Melleson Davenport, May 8, 1765

MARRIAGES.

John Howard & Huldah Sibley,	June 26, 1765
Jacob Nelson & Annabel Harback,	July 4, 1765
Archelaus Putnam & Sarah Putnam,	Oct. 10, 1765
David Keith of Uxbridge & Ruth Bacon,	Nov. 5, 1765
Josiah White of Uxbridge & Hannah Gould,	Nov. 14, 1765
John Carriel & Tamar King,	Dec. 12, 1765
Jacob Cummings, Jr., & Bridget Lilley,	Dec. 19, 1765
Ebenezer Putnam & Hannah Dike,	Jan. 16, 1766
Thomas Chase & Deborah Killum,	Feb. 20, 1766
Jeremiah Stockwell of Chesterfield & Sarah Stockwell,	Feb. 27, 1766
Obadiah Brown of Uxbridge & Mary Barton,	April 3, 1766
Joshua Weatherell of Dudley & Hannah William,	April 17, 1766
Asa Grosvenor of Pomfret & Hannah Hall,	April 24, 1766
Benjamin Hicks & Mary Woodbury,	Sept. 4, 1766
Adonijah Putnam & Mary Wilkins,	Nov. 27, 1766
Bartholomew Town, Jr., & Betty Rice,	Jan. 22, 1767
John Barnard & Sarah Fisk,	Oct. 30, 1766
Samuel Holman & Hannah Commings,	Dec. 18, 1766
Edward Goddard of Shrewsbury & Eunice Walker,	June 11, 1764
Ebenezer Marsh & Mary Bullen,	Jan. 29, 1765
Thomas Moor of Brookfield & Priscilla Holland,	Sept. 25, 1766
John Singletary & Sarah Jennison,	April 15, 1767
Jonathan Gale of Oxford & Violetty Kinny of Brookfield,	April 21, 1768
John Adams, Jr., of Uxbridge & Elisabeth Newton,	Nov. 28, 1768
Joseph Gleason, Jr., & Marcy Streater, both of Oxford,	Feb. 10, 1769
Samuel Woodward of Worcester & Submit Hagar,	Feb. 8, 1769
Joel Johnson & Elanor Park, both of Hardwick,	Sept. 27, 1768
Reuben Park & Molly Barton,	Sept. 27, 1768
Elisha Holman & Jerusha Snow,	May 21, 1767
Jedidiah Bugbee of the Union & Molly Hiscock,	Oct. 29, 1767

Timothy Carter, Jr., & Sarah Walker,	May 29, 1768
Daniel Bucknam, Jr., & Rebecca Boyden,	June 11, 1768
Asa Taft & Molly Stone,	Nov. 24, 1768
Ebenezer Gould & Tabitha Kinny,	Feb. 25, 1768
Joseph Bullen & Phebe Garfield,	June 20, 1768
Bartholomew Carriel (?) & Rebecca Harbach,	Aug. 11, 1768
Abel Chase, the 3d, & Elisabeth Eliot,	Nov. 30, 1768
Joseph Newell of Thompson & Elisabeth Ames,	Sept. 1, 1768
Solomon Cook & Keziah Holton,	Nov. 29, 1768
Stephen Sibley & Eleanor Lillie,	Dec. 29, 1768
Joshua Lillie & Betty Cummings,	April 28, 1768
Ambrose Stone & Mary Everdan,	May 22, 1768
Stephen Rice & Ruth Stone,	May 12, 1768
Samuel Wakefield & Mary Davenport,	May 25, 1768
Asa Hazeltine of Upton & Mary Woodward,	May 26, 1768
John Dudley & Molly Morss,	Oct. 13, 1768
David Fisk & Sarah Goodale,	June 24, 1769
Peter Jennison & Mehitable Singletary,	March 31, 1769
William Brown & Grace Wadsworth,	Jan. 22, 1769
Moses Huse of Methuen & Elisabeth Barton,	April 20, 1769
John Gould of Lyndesboro & Susanna Chase,	Oct. 31, 1769
Ezra (?) Harwood & Lydia Hiscock,	Feb. 16, 1769
Joseph Lillie & Prudence Kinny, both of Charlton,	Oct. 12, 1769
Levi Newton & Elisabeth Woodward, both of Worcester,	Oct. 26, 1769
Abner Gleason & Abigail Rich of Oxford,	Jan. 18, 1770
Simon Chase & Hannah Chase,	May 11, 1769
John Gould & Mary Gould,	Aug. 17, 1769
Malachi Willson of Wrentham & Hannah Burdon,	Aug. 22, 1769
David Sibley & Phebe Lillie,	Jan. 25, 1770
Samuel Goddard & Elizabeth King,	May 25, 1769
William Dike (?) & Abigail Jennison,	Sept. 21, 1769
Abraham Taylor & Mary Leland,	Sept. 21, 1769
John Burley of the Union & Percis Harwood,	Oct. 28, 1769
Benjamin Hutchinson & Judith Lillie,	Nov. 2, 1769

Simonds Whipple & Mary Sibley,	Nov. 16, 1769
Noah Stockwell & Mercy Wright,	Dec. 12, 1769
Benjamin Swinnerton & Elisabeth Hall,	Dec. 21, 1769
Daniel Stone, Jr., & Hannah Gould,	Jan. 9, 1770
Gershom Biglo, Jr., & Lydia Stockwell,	Jan. 11, 1770

[*Sutton continued p. 144*].

LANCASTER.

May 18, 1653, "Nashaway" to be a township to be called Lancaster. Mass. Rec., Vol. IV, Part. I, p. 139. First (Unitarian) Church organized 1653. Officiating clergymen mentioned: Rev. Timothy Harrington, Rev. John Mellen, Rev. Samuel Harrington.

Ebenezer Taylor & Mary Houghton,	March 9, 1749
Nathaniel White & Lydia Phelps,	Nov. 9, 1749
Rev. John Mellen & Rebeckah Prentice,	March 27, 1749
John Rogers of Leominster & Relief Prentice,	March 27, 1750
Jotham Biglow of Holden & Mary Richardson,	May 23, 1750
David Taylor of Lunenburg & Elizabeth Houghton,	Nov. 29, 1750
Rev. John Rogers of Leominster & Mrs. Releafe Prentice,	March 27, 1750
Gershom Flagg & Mary Willard,	Dec. 6, 1750
William Phelps & Mary Nichols,	April 25, 1751
Jonas Fletcher of Groton & Ruth Fletcher,	May 23, 1751
John Beaman & widow Sarah Page,	May 22, 1751
David Wilder & (Mrs.) Martha White,	Dec. 4, 1751
Josiah Cutting of Shrewsbury & Orpah Houghton,	Jan. 2, 1752
Joseph Kilbourn & Mary Sawyer,	Jan. 22, 1752
George Mcfarling of Lunenburg & Margaret Terrance,	April 16, 1752
David Baldwin of Billevica & Keziah Bennet,	June 18, 1752
Reuben Lipunwell & Anna Wyman,	June 18, 1752
Primas Law & Ross Canterbery (negroes),	Oct. 18, 1752
Enoch Hill & Sarah Rugg,	Oct. 24, 1752
Abijah Willard & Anna Prentice,	Nov. 15, 1752

Nathaniel Joslin & Martha Fairbanks,   Nov. 30, 1752
James Richardson of Leominster & Hannah House,
       Jan. 10, 1753
Asa Harris & Abigail Bennet,   Jan. 10, 1753
Phinehas Houghton & Ruth Osgood,   Jan. 6, 1753
Thomas Heywood of Lunenburg & Elizabeth Richardson,   July 11, 1753
William Smith (Townsend) & Martha Dunsmore,
       Nov. 27, 1753
Joshua Read of Lexington & Susannah Houghton,
       Nov. 27, 1753
Benjamin Osgood, Jr., & Mary Carter,   Dec. 5, 1753
John Divol & Elizabeth Beman,   Dec. 26, 1753
Aaron Osgood, Jr., & Hannah Warner,   March 6, 1754
Dr. William Dunsmore & Hannah Sumner of Killingsly,   Jan. 7, 1754
Amos Sawyer, Jr., & Mary Rugg,   Jan. 9, 1755
Tyrus Houghton & Rachel Honn (?),   Jan., 1755
Samuel Prentice & Prudence Osgood,   Feb. 13, 1755
William Tucker & Mary Kendall,   Feb. 20, 1755
Nathaniel Wilder, Jr., & Lydia Kendall,   Feb. 27, 1755
George Parkhurst & Keziah Whitcomb of Bolton,
       March 13, 1755
Converse Richardson & Mercy Nichols,   March 27, 1755
David Thomas of Pelham & Elizabeth Harper, Nov. 18, 1755
Ephraim Wilder (Tert[s]) & Lucretia Lock,   April 3, 1755
Jabez Fairbank & widow Naomi Dupee,   Jan. 22, 1756
Benjamin Shead of Lunenburg & Elizabeth Bloors (?),
       July 19, 1756
Isaac Eveleth of Brookfield & Eunice Hudson, Sept. 2, 1756
William Deputron of Lancaster & Sarah Rice of
    Shirley,   Oct. 12, 1756
Rev. Elisha Marsh of No. 2 & Susannah Willard,
       July 25, 1757
William Kendall & Mary Lipinwell,   Aug. 15, 1757
Samuel Gamble & Eunice Dunsmore,   Oct. 11, 1757
Mark Lincoln & Mary Carter,   Oct. 20, 1757
Josiah Whitcomb of Bolton & Dorothy Osgood,
       Oct. 24, 1757

MARRIAGES.

Joseph Woods & Lucy Butler, Nov. 30, 1757
Elijah Woods & Mary Goodfree, Feb. 2, 1758
Jonathan Wheelock of Leominster & Thankful Haskell, Dec. 27, 1757
Phineas Carter & Mary Sawyer, Feb. 22, 1758
Philemon Houghton & Rebeckah Gates, Feb. 23, 1758
Paul Sawyer & Lois Houghton, March 7, 1758
John Brooks & Katherine Dunsmore, March 8, 1758
Ephraim Sawyer & Susanna Richardson, June 11, 1752
Ezekiel Kendall & Mary May, Dec. 21, 1752
Josiah Bayley & Lydia Parker, Feb. 13, 1753
Nathan Burpee, Jr., & Azubah Sawyer, March 14, 1753
Nathan Burpee & Azubah Osgood, Jan. 24, 1754
Josiah Jackson & Mary Darby of Narraganset No. 2, Jan. 30, 1755
Oliver Hoar & Silence Houghton, Feb. 28, 1754
Levi Moore & Rebeckah Sawyer, March 7, 1754
Samuel Rice & Mary Bennet, April 10, 1754
Aaron Sawyer & Abigail (Sawyer), April 25, 1754
Dorchester & Pegg (negroes) married in hay time, 1754
Asa Wilder & Lydia Rugg, Dec. 12, 1754
Jonathan Fairbank & Ruth Houghton, Feb. 3, 1754
Joseph Stuart & Mary Snow, Aug. 28, 1755
John Curtis & Elizabeth Robbins, Nov. 13, 1755
Josiah Houghton & Grace Whitney, Jan. 6, 1756
Israel Moore & Abigail How, Jan. 15, 1756
Joseph Osgood & Katherine Sawyer, Jan. 29, 1756
Elisha Sawyer & Susanna Husk, March 8, 1756
Thomas Gary, Jr., & Jane Wilder, April 22, 1756
Samuel Burpee, Jr., & Martha Brocklebank, June 10, 1756
Charles Morris & Elizabeth Lagget, Sept. 5, 1756
Jabez Brooks & Lucy Sawyer, Jan. 27, 1757
James Cowey & Mary Parsons, March 3, 1757
Christian Angell & Hannah Bennet, April 14, 1757
John May, Jr., & Keziah Sawyer, June 1, 1757
Benjamin Houghton (Tert[s]) & Priscilla Wilder, Nov. 17, 1757
Tilly Littlejohns & Hannah Brooks, Dec. 1, 1757
John Benney & Dinah Beman, Dec. 26, 1757

David Nelson & Hannah Bailey, Dec. 29, 1757
John Farrar & Ann Chandler, Jan. 11, 1758
Lemuel Houghton & Dinah Osgood, May 1, 1758
Thomas Ross, Jr., & Priscilla Cooper, June 8, 1758
Nathaniel Houghton & Mary Richardson, June 29, 1758
Lewis Conguerett & Abigail Wheeler, July 23, 1758
Daniel Rice & Keziah Snow, Nov. 2, 1758
Barzillai Holt & Lois Allerd, Feb. 22, 1759
David Osgood, Jr., & Sarah Bailey, April 12, 1759
Samuel Snow & Sarah Bernett (?), July 19, 1759
Jonathan Bailey & Eunice Houghton, Jan. 16, 1760
Elisha Wilder & Mehitabel Dresser, Jan. 17, 1760
Jonathan Osgood & Joanna Bearnon, Jan. 17, 1760
Israel Moore & Katherine Sawyer, Oct. 9, 1760
Josiah Kendall, Jr., & Esthar Sawyer, Mar. 26, 1760
Samuel Ross & Katherine Gary, Nov. 27, 1760
Ezra Sawyer & Keziah Sawyer, Dec. 11, 1760
Joseph Sawyer & Agnes Dunsmore, Aug. 20, 1761
Roger Ross & Molly Rugg, Sept. 3, 1761
Jonathan Whitcomb & Tamar Ross, Sept. 3, 1761
John Boynton & Elizabeth Jewitt, Nov. 26, 1761
Peter Goodenow & Ann Mosemon, Dec. 17, 1761
Asa Whitcomb & Bettey Sawyer, Jan. 26, 1762
Joseph Houghton & Martha Snow, March 11, 1762
Richard Proutee & Ephe Smith, May 6, 1762
Nathaniel Jones & Phebe Burpee, May 11, 1762
Josiah Wilder & Abigail Osgood, June 3, 1762
Phinehas Wilder & Lois Brown, Sept. 8, 1756
Jonathan Osgood, Jr., & Abigail Whitcomb, June 20, 1758
Jonathan Coborne & Sarah Harvey, April, 1759
Peter Snow & Eunice Goodfree, Dec. 19, 1754
Henry Haskel, Jr., & Rebeccah Willard, Jan. 6, 1757
Jacob Williams & Abigail Wyman, Nov. 29, 1759
James Willard & Sarah Longley, March 31, 1761
James Ballard & Mary Robbins, May 11, 1756
Ebenezer Maynard & Sarah Knight, both of Westboro, July 16, 1756
Phinehas Willard & Rebeckah Willard, both of Harvard, Jan. 5, 1758

MARRIAGES.

Sherebiah Hunt & Deborah Wilder, April 2, 1758
Luke Richardson & Demarius Carter, both of Leominster, Sept. 7, 1758
Daniel Knight & Elizabeth Houghton, May 12, 1758
Levi Nichols & Elizabeth Sawyer, Nov. 29, 1759
Gardner Wilder & Martha Wilder, Nov. 13, 1760
John Heywood of Lunenburg & Silence White, Dec. 31, 1761
Benjamin Priest & Hannah Johnson, Jan. 20, 1761
Joshua Johnson, Jr., & Hannah Avery of Groton, Jan. 20, 1761
Mitchel Richards of Shirley & Esthar Mitchel of Lunenburg, July 2, 1761
Timothy Kendall & Anna Houghton, both of Leominster, Jan. 20, 1762
James Lock & Rebeckah Wilder, Feb. 2, 1762
John Gibbs & Elizabeth Kendall, Sept. 3, 1760
Samuel Titus of Ipswich-Canada, N. H., & Ann Biglow of Westminster, Sept. 11, 1760
Samuel Osgood of Naraganset No. 6 & Thankfull Mathews, Sept. 18, 1760
Seth Harrington of Westminster & Priscillai Houghton, Nov. 13, 1760
Josiah Osgood & Jane Boynton, Dec. 9, 1760
Zaccheus Bemis & Elizabeth Lyon, both of Westminster, Feb. 10, 1761
Joel Houghton & Sarah Parson of Shrewsbury, Feb. 25, 1761
Gideon Smith & Mary Biglow, both of Westminster, April 16, 1761
Jeremiah Stewart of Leominster & Hannah Stewart, Feb. 4, 1762
Samuel Bixby of Princetown & Hannah Powers, March 4, 1762
George Peterson & Margaret Dorchester, Feb. 26, 1762
William Gibbs & Joanna Gleason, both of Princetown, April 14, 1762
James Houghton (tert[s]) & Ann Eveleth, Sept. 10, 1762
John Boynton of Shrewsbury & Elisabeth Bemon, Jan. 13, 1763

Josiah Jackson & Mary Darby, both of Narraganset
  No. 2,   Jan. 30, 1755
Warren Snow of Leicester & Anna Harvey,   Oct. 25, 1759
Edward Houghton & Lucretia Richardson,   Oct. 16, 1760
William Phelps & Mary Flagg,   Sept. 17, 1761
Dr. Nathan Raymond of Littleton & Rebeckah Richardson,
                                            Dec. 1, 1762
Thomas Gates & Abigail Wilder,   April 23, 1761
Nathaniel Turner & Anna Goss,   Sept. 12, 1758
Simon Willard & Elizabeth Willard of Harvard, Oct. 5, 1758
Richard Baker of Narraganset No. 2 & Mary Sawyer,
                                            Nov. 16, 1758
Elijah Beaman & Thankful Nichols,   April 16, 1759
Edward Parmenter of Sudbury & Sarah Beaman,
                                            June 5, 1759
Hooker Osgood, Jr., & Susanna Sawyer,   June 29, 1759
Thomas Page of Leominster and Mary Knight,
                                            Aug. 16, 1759
John Cobley of Narraganset No. 6 & Mary Wilder,
                                            Nov. 18, 1759
Thomas Grant & Hannah Churchill,   Feb. 7, 1760
Edmund Larkin & Abigail Albert,   May 21, 1760
Elijah Osgood & Mary Wallingsford,   Nov. 19, 1760
Joseph Wilson of Petersham & Hannah Osgood, Jan. 1, 1761
Josiah Fairbank & Abigail Carter,   Jan. 22, 1761
John Ball of Westboro & Abigail Wilder,   Jan. 22, 1791
John McCarty & Margaret Mcfarling,   March 16, 1761
Fortunatus Eager & Thamar Houghton,   June 18, 1761
Peter Thurston & Dorothy Gates,   Dec. 3, 1761
Matthew Knight of Leominster & Dinah Carter,
                                            March 18, 1762
Nath. Wilder & Lucy Knight,   April 17, 1762
John Phelps & Elizabeth Walker,   May 12, 1762
Joel Phelps & Prudence Brown,   May 26, 1762
Stanton Carter & Peninnah Albert,   May 27, 1762
Ens. Tilly Moore & Mrs. Zilpah Whiting,   Aug. 26, 1762
Eben^r Hills of Swansey, N. H., & Abigail Nichols,
                                            Oct. 19, 1762
Cyrus Fairbanks & Lucy Wilder,   Dec. 9, 1762

MARRIAGES.

Stephan Smith & Lucy Kendall,	July 8, 1762
Enoch Dole & Eunice Richardson,	Oct. 26, 1762
Oliver Dresser & Olive Osgood,	Nov. 4, 1762
Daniel Greenleaf & Dorothy Richardson,	Nov. 18, 1762
Moses Sawyer & Mary Sawyer,	April 27, 1763
David Moors & Elizabeth Whitcomb,	Aug. 11, 1763
William Brown & Elizabeth Houghton,	Oct. 20, 1763
Nathaniel Hastings & Elizabeth Goodenow,	March 8, 1764
Nathan Gary & Hepsibeth Wilder,	April 11, 1764
Elijah Houghton & Mary Allen,	Oct. 3, 1764
Peter Hilt of Worcester & Margaret Z——red (?),	Feb. 7, 1763
William Willard of Petersham & Katherine Wilder,	Nov. 22, 1763
Josiah Locke & Esther Kitteridge of Tewksbury,	Feb. 29, 1764
Robert Phelps & Rachel Richardson of Billerica,	Jan. 24, 1765
Dr. Stephen Ball of Westboro & Mary Fairbank,	May 23, 1765
James Goodwin & Bathsheba Robbins,	May 28, 1765
Daniel Warner & Susanna Rugg,	Oct. 30, 1765
Jonathan Whitney & Mary Wyman,	Oct. 31, 1765
Daniel Rugg, Jr., & Elizabeth Divoll,	Oct. 31, 1765
Paul Dickinson of Groton & Damaris Knight,	March 10, 1766
Joseph Wheeler & Mrs. Sarah Allen,	Aug. 14, 1766
William Kendall & Mary Knight,	Sept. 18, 1766
James Godfry & Mrs. Mary Pratt of Harvard,	May 19, 1767
Ephraim Carter, Jr., & Abigail Carter, Jr.,	Dec. 3, 1767
David Nims, Jr., of Keene, N. H., & Jemima Carter,	Jan. 12, 1768
Silas Carter & Lucy Sawyer,	Jan. 12, 1768
Jonathan Kendall, 4th, & Hannah Johnson,	Feb. 9, 1768
Capt. Samuel Wilder of Ashburnham & Mrs. Dorothy Carter,	Feb. 18, 1768
Benjamin Warren of Littleton & Elizabeth Haywood,	Sept. 19, 1764

Zach. Harvey, Jr., & Mary Norcross, both of Prince-
    town,   Nov. 15, 1764
Samuel Hancock of Harvard & Abigail Snow,
                                                        July 21, 1763
Levi Houghton & Ame Richardson,   Nov. 21, 1763
Jonathan Townsend & Hulda Newton, both of West-
    minster,   March 24, 1765
Jotham Rice of Rutland & Hannah Snow,   Feb. 11, 1767
William Williams of Marlboro & Zilpah Wilder,
                                                        Feb. 12, 1767
Kendall Boutell (or Routell) of Lunenburg & Mary
    Wilder of Leominster,   April 1, 1762
Sol. Shed & Elizabeth Boynton, both of Lunenburg,
                                                        May 24, 1763
Benjamin Houghton & Achah Whetcomb,   Oct. 14, 1763
Josiah Sawyer of Bolton & Mary Tooker,   Jan. 14, 1764
Joseph Russ & Susanna Priest,   July 1, 1764
Gardener Wilder & Dorothy Richardson,   March 8, 1765
John Lock & Lucy Wilder,   March 8, 1765
Jacob Bennet & Anna Boynton,   Dec. 11, 1763
Enoch Jewett of Templeton & Mary Moore of Shrews-
    bury,   March 8, 1764
Jedediah Woods of Warwick & Mary Bixby, Jan. 11, 1765
Hannaniah Rand of Westminster & Martha Osgood,
                                                        Dec. 20, 1765
Josh. Church & Kezia Goss,   Feb. 21, 1765
Manassah Bixby of Shrewsbury & Elizabeth Duns-
    moor,   Nov. 12, 1765
Amos Powers & Molly Parmenter, both of Prince-
    town,   Jan. 21, 1766
Aaron Stearns of Princetown & Esther Glazier of
    Westminster,   Feb. 16, 1766
Joseph Houghton, Jr., & Lois Ross, both of Bolton,
                                                        Nov. 29, 1770
Ethan Kendall & Thankfull Moor,   July 4, 1771
Jonathan Carter of Leominster & Damarius Whit-
    comb,   April 3, 1765
Ephraim Robins of Petersham & Joanna Holden
    of Harvard,   July 25, 1765

MARRIAGES.

Elkenah Woodcock of Swansey & Susanna Nichols,
                                          Sept. 24, 1765
Wyat Gun of Swanzey & Martha Houghton,   Feb. 25, 1766
Daniel Spooner of Petersham & Bethia Nichols.
                                          Sept. 3, 1767
Samuel Joslin & Abigail Wilder,   Oct. 1, 1767
William Alexander, Jr., of Lunenburg & Ruth Putnam of Harvard,   May 31, 1759
James Digens & Lydia Hale, both of Leominster,
                                          June 1, 1769
Abisha Phelps & Katharine Richardson,   April 22, 1770
Jonathan Carter of Sudbury & Deborah Hunt, Oct. 25, 1771
Silas Church & Mary Osgood of Templeton, Nov. 25, 1771
John Wilder & Abigail Kendall,   Dec. 1, 1771
Thomas Meriam & Sarah Wilder, both of Westminster,   Nov. 24, 1762
Robert Crawford of Worcester & Elizabeth Leitch of Lunenburg,   Jan. 13, 1763
Levi Woods of Petersham & Tamar Houghton of Leominster,   April 20, 1763
Nathaniel Willard & Eunice Farwell of Stow, May 25, 1763
William Longley of Shirley & Lydia Wallingsford,
                                          Aug. 8, 1763
Robert Proctor & Ruth Fowl,   Oct. 7, 1764
David Hastings & Dinah Williams, both of Shrewsbury,   May 25, 1763
John Richardson of Petersham & Eunice Green,
                                          Dec. 18, 1765
Thomas Bennett & Lydia Longley,   Dec. 29, 1765
Samuel Norcross & Rachel Harvey, both of Princetown,   May 2, 1766
Moses Russell of Littleton & Sarah Phelps, Nov. 27, 1767
Andrew Poor & Esther Snow,   Nov. 1, 1767
John Hammond & Lucy Powers,   Nov. 3, 1768
Andrew Haskell & Lois Bullin,   Aug. 10, 1769
Joseph Moor, Jr., & Hepzibeh Bush of Shrewsbury,
                                          Oct. 26, 1769
Moses Smith & Abigail Green,   Jan. 24, 1771
Timothy Blodget & Lydia Walker,   June 3, 1771

LANCASTER.

Eliphalet Rogers of Princetown & Eunice Bennet,
                                                Aug. 14, 1771
William Tinney & Mehitable Jones, both of Bolton,
                                                Oct. 15, 1771
Jedidiah Boynton & Elizabeth Holt,   Feb. 10, 1772
Nathaniel Wright, Jr., & Ruth Richardson,   May 22, 1770
William Thompson & Elizabeth Jewett,   May 30, 1770
Joshua Piper & Betty Proctor,   June 11, 1770
Thomas Rugg & Mehitabell Houghton,   July 26, 1770
Daniel Norcross & Thankful Sawyer,   Oct. 9, 1770
Elijah Ball & Rebecca Moors,   Oct. 18, 1770
Solomon Goodale & Persis Bayley,   Oct. 30, 1770
Ephraim Willard, Jr., & Lois Geary,   Nov. 29, 1770
Rev. Caleb Prentice & Pamela Mellen,   Jan. 1, 1771
Stephen Haywood & Ruth Dunsmoor,   March 6, 1771
Joseph Whitaker & Mary Whitney,   April 25, 1771
Jonathan Buss & widow Mary Stewart,   July 4, 1771
David Holt & Hannah Kendall,   Sept. 25, 1771
Jonas Johnson & Damaris Rugg,   Oct. 17, 1771
Samuel Gerrish & Abigail Moor,   Dec. 26, 1771
Asa Smith & Sarah Stewart,   March 29, 1772
David Goodale & Dorothy Newton,   April 8, 1772
Giles Wills & Relief Wilder,   May 5, 1772
Ezra Hale & widow Thankful Brabrook,   June 23, 1772
Jonathan Butterick & Hannah Wilder Sawyer,   July 2, 1772
Joseph Seaver & Abigail Sawyer,   July 7, 1772
Jonathan Moor & Elizabeth Richardson,   July 8, 1772
Luther Graves & Phebe Jewett,   Aug. 13, 1772
Samuel Mason & Sarah Whitney,   Oct. 8, 1772
Obadiah Gross & Lucy Houghton,   April 1, 1773
Lemuel Beman & Prudence Rowe,   May 19, 1773
Elias Farnsworth & Lois Willard,   Nov. 25, 1773
Abner Farrington & Joanna Kilburn,   Dec. 7, 1773
Joseph Lewis & Martha Lock,   Dec. 14, 1773
Moses Newhall & Hannah Robbins,   Dec. 16, 1773
Levi Carter & Silence Beman,   Jan. 20, 1774
Nathaniel Brown & Esther Smith,   Feb. 1, 1774
John Phelps & Lois Davis,   Feb. 10, 1774
Silas Fairbanks & Mrs. Lydia Prouty,   March 17, 1768

MARRIAGES.

Jacob Bennet of Leominster & Mrs. Elizabeth
    Wilder,　　　　　　　　　　　　　　April 7, 1768
Joseph Page & Mrs. Eunice White,　　　July 21, 1768
Samuel Wilder & Mrs. Sarah Ballard,　　Aug. 1, 1768
Timothy Temple & Mrs. Deborah Ball,　　Aug. 31, 1768
James Crosman of Monadnock & Mrs. Mary Preist,
　　　　　　　　　　　　　　　　　　　Oct. 17, 1768
Abel Shead of Groton & Mrs. Ruth Haskell, Nov. 29, 1768
Francis Eager of Paxton & Sarah Frairbank, Dec. 1, 1768
Paul Richardson of Winchester, N. H.; & Mrs. Euse-
    bius Harrington,　　　　　　　　　　Jan. 5, 1769
Joseph House & Mrs. Alice Houghton,　Jan. 31, 1769
Joseph Carter & Mrs. Bulah Carter,　　Feb. 22, 1769
Deacon Israel Houghton & Mrs. Elizabeth Wilder,
　　　　　　　　　　　　　　　　　　　March 14, 1769
John Wilder & Mrs. Catherine Sawyer of Bolton,
　　　　　　　　　　　　　　　　　　　June 1, 1769
John Jonus (?) of Colrain & Mrs. Abigail Atherton,
　　　　　　　　　　　　　　　　　　　July 12, 1769
William Shaw of Peterboro & Mrs. Barbara Zwier (?),
　　　　　　　　　　　　　　　　　　　July 20, 1769
William Heywood of Lunenburg & Mrs. Rebecca
    Kendell,　　　　　　　　　　　　　　Oct. 12, 1769
Edward Poor of Worc. & Mrs. Eunice Goodridge,
　　　　　　　　　　　　　　　　　　　Nov. 11, 1769
James Pratt & Mrs. Zerniah (?) Rugg,　Nov. 16, 1779
Sampson Ayner & Lucy Lew of Littleton (free
    negroes),　　　　　　　　　　　　　Dec. 14, 1769
Joseph Goodridge of Lunenburg & Mrs. Elizabeth
    Phelps,　　　　　　　　　　　　　　Dec. 28, 1769
James Elder of Worcester & Mrs. Sarah Gates, Jan. 16, 1770
James Foster of New Ipswich & Hannah Priest, April 10, 1770
Joseph Brown & Mrs. Annice Knight,　　May 29, 1770
John Priest, Jr., & Mrs. Mary Longley,　May 5, 1770
William Grimes, Jr., of Swanzey, N. H., & Mrs.
    Mary Willard,　　　　　　　　　　　May 31, 1770
John Townsend of Bolton & Mrs. Eunice Fairbank,
　　　　　　　　　　　　　　　　　　　July 25, 1770

    ED.—The title "Mrs." applied evidently to maidens as well as widows, but no distinction on the Record.

LANCASTER.

Salmon Goodfrey & Mrs. Rebecca Phelps,	Aug. 20, 1770
John Brown of Charlemont & Mrs. Lucy Rugg,	Oct. 1, 1770
Nathaniel Joslyn & Mrs. Mary Bennet,	Sept. 5, 1770
Micah Brian & Mrs. Rebecca Ball,	Nov. 27, 1770
Jonas Fairbank & Mrs. Elizabeth Wilder,	Dec. 6, 1770
Thomas Stearns of Fitchburg & Mrs. Molley White,	Jan. 9, 1771
Joshua Smith of Southboro & Mrs. Abigail Wilder,	Jan. 31, 1771
John Bennett & Mrs. Lucy Phelps,	Feb. 7, 1771
Jacob Zwier (?) & Mrs. Abigail Priest,	March 21, 1771
Daniel Bigelow of Worcester & Mrs. Mary Ballard,	May 2, 1771
Antipas Bartlet of Northboro & Mrs. Lois White,	June 13, 1771
Aaron Kendall of Leominster & Mrs. Katherine Wyman,	Nov. 21, 1771
John Robbins & Mrs. Lydia Haskell,	Nov. 27, 1771
Lemuel Haskell of Harvard & Mrs. Lucy Green,	Nov. 28, 1771
Daniel Goss & Mrs. Eunice Wilder,	Dec. 20, 1771
Samuel Wilder & Mrs. Martha Rugg,	Jan. 15, 1772
Samuel Crosby of Billerica & Mrs. Abigail Bailey,	Feb. 6, 1772
Joshua Whitcomb of Templeton & Mrs. Eunice Prescott,	Feb. 26, 1772
William Locke & Mrs. Mary Fowle,	June 18, 1772
Jonathan Bosworth & Mrs. Mary Holt,	Aug. 6, 1772
Moses Wilder & Mrs. Eunice Furbush,	Aug. 26, 1772
Dr. Israel Atherton & Mrs. Rebecca Prentice,	Sept. 6, 1772
Elijah Rice of Holden & Mrs. Leafy Williams of Princetown,	Nov. 10, 1772
Samuel Kilbourn of Lunenburg & Mrs. Sarah Cook,	Dec. 7, 1772
John Locke of Templeton & Mrs. Henrietta Harrington,	Dec. 23, 1772
Titus Wilder & Mrs. Mary Allen,	April 21, 1773
Jotham Woods & Mrs. Mehatable Aldis,	Aug. 19, 1773
Moses Russell & Mrs. Hannah Kendall,	Aug. 21, 1773

MARRIAGES.

William Brooks & Mrs. Bulah Wilder,	Nov. 10, 1773
Reuben Geary & Mrs. Lucy Cutter Brooks,	Nov. 17, 1773
Timothy Knight, Jr., & Mrs. Lydia Wilder,	Nov. 18, 1773
Dr. Abraham Haskell of Lunenburg & Mrs. Sarah Green,	Nov. 25, 1773
Lemuel Fairbank & Mrs. Phebe Winn,	Dec. 9, 1773
Joseph Wilder, Jr., of Leominster & Mrs. Susanna Phelps,	Dec. 16, 1773
Benjamin Turner & Mrs. Sarah Lypenwell,	Dec. 22, 1773
Phinehas Sawyer, Jr., of Fitchburg & Mrs. Mary Prescott,	Jan. 4, 1774
Joel Osgood & Mrs. Lois Rugg,	Jan. 6, 1774
Jeremiah Sackwell & Mrs. Hannah Ross,	March 2, 1774
John Abbott & Lois Burnett,	March 22, 1775
Moses Mosman of Sudbury & Mary Willard,	April 2, 1775
Ephraim Kendall & Elizabeth Knight,	May 30, 1775
Joseph Joslyn & Dorothy Osgood,	July 20, 1775
Lemuel Sawyer & Anna Pratt,	Sept. 10, 1775
Eleazer Brown of Swansey, N. H., & Susanna Rugg,	Oct. 5, 1775
John Prescott, Jr., & Mary Ballard,	Oct. 25, 1775
Nathaniel Haskell & Abigail Sawyer,	Oct. 31, 1775
Rev. Jacob Biglow of Sudbury & Elizabeth Wells,	Nov. 23, 1775
Capt. Israel Jennison of Worcester & Margaret Coolidge of Boston, resident in Lancaster,	Dec. 26, 1775
Colonel Joseph Wilder & Rebecca Lock,	Dec. 27, 1775
Samuel Moor & Abigail Hasting,	Jan. 6, 1776
Jonathan Osgood & Rebecca Divoll,	Jan. 11, 1776
Capt. Samuel Mower of Wor. & Esther Lock,	Jan. 18, 1776
John Hoar of Westminster & Abigail White,	Feb. 21, 1776
John Chandler & Katy Holman,	Feb. 29, 1776
Henry Willard (farmer) & Sybal Knights,	July 16, 1776
Daniel Knights & Mary Woods,	Feb. 27, 1777
Luther Fairbank & Thankful Wheelock,	March 5, 1777
Moses Sawyer & Betty Larkin,	April 23, 1777
Samuel Adams & Mrs. Elizabeth Nowell,	May 1, 1777
Josiah Sawyer & Mrs. Susanna Green,	May 8, 1777
Joseph Willson of Keene & Mrs. Sarah Wilder,	June 2, 1777

Samuel Dickerson & Mrs. Lois Willard,	June 19, 1777
Mr. Israel Butler & Mrs. Anna Phillips,	June 26, 1777
Deacon Cyrus Fairbank & Mrs. Elizabeth Wynne,	July 2, 1777
Zebediah Wyman of Woburn & Mrs. Eunice Wyman,	Aug. 6, 1777
William Wilder & Mrs. Relief Carter,	Dec. 18, 1777
Ephraim Munrow & Mrs. Mary Atherton, both of Harvard,	June 12, 1778
Samuel Thompson & Mrs. Eunice Dole,	April 1, 1778
Joseph Farnsworth & Mrs. Mary Hersey,	April 8, 1778
Abel Phelps & Mrs. Lois Willard,	May 7, 1778
Jonathan White & Mrs. Rebeccah Haskell,	May 28, 1778
Thomas Cummings & Mrs. Dolly Case,	Sept. 7, 1778
Nathaniel Eaton & Mrs. Lucy Bennett,	Dec. 30, 1778
Dr. R. P. Bridge & Mrs. Anna Harrington,	Jan. 24, 1772
Jacob Fowle & Mrs. Elizabeth Abbott,	Jan. 31, 1772
Jonathan Wallas of South Brimfield & Mrs. Elizabeth Osgood,	March 4, 1772
Jeremiah Ballard & Mrs. Rebecca Joslyn,	March 4, 1772
Dr. Jonas Prescott of Rindge & Mrs. Susanna Wilder,	March 31, 1772

HARDWICK.

Jan. 10, 1739, the plantation of Lambstown established as Hardwick. Prov. Laws, Vol. II, p. 971. First (Congregational) Church organized 1736. Officiating clergyman mentioned: Rev. David White.

Elisha Field & Betty Pratt,	Jan. 11, 1753
John Haskell & Elizabeth Lawrence,	March 4, 1753
Jacob Gibbs & Bethiah Bacon,	March 13, 1753
Gideon Carpenter & Jemima Jennis,	May 31, 1753
Samuel Atwood & Peace Steward,	Aug. 30, 1753
Joseph Safford & Martha Powers,	Oct. 26, 1753
Benjamin Stearns & Mary Warren,	Nov. 12, 1753
Solomon Emmons & Mary Marsh,	Jan. 31, 1754
Jacob Pepper & Abigail Foster,	Feb. 28, 1754
Elisha Temple & Abigail Thompson,	Feb. 3, 1755

MARRIAGES.

Nathaniel Merrick & Susanna Lawrence,	Feb. 13, 1755
James Bacon & Abigail Aikens,	June 5, 1755
Nathaniel Whitcomb & Margaret Aikens,	June 19, 1755
Ichabod Stratton & Hannah Goodenow,	July 1, 1755
Chellis (?) Safford & Rebekah Winslow,	July 10, 1755
Zeru Shaddai (?) Doty & Mary Warner,	Dec. 4, 1755
Phillip Spooner & Elizabeth Winslow,	Dec. 25, 1756
Joseph McMichaell & Thankful Olmstead,	Jan. 21, 1756
James Fay, Jr., & Mary Winslow,	March 18, 1756
Timothy Pratt & Ruth Abbott,	Oct. 14, 1756
Zebu. (?) Johnson & Ellis Mirick,	Nov. 25, 1756
Israel Olmstead & Anna Safford,	Nov. 25, 1756
Jonathan Farr & Mercy Winslow,	Jan. 19, 1757
Nathan Billing & Lydia Wells,	Feb. 24, 1757
Jeremiah Anderson & Isabell Partrick,	Nov. 15, 1757
Isaac Morgan & Lucretia Downing,	Dec. 6, 1757
Daniel Billing & Mary Rugles,	Feb. 23, 1758
Stephen Ghoram & Sarah Freeman,	March 16, 1758
David Gilbert & Esther Ginne,	March 23, 1758
Moses Whiple & Katherine Forbush,	May 20, 1758
Noah Emmonds & Mary Farr,	May 20, 1758
Daniel Warner & Mary Wright,	May 31, 1758
Stephen Fisk & Anna Green,	June 29, 1758
Lieutenant Nathaniel Kellog & Martha Hamond,	July 19, 1758
Lenard Robinson & Rebecca Billing,	Aug. 31, 1758
Abell Benjamin & Susanna Carpenter,	May 22, 1759
Thodorus Doty & Jane Dunsmore,	May 30, 1759
Daniel Fay & Mary Crosby,	March 10, 1757
Ebenezer Safford & Abigail Higgins,	Nov. 24, 1759
Samuel Dexter & Thankfull Freemon,	Nov. 25, 1759
Dr. Chilles Safford & Lydia Warner,	Feb. 8, 1760
Capt. Jonathan Fletcher & Mary Sears,	May 1, 1760
Ensign Jonas Fay & Sarah Fasset,	May 1, 1760
Isaac Abbot & Elizabeth Goodenow,	Aug. 14, 1760
Benjamin Rogers & Mehitable Fay,	Sept. 10, 1760
Benjamin Winchester & Sarah Allen,	Feb. 19, 1761
Wilson Freeman & Dorcas Fish,	Feb. 28, 1761
Simon Giffen & Abigail Higgens,	March 24, 1761

Elkanah Slevant (?) & Lydia Cobb,	Sept. 7, 1761
Freemon Sears & Mehitabel Haskel,	Oct. 22, 1761
Rev. Lamuel Hedge & Mrs. Sarah White,	Nov. 5, 1761
David Allen & Elisabeth Fisk,	Nov. 12, 1761
Edward Clafford & Abigail Winslow,	Nov. 30, 1761
Israel Johnson & Abial Safford,	Dec. 29, 1761
Edward Foster & Deborah Bangs,	Jan. 13, 1762
Elijah Warner & Submitt Wells,	Jan. 14, 1762
Ebenezer Chipman & Susanna Ruggles,	March 4, 1762
Abijah Edson & Hannah Ruggles,	June 10, 1762
Azariah Wright & Mary Safford,	June 29, 1762
Nathan Wheeler & Hannah Hunt,	July 1, 1762
Jacob Hastings & Mary Bangs,	July 22, 1762
Thomas Wheeler & Sarah Warner,	Sept. 8, 1762
Lieut. John Granger & Rebecca Hascall, both of New Brantree,	June 16, 1763
Noah Houghton of Palmer & Rachel Thompson of New Brantree,	Sept. 7, 1763
Ebenezer Lawrence & Lydia Richmond of New Brantree,	Dec. 18, 1763
Moses Whitcomb & Sarah Powers,	Nov. 4, 1762
Solomon Johnson & Sarah Dexter,	Dec. 28, 1762
Benjamin Rogers & Temperance Finney,	April 5, 1763
Jonathan Farr, Jr., & Lucy Fay,	Oct. 27, 1763
Enoch Babcock & Katherine Densmore,	Dec. 15, 1763
Solomon Green & Elizabeth Page,	Dec. 29, 1763
Benjamin Robarts & Martha Abbot,	Feb. 29, 1764
Abraham Knolton & Susanna Jorden,	March 12, 1764
Henry Gilbert & Patience Marsh,	April 5, 1764
Samuel Billings & Buelah Fay,	June 28, 1764
John Cobb & Thankfull Sears,	July 19, 1764
Benjamin Green & Hannah Robinson,	Aug. 31, 1764
Ebenezer Lyscomb & Mary Hooker,	Oct. 8, 1764
Edward Higgins & Thankful Rice,	Oct. 17, 1764
Edward Goodspeed & Judith Winslow,	Oct. 19, 1764
Nathaniel Dickinson & Elizabeth Fisk,	Nov. 7, 1764
Stephan Belding & Martha Johnson,	Nov. 7, 1764
Joseph Warner & Mary Whipple,	Nov. 13, 1764
Isaac Fay & Keziah Doan,	Nov. 22, 1764

MARRIAGES.

Joseph Nye & Sarah Bradish,	Dec. 27, 1764
John Dunsmore & Elizabeth ———,	April 15, 1765
John Burt of Springfield & Bathsheba Warner,	June 4, 1765
David Aken & Hannah Simons of Ware,	July 18, 1765
Aaron Hunt & Sarah Robinson,	Oct. 24, 1765
William Thomas & Abiel Collins,	Aug. 23, 1765
John Tufts & Martha Ruggles,	Nov. 11, 1765
Abel Harwood & Sarah Ruggles,	Nov. 27, 1765
Lemuel Cobb & Lydia Allen,	Oct. 10, 1765
John Hunt & Patience Wright,	Dec. 25, 1765
David Glazier & Sarah Pratt,	Feb. 6, 1766
Asa Hatch & Lucy Warner,	Jan. 23, 1766
Samuel Hunt & Abigail Fisk,	Feb. 20, 1766
Jonathan Warner & Hannah Mandell,	Feb. 5, 1766
John Tufts & Martha Ruggles,	Nov. 11, 1763
Leonard Robinson & Mercy Newton,	March 13, 1766
James Wright & Mary Hunt,	June 18, 1766
Job Dexter & Mary Hinkley,	July 17, 1766
William Sherman & Hannah Steward,	Sept. 10, 1766
Shearjashub Goodspeed & Elizabeth Ruggles,	Nov. 20, 1766
Benj. Ruggles, 3d, & Elizabeth Fay,	Nov. 26, 1766
Sol. Bush & Content Whetcomb,	Nov. 27, 1766
Asa Curtis & Lois Goss,	Nov. 27, 1766
Silas Johnson & Patience Walker,	Nov. 27, 1766
Silas Nye & Patience Carpenter,	Nov. 27, 1766
Philip Washburn & Sarah Carpenter,	Jan. 8, 1767
Abiel Stetson & Ruth Bonny,	Feb. 24, 1767
Eli Freeman & Mary Rice,	March 26, 1767
Zachariah Harwood & Levina Rice,	April 30, 1767
Samuel Beak & Abigail Thomas,	July 30, 1767
Samuel Billing & Sarah Crosby,	Nov. 26, 1767
William Fuller & Mercy Powers,	Dec. 3, 1767
Aaron Power & Hannah Goodenow,	March 10, 1768
Abner Marble of Petersham & Zerniah Rice,	April 19, 1768
John Stone & Susanna Mundell,	May 12, 1768
Stephen Warner & Lois Goss,	May 25, 1768
Timothy Moore & Mary Warner,	May 25, 1768
Joseph Smith & Jane Smith of Petersham,	Aug. 26, 1768
Daniel Steward & Eunice Allen,	Sept. 5, 1768

William Page, Jr., & Mercy Raymond,	Oct. 6, 1768
James Page, Jr., & Thankfull Raymond,	Oct. 6, 1768
John Foster of ——chester & Rebecca Page,	Oct. 6, 1768
Benjamin Robinson of New Braintree & Hannah Nye,	Nov. 2, 1768
Henry Higgins & Mary Fisk,	Nov. 9, 1768
Elisha Gilbert of Oakham & Submit Glaizer,	Nov. 16, 1768
Nathaniel Rice of Rutland & Elisabeth Lawrence,	Nov. 24, 1768
Silas Dean & Elisabeth Randell of Greenwich,	Nov. 30, 1768
Luke Brown, Jr., & Mary Adams, both of Worcester,	Jan. 26, 1769
Reuben Snow & Mercy Sears,	May 11, 1769
Eleazer Packard & Mary Woodbury,	June 9, 1769
John Griffin & Mary Weeks,	Sept. 7, 1769
Eliphalet Washburn & Anna Benjamin,	Sept. 19, 1769
Paul Knowlton & Lucy Forbush,	Nov. 8, 1769
David White & Bathsheba Crowell,	Nov. 23, 1769
Experience Luce & Anna Lawrence,	Nov. 30, 1769
Jabez Elwell & Thankfull Clark,	Dec. 21, 1769
Ebenezer Chiles & Abigail Wellis,	Dec. 16, 1769
Nathan Billing & Relience (?) Bangs,	Dec. 26, 1769
Jonathan Fisk & Hannah Rice,	Jan. 18, 1770
John Raymond & Mercy Jordan,	March 7, 1771
Lemuel Willis & Rebecca Berry,	May 27, 1771
Daniel Munden & Rebecca Wheeler,	Aug. 8, 1771
Daniel Clarke & Lydia Carpenter,	July 3, 1771
Elisha Sears & Hannah Sears,	Oct. 31, 1771
Stephen Warner & Damaris Church,	Nov. 13, 1771
Richard Waite & Submit Thomas,	Nov. 14, 1771
Richard Sears & Mary Lee,	Dec. 19, 1771
Ezra Alden & Sarah Harwood,	Jan. 2, 1772
John Hamilton & Isabel Burnet,	Feb. 27 (?), 1772
Edward Ruggles, Jr., & Anna Dean,	March 25, 1772
Elias Walker & Sarah Aiken,	Feb. 25, 1772
Silvanus Cobb & Elizabeth Warren,	March 9, 1772
Samuel Linds & Deborah Perkins,	March 19, 1772
Joseph Clawland & Betty Wheeler,	May 4, 1772
Roger Haskell & Joanna Haskell,	May 28, 1772

MARRIAGES.

Joanna Flint & Marcy Leonard,	June 18, 1772
James Wing & Rebecca Willis,	Aug. 13, 1772
Benjamin Stebbins & Marcy Aikens,	Sept. 24, 1772
Luke Bonney & Marcy Thomas,	Nov. 5, 1772
Benajah Putnam & Eliz^a Livermore,	Nov. 19, 1772
Robert McIntyre & Rhoda Warner,	Nov. 26, 1772
John Amidown & Mercy Allen,	Feb. 14, 1771
John Nims & Betty Rice,	Feb. 14, 1771
John Hunt & Elizabeth Webster,	Dec. 23, 1772
Benjamin Ruggles & Jerusha Aikens,	Feb. 11, 1773
David Leonard & Hannah Whipple,	Feb. 15, 1773
John Bradish & Hannah Warner,	March 4, 1773
Stewart Southgate & Deborah Rayment,	July 22, 1773
Ezra Conant & Anna Fisk,	March 21, 1770
Thomas Wheet & Abigail Hearns,	March 22, 1770
Jonathan Danforth & Susanna White,	April 19, 1770
Benjamin Fisk & Hannah Winslow,	Aug. 15, 1770
Stephen Rice & Thankful Gleazer,	Oct. 23, 1770
James Page & Anna Warren,	Oct. 25, 1770
Elisha Cobb & Elisabeth Burnet,	Nov. 8, 1770
Southworth Jenkins & Hulda Wright,	Nov. 15, 1770
Ephraim Cleveland & Lydia Whipple,	Nov. 15, 1770
Isaac Nye & Hannah Walker,	Nov. 29, 1770
Amos Thomas & Eunice Bangs,	Dec. 20, 1770
Ephraim Titus & Hannah Cobb,	Dec. 20, 1770
James Lawton & Mary Rayment,	Jan. 3, 1771
Nathaniel Leason & Sarah Johnson,	Jan. 14, 1771
Gideon Wheeler & Sarah Forbush,	Jan. 14, 1771
Nathan Carpenter & Anna Cox,	March 15, 1773
Joseph Robinson & Sarah Clark,	Sept. 30, 1773
Paul Dean & Elizabeth Ruggles,	Sept. 19, 1773
Timothy Nichols & Joanna Dean,	Jan. 13, 1774
Edward Taylor & Lydia Haskell,	Nov. 23, 1775
William Johnson & Hannah Johnson,	Jan. 25, 1776
James Hawkes & Olive Willis,	March 7, 1776
Thomas Robinson, Jr., & Rebecca Paige,	April 11, 1776
Joseph Chamberlain & Deborah Nye,	April 18, 1776
Calvin Fairbanks & Jenney Ayres,	June 20, 1776
Dudley Jordan & Bathsheba Rice,	Aug. 8, 1776

Jesse Kinney & Hannah Stearns, Aug. 11, 1776
Jabez Cobb & Content Clark, Dec. 8, 1776
Paul Mandell, Jr., & Mary Briggs, Nov. 28, 1776
Thomas Martin Wright & Elizabeth Newton, Dec. 19, 1776
Jesse Byam & Sarah Chamberlain, Jan. 30, 1777
Edmund Willis & Mary Fuller, Feb. 23, 1777
Rufus Carpenter & Olive Whitcomb, Feb. 27, 1777
Lemuel Cobb & Abigail Ammidown, March 27, 1777
Stephen Woodward & Molly Sibley, May 13, 1777
Moses Mandell & Mary Wheeler, May 28, 1777
Judah Simonds & Thankful Allis, May 28, 1777
Nathaniel Graves & Marcy Paige, May 29, 1777
John Ruggles & Mary Caldwell, May 29, 1777
Andrew Haskell & Susannah Paine, July 10, 1777
John Perkins & Sarah White, July 23, 1777
James Thompson & Polly Sellon, Aug. 20, 1777
John Hedge & Mary Haskell, Sept. 7, 1777
Hon. Jonas Fay, Esq., of Bennington, Vt., & Mrs.
    Lydia Safford, Nov. 20, 1777
Thomas Shaw & Elizabeth Finney of Petersham, Jan. 7, 1778
Jonathan Lynds of Petersham & Mrs. Rhoda Mc-
    Intyer, April 26, 1778
Pauz (?) Rice & Chloe Lincoln, April 8, 1779
Lieut. John Hastings & Mehitable Berry, April 11, 1779
Capt. Edward Clark of Hubbardston & Susanna Rice,
    April 22, 1779
Seth Babbit & Betty Blanchard, April 22, 1779
Martin Rice of Charlemont & Lucy Rice, July 6, 1779
John Dotey & Mary Mandell, Sept. 19, 1779
Ephraim Hodges & Katharine Johnson, Nov. 25, 1779
Atwood Aiken & Hannah Willis, Dec. 9, 1779
Benjamin Ruggles, 4th, & Betty Parks, Dec. 15, 1779
Levi Babbit of Norton & Betty Babbit, Dec. 21, 1779
Daniel Ruggles & Lucy Paige, Dec. 30, 1779
Moses Haskell, Jr., & Priscilla Hinkley, Jan. 12, 1780
Benjamin Holmes of Princeton & Elizabeth Weeks,
    Feb. 10, 1780
Joseph Robinson of New Braintree & Lucy Ruggles
    of Barre, Feb., 1780

MARRIAGES.

Asa Hodge & Meriam Dexter,	May 31, 1780
Peter Ford & Mary Fothergill,	June 25, 1780
Seth Woodward of Petersham & Ruth Ayres,	Aug. 25, 1778
Jonathan Richardson of Barre & Temperence Nye of Oakham,	Nov. 12, 1778
Samuel Hopkins & Elizabeth Hastings,	Dec. 17, 1778
Silvanus Nye of Barre & Mary Banks of Keene, N. H.,	March 2, 1779
Timothy Newton, Jr., late of Hardwick, & Abigail Earl,	March 4, 1779
Aaron Hudson & Sarah Webster,	Nov. 3, 1777
Jacob Whipple & Edna Furbush,	Dec. 30, 1777
Elijah Washburn & Mary Winchester,	Jan. 1, 1778
Jonathan Child & Deliverance Freeman,	Jan. 15, 1778
John Newton & Lydia Freeman,	Jan. 15, 1778
Daniel Fay, Jr., & Mary Paige,	Aug. 23, 1778
Asa Hull of Montague & Martha Furbush,	Oct. 12, 1778
Jedidiah Fay & Jerusha Aiken,	Nov. 12, 1778
Thomas Fuller & Lydia Paige,	Nov. 26, 1778
Moses Hunt & Esther Jinney,	Dec. 10, 1778
Jonathan Gilbert of New Braintree & Sarah Ammidon,	Jan. 5, 1779
Benjamin Stetson & Mary Johnson,	Aug. 24, 1780
Joseph Hews of Lime & Mary Rice,	Oct. 5, 1780
Ebenezer Cobb & Martha Hastings,	Oct. 5, 1780
David Prat & Hannah Hammond of Petersham,	Oct. 12, 1780
Deacon Daniel Spooner of Petersham & Mrs. Mary Dean,	Oct. 16, 1780
Theodoras Forbes & Elizabeth Winchester,	Jan. 22, 1781
James Biram & Elizabeth Cox,	Feb. 8, 1781
Henry Rixforth & widow Sarah Stanford,	Feb. 2, 1781
Nathaniel Harriman of Chesterfield & Bethany Snow,	March 14, 1781
Oliver Harris & Mehitable Shaw,	April 4, 1781
Ephraim Hunt, Jr., of Greenwich & Rhod Furbush,	April 5, 1781
Robert Sprout & Betsey Lincoln,	Sept. 17, 1781
Isaac Parmeter & Lydia Furnas, both of Oakham,	Oct. 4, 1781

Antipas How of Swanzey, N. H., & Joanna Larrance,
    Jan. 20, 1782
Gamaliel Ellis & Jemima Nye,   Feb. 21, 1782
John Rice of Charlemont & Ruth Rice,   March 6, 1782
George Haskell & Comfort Knowlton,   April 25, 1782
Seth Hinckley, Jr., & Lydia Berry,   May 12, 1782
Stephen Chandler & Meribah Nye,   May 23, 1782
Moses Cheney, Jr., of Warwick & Lucy Dexter, July 4, 1782
Samuel Haskins, Jr., & Percis Johnson,   Sept. 5, 1782
John Terry, Jr., & Sarah Ramsdel,   Sept. 26, 1782
John Keith & Lerviah Willis,   Oct. 21, 1782
William Nye & Molly Purrington,   Dec. 26, 1782
Tilly Foster & Abigail Hammond, both of Petersham,
    Dec. 29, 1782
Benjamin Woodward & Molly Woodward,   Jan. 17, 1783
Solomon Mason, Jr., of Greenwich & Margaret Harris,
    Jan. 30, 1783
Edward Allen of New Windsor & Sarah Snow,
    Jan. 30, 1783
Noah Patch & Jemima Cox,   Feb. 4, 1783
David Barnard of Shelburne & Rhoda Allen, March 4, 1783
Ephraim Ruggles & Olive Powers,   March 20, 1783
Nathan Rozer of Rutland & Abigail Mead of Hub-
    bardston,   April 5, 1783
David Weeks & Betsey Robinson,   May 22, 1783
John Giffin & Kezia Smith,   July 22, 1783
Phinehas Meigs of Sunderland & Susanna Winslow,
    Aug. 3, 1783
Silvanus Brimhall of Barre & Triphena Johnson,
    Sept. 14, 1783
Nathaniel Johnson, Jr., & Mary Nye,   Sept. 5, 1783
Peter Rainheart of Greenwich & Polly Crose, Nov. 2, 1783
Henry Butterfield of Greenwich & Rachel Thayer,
    Nov. 20, 1783
David Basset & Phebe Terry,   Dec. 11, 1783
Ebenezer Sprout & Mary Thayer of Petersham,
    Dec. 11, 1783
Joseph Parks of Norwich & Dorothy Bartlett,
    Dec. 11, 1783

MARRIAGES.

Asa Brigham of Barnard & Sarah Newton,	Dec. 25, 1783
Elijah Carpenter & Sarah Wing,	Feb. 1, 1784
Eleazar Dexter & Abigail Dexter,	April 8, 1784
Nathan Paige & Hanna Cobb,	April 25, 1784
John Gorham & Polly Dexter,	June 3, 1784
Frederick Wicker & Susanna Newton,	June 24, 1784
Lot Jenny of Hartland & Olive Hatch,	Aug. 4, 1784
Israel Lawton & Dolly Billing,	Aug. 26, 1784
Timothy Hathaway & Rhoda Clark,	Sept. 23, 1784
Israel Aiken of Windsor & Susanna Smith,	Sept. 23, 1784
John Hunt & Sarah Fay,	Oct. 1, 1784
Silas Gorham & Cynthia Hanmer,	Nov. 14, 1784
Robert Dean of Barnard & Unice Billing,	Dec. 23, 1784
Foster Paige & Amittia Page,	Jan. 6, 1785
Moses Forbush & Patty Marble of Petersham,	Jan. 9, 1785
Samuel Warden of Petersham & Betsey Sibley,	June 30, 1785
Simon Oliver of Barre & Mary Morgan,	July 24, 1785
Abijah Sibley & Patty Korey,	Sept. 29, 1785
John Earl & Unice Allen,	Oct. 2, 1785
Abel White & Abigail Babbit, both of Barre,	Oct. 5, 1785
James Pierce & Susanna Mirick,	Nov. 20, 1785
James Bailey & Silence Humphrey of Sheutesbury,	Nov. 24, 1785
Judah Hinckley & Sally Ruggles,	Dec. 15, 1785
Silas Johnson, Jr., & Hanna Nye,	Dec. 15, 1785
John Jameson & Rhoda Smith of Petersham,	Dec. 15, 1785
Thomas Spooner & Martha Smith,	Dec. 15, 1785
Abraham Bell of New Braintree & Elizabeth Joslyn,	Dec. 29, 1785
Joseph Bowman, Jr., of Barnard & Fanny Spooner,	Jan. 26, 1786
Joseph Harvey & Polly Arnold,	Feb. 2, 1786

OXFORD.

May 31, 1693, "Daniel Allen is recorded as Representative from Oxford." Mass. Archives, Vol. VI, p. 278. First (Congregational) Church organized 1721. Officiating clergymen mentioned: Rev. Jonathan Campbell, Rev. John Campbell, Rev. Joseph Bowman.

Oliver Shumway of Oxford & Elisabeth Holman of
    Sutton, April 15, 1747
Elias Tenison & Hannah Twist, both of Sutton,
    June 16, 1748
John Eddy & Patience Town, June 18, 1747
Ebenezer Merriam & Elisath Lock, both of County
    Gore, Sept. 17, 1747
Joseph Robbins of Douglass & Mary Chamberlain,
    Nov. 3, 1748
Ebenezer Learned & Jerusha Baker, Oct. 5, 1749
Job Mackintire & Abigail Mackintire, May 29, 1750
John Boyle & Mary Hunkins, June 7, 1750
John Thomas of Worcester & Elizabeth Wiley,
    Nov. 12, 1747
Caleb Barton of Oxford & Susannah March of Sutton,
    Jan. 13, 1747
Ichabod Stockwell of Sutton & Experience Gleason,
    Feb. 2, 1747-8
Nehemiah Stone & Hannah Lock, both of County
    Gore, Dec. 1, 1748
Ebenezer Barton & Hannah Barton, both of Dudley,
    Jan. 24, 1748-9
Samuel Curtis of County Gore & Mary Town,
    Sept. 19, 1751
Tabez Holden & Rebekah Ward, Oct. 3, 1751
James Town & Ann Blood, Dec. 10, 1747
Samuel Robinson of Dudley & Hannah Learned,
    Aug. 25, 1748
Jonathan Streeter & Olive Gleason, March 3, 1748-9
Samuel Mower of Worcester & Comfort Learned,
    May 18, 1749

MARRIAGES.

Thomas Read & Experience Shumway,	Aug. 2, 1749
John Wilson & Lois Town,	Sept. 7, 1749
Elnathan Beers (?) of Leicester & Bulah Pratt,	Nov. 24, 1749
Jonathan Wart of Sutton & Mrs. Mercy Gleason,	—— 19, 1749
Joseph Pratt & Katherine Read,	7 mo. 27 da., 1750
Jonathan Fuller & Mary Whiple,	Oct. 5, 1750
John Learned & Miriam Smith,	Jan. 31, 1750
Samuel Edward & Prudence Miriam of Gore,	June 25, 1751
Elisha Davis & Mary Harris,	July 11, 1751
John Jones & Mary Rockett,	Oct. 17, 1751
Alexander Nickoll & Joan Hart of Leicester,	Oct. 30, 1751
Josiah Wolcott & Mrs. Isebell Campbell,	Feb. 13, 1751–2
Thomas Town & Hannah Ballad (?),	Feb. 13, ——
Phinehas Ward & Sarah Rockett,	April 1, 1752
Levi Shumway & Priscilla Gleason,	Sept. 3, 1752
Joseph McIntyre & Rebonah Harwood,	Sept. 3, 1752
Solomon Harwood & Sarah Taylor,	Dec. 4, 1752
Samuel Lamb & Sarah Dana,	April 5, 1753
John Rocket & Hannah Frost,	June 4, 1753
John Stone of Palmer & Estor Spencer (?),	June 19, 1753
Jonathan Phillips of County Gore & Rachel Humphy (?),	Oct. 4, 1753
Nathan Shumway & Judith Whitney,	Feb. 7, 1754
John Adams of Brookfield & Mary Brown,	Oct. 3, 1754
Joseph Lafflin (?) & Martha Cumins (?),	Nov. 21, 1754
William Learned of Killingly & Mrs. Elizabeth Maya (?),	Dec. (?) 12, 1754
Ephraim Ballard & Martha Moore,	Dec. 29, 1754
Nathaniel Gleason & Susanna Streeter,	Jan. 2, 1755
Hezekiah Meriam of County Gore & Sarah Claflin (?),	April 3, 1755
David Town & Kezia (?) Shumway,	Aug. 26, 1755
John Marvin & Rebona Ballard,	Oct. 23, 1755
Abijah Kingsbury & Mary Chamberlain,	Oct. 23, 1756
Joseph Phillips & Lydia Wilson,	Nov., 1756
John Wyman & Experience Read,	April 23, 1752
John Wyley & Rachell Curtis,	June 18, 1752
Samuel Harris & Margaret Robins,	Aug. 27, 1752

William Lamb & Rebecca Hovey, Feb. 12, 1753
Joseph Lafflin & Phebie Wilson, July 12, 1753
Job Welds & Eunice Thayer, both of County Gore,
 May 23, 1754
John Nickolls & Jerusha Moore, May 15, 1755
Jonathan Ballard & Ellis Moore, July 15, 1755
Joseph Twiss, Jr., & Esther Frost, both of Charlton,
 July 24, 1755
Josiah Town & Susanna Rich, both of Charlton,
 Aug. 13, 1756
Edmund Town & Hannah Sparhawk, Aug. 13, 1756
Edward Davis & Abigail Learned, Nov. 11, 1756
Southwick Hebberd of Dudley & Abigail Coller (?)
 of Shrewsbury, March 24, 1757
Samuel Learnard & Mehitable Town, June 12, 1760
Zebulon Streeter & Tabitha Hovey, July 16, 1760
Thaddus Rich & Abial Frost, both of Charlton, Aug. 19, 1760
Abel Levins & Esthar Muneil, Aug. 28, 1760
Israel Phillips & Huldah Town, Sept. 18, 1760
David Pratt, Jr., & Sarah Shumway, Oct. 23, 1760
Joseph Phillips & Mrs. Bethsheba Town, Dec. 10, 1760
Noah Dodge of Dudley & Mary Wiley, March 12, 1761
John Town, Jr., & Dorothy Pratt, April 9, 1761
Ebenezer Humphrey & Ruth Shumway, April 9, 1761
Deacon Jonathan Town & Mrs. Martha Rogers,
 April 28, 1761
Southwick Hibberd of Dudley & Abigail Coller of
 Shrewsbury, March 21, 1757
Noah Hall of Killingsley & Lydia Brown, April 24, 1759
William Simpson & Susannah McKnight, Oct. 3, 1759
Nehimiah Houghton of Sturbridge & Eunice Curtis
 of Gore, Dec. 19, 1759
Isaac Putnam & Rachel Pratt, May 28, 1760
Abijah Harris & Sarah Lamb, Dec. 18, 1760
Asa Conant & Sarah Edwards, March 30, 1761
Jacob Peirce of Township No. 1 & Abigail Meriam
 of said township, June 18, 1761
Reuben Barton & Katherine Learnard, June 29, 1761
Isaac Barton & Sarah Covel, July 29, 1761

MARRIAGES.

Jabez Tatman & Mary Dudley, both of Worcester,
                                            Sept. 23, 1761
Isaac Mophit of Dudley & Sarah Learnard of Oxford,
                                            Nov., 1761
John Dana & Hannah Humphrey,   Dec. 15, 1761
Thomas Eddy and Hannah Eddy,   May 10, 1762
Richard Moore, 3d, & Mary Eddy,   Aug. 19, 1761
John Crowl (?) of Leicester & Sarah Meriam, Jan. 13, 1763
Benjamin Fitts & Mary Cook, both of Sutton, Oct. 19, 1762
Andrew Crowl of Leicester & Mary Claflin, Dec. 9, 1762
Samuel Moore & Zeriah Levins,   Dec. 16, 1762
Joseph Gleason of Sandisfield & Sarah Eddy, Dec. 20, 1762
Ebenezer Robbins & Susanna Kingsbery, Jan. 12, 1763
Edward Davis, Jr., & Elizabeth Davis, Jan. 19, 1763
William Davis, Jr., & Sibbel Davis, July 5, 1764
Jacob Davis of Charlton & Rebecca Davis, Jan. 9, 1765
James Gray & Molley Lamson of Gore, Jan. 24, 1765
Henry Burnet & Ruth Merriam of County Gore,
                                            March 26, 1765
Reuben Lamb of Leicester & Rebecca Nichols,
                                            April 4, 1765
Henry King & Abigail Timsdell, both of Sutton,
                                            Oct. 24, 1765
Jonah Titus & Thankfull Parker, both of Douglas,
                                            Oct. 29, 1765
Jacob Kingsbery & Hannah Parker of Douglas,
                                            March 10, 1766
Abel Sibley & Abigail Nickols, both of Sutton,
                                            May 22, 1766
Abner Sibley & Betty Lilley, both of Sutton, May 28, 1766
Samuel Lamb of Spencer & Elizabeth Davis, April 16, 1766
Nathaniel Davis & Sarah Stone,   May 13, 1765
Stephen Barton & Mrs. Dorothy Moore, Jr., May 28, 1765
Jedidah Barton & Mrs. Mary Rackit, May 29, 1765
James Freeland of Brimfield & Mrs. Elizabeth Thomas,
                                            Sept. 5, 1765
Jonathan Baldwin of Spencer & Mary Hunt, Oct. 28, 1766
John Ballard & Mrs. Mary Marsh of Douglas, Dec. 18, 1766
William Burnit & Lucy Gleason,   Jan. 22, 1766

Nathaniel Rich of Royalston & Phebe Putnam of
    Sutton, Sept. 25, 1766
Paul Sibley & Sarah Putnam, both of Sutton, Dec. 2, 1766
Nathaniel Cummings & Molly Robins, both of
    Douglas, Dec. 11, 1766
Noah Amidown & Abigail Putney, Feb. 19, 1767
Benjamin Keyes of Shrewsbury & Lucy Miriam,
    April 13, 1767
Daniel Hood & Sarah Hovey, April 22, 1767
Isnath (?) Pratt, Jr., & Abigail Davis, Jr., April 30, 1767
John Darby & Hannah Earcy (?), May 1, 1766
John Rand & Mrs. Tabitha Stedman, June 5, 1766
Jacob Emerson & Sarah Dole (?), July 3, 1766
Joseph Hosley, Jr., & Abigail Kendall, July 24, 1766
Jeremiah ———— & Elizabeth Warren, Sept. 7, 1766
Elijah ———— & Bethnia Hosley, June 1, 1767
Samuel Davis, Jr., & Mary Rich of Sutton, Aug. 17, 1767
Stephin Bullen & Elizabeth Rich, Sept. 3, 1767
Jonathan Day of Needham & Mary Mayo, May 21, 1767
Thomas Fisk & Naomi Mixter of Sutton, June 25, 1767
Elias Pratt & Lydia Holl, Aug. 6, 1767
Isaac Burnitt of Warwick & Esther Meriam of
    County Gore, Oct. 15, 1767
Elijah Moore, Jr., & Jemima Kingsbury, Oct. 29, 1767
John Campbell & Elizabeth Stone of Gore, Nov. 26, 1767
James Brown & Mary Shumway, Feb. 16, 1768
David Gleason & Lydia Meriam of County Gore,
    March 17, 1767
John Learned, Jr., & Abigail Davis, Sept. 29, 1768
Josiah Blood of Charlton & Mrs. Thamazin Hudson,
    Nov. 9, 1768
Ebenezer Coburn, Jr., & Dorcas Shumway, Nov. 10, 1768
Joseph Pratt, the 3d, & Mary Hudson, Sept. 29, 1768
Nathan Prat & Mary Pratt of Gore, Oct. 23, 1768
Jason Collar & Mary Bogle, Nov. 24, 1768
Jonathan Stone of Dudley & Elizabeth Gros,
    Nov. 29, 1768
James Hill of Douglas & Dorothy Learned, Feb. 16, 1769
Samuel Town & Tabatha Eddy, March 9, 1769

MARRIAGES.

Jeremiah Ammedown & Elizabeth Martin of Douglas,
            Feb. 23, 1769
Micah Pratt & Lucy Shumway,   Feb. 23, 1769
Bartholomew Putnam & Molly Putnam, both of
 Sutton,   March 1, 1769
Uriah Stone, Jr., of ye Country Gore & Lois Stone,
            July 25, 1769
Asa Pratt & Susanna Bemis of Charlton, Sept. 6, 1769
Philip Amidown & Eunice Shumway,   Nov. 2, 1769
Jacob Peirce & Mrs. Abigail Shumway,   Nov 7, 1769
Joshua Meriam & Mrs. Hannah Lovell,   Nov. 14, 1769
Isaac Shumway & Rebecca Gros of Douglas, Nov. 14, 1769
Jonathan Smith of Warwick & Elisabeth Harbridge
 of Dudley,   Nov. 30, 1769
Aaron Wakefield & Olive Wright of ye Country Gore,
            Nov. 16, 1769
Collins Moor & Hannah Town,   March 26, 1770
Abner Shumway of Sutton & Lucy How, April 19, 1770
Benjamin Tewel of Warwick & Elizabeth Merriam,
            May 30, 1770
Jonas Pratt, Jr., & Jenny Foster,   July 5, 1770
Ichabod Stockwell & Mary Snow,   Sept. 17, 1770
Benjamin (or Benajah) Putnam & Mrs. Sarah Fitts,
 both of Sutton,   Dec. 13, 1770
John Allen & Mrs. Kezia Amidown,   Jan. 16, 1771
Aaron Grant of Royalston & Mrs. Mary Town of
 Sutton,   Feb. 20, 1771
Joseph Davis & Hannah Lamb,   Jan. 15, 1771
Benjamin Jewell of Warwick & Eliza Merriam of ye
 County Gore,   May 30, 1770
Ichabod Stockwell & Mary Snow,   Sept. 1;, 1770
Samuel Robertson of Sutton & Hannah Shumway,
            Nov. 25, 1771
William Mills, Jr., of Needham & Eunice Eddy,
            March 4, 1772
Joseph Pratt, the 3d, & Esther Blood of Charlton,
            May 29, 1772
Salem Town of Charlton & Elizabeth Mayo, July 11, 1771
Reuben Robinson of Dudley & Rebecca White, Aug. 29, 1771

Daniel Whitney of Shrewsbury & Katy Stone of
    Gore, Sept. 26, 1771
Moses Fay of New Rutland & Eliz^a Learned, Nov. 7, 1771
Craft Davis & Katherine Streeter, Jan. 16, 1772
Gideon Sibley & Tamar Fitts, April 28, 1772
Edmund Eddy & Phebe Nichols, Oct. 15, 1772
Gideon Smith of Springfield & Mrs. Mary Freeland,
    Nov. 4, 1772
Daniel Fisk & Mrs. Susanna Thurston, Nov. 10, 1772
Ephraim Amidown, Jr., & Jane Robins, Dec. 17, 1772
Douglass Robins of Dudley & Esther Kingsbury,
    May 4, 1772
Joseph Sparhawk & Patience Lamson, May 12, 1772
James Gleason, Jr., & Huldah Wite of the Gore,
    May 28, 1772
Stephen Pratt & Phebe Meriam of the Country Gore,
    Nov. 26, 1772
John Ives & Eunice Collar, Dec. 1, 1772
Reuben Davis of Charlton & Sarah Moore, March 3, 1772
Amasa Allen & Esther Fish, June 23, 1773
Ezekiel Gleason & Esther Streeter, Oct. 5, 1773
William Watson & Mrs. Abigail Peirce, June 8, 1773
Jacob Shumway, Jr., & Cloe Hancock, June 16, 1773
Capt. Isaac Hartwell & Mrs. Phebe Brewer, both
    of Gore, July 14, 1773
Reuben Eddy & Sibbele Moore, Nov. 25, 1773
Jonathan Underwood & Thamazin Hudson, Feb. 17, 1774
Charles Hart of Worcester & Olive Fish, March 10, 1774
Salem Town of Charlton & Ruth Moore, April 11, 1774
William Nichols, the 3d, & Lydia Town, May 5, 1774
Samuel Campbell & Ruth Nichols, Dec. 15, 1774
Anthony Dike of Sutton & Ann Jennison, Jan. 16, 1775
George Robinson & Deborah Learned, Feb. 7, 1775
Solomon Cook & Sarah Hancock, March 29, 1775
Silvanus Town & Margaret Watson, March 29, 1775
Levi Davis & Deborah Moore, April 3, 1775
Ephraim Meriam & Ruth Gleason, both of Country
    Gore, April 10, 1775
Joseph Read & Hannah Learned, May 7, 1775

MARRIAGES.

William Hudson, Jr., & Ruth Shumway, June 28, 1775
John Hart of Leicester & Sarah Singletarry, Oct. 26, 1775
John Barton & Persis Eddy, April 3, 1776
Curtis Dixon & Lydia Wight of the Gore, April 4, 1776
Deacon Edward Davis of Dudley & widow Abigail Watson, April 22, 1776
Asa Learned & Mary Child, May 7, 1776
Frost Rockwood & Sarah Pratt, May 16, 1776
Thomas Pratt & Lydia Phillips, May 28, 1776
Elihu Thurston & Deborah Stevens of Worcester, Aug. 14, 1776
Obadiah Allen & Mehitable Amidown, Sept. 19, 1776
Smith Johnson & widow Abigail Amidown, Nov. 5, 1776
Ambrose Stone & Mercy Hovey, Dec. 12, 1776
Israel Stone & Tryphena Boyden of Worcester, July 4, 1776
David Stone & Sarah Treadwell of Sutton, July 25, 1776
Joshua Rawson of Upton & Rebecca Griffeth, Oct. 23, 1776
William Talle & Jemima Eddy, both of Leicester, Aug. 20, 1776
Edward Gros & Joanna Nichols, Nov. 15, 1774
John Harwood, Jr., & Lydia Sibley, both of Sutton, Aug. 28, 1777
Ebenezer Farr of Chesterfield & Mary Titus of Douglass, Feb. 6, 1777
Timothy Sparhawk & Mary Conant, Feb. 4, 1778
Moses Rowel of Oxford & Elizabeth Baker of Charlton, March 19, 1778
Robert Fitts, Jr., & Phebe Patch, Aug. 25, 1778
Jedidiah Barton & Sarah Miller, Oct. 7, 1778
Jeremiah Davis & Hannah Davis, Nov. 19, 1778
Benjamin Upham of Dudley & Hepzibah Learned, Nov. 26, 1778
William Smith & Esther Delaney of Ward, Dec. 30, 1778
Samuel Carriel of Sutton & Elizabeth Shumway, Dec. 31, 1778
David Dana Town & Elizabeth Breed of Sutton, Dec. 31, 1778
Nathan Taft of Northbridge & Judith Sibley of Sutton, Oct. 1, 1778

OXFORD. 135

Daniel Carriel & Betty Gould, both of Sutton, Dec. 3, 1778
Daniel Sibley & Phebe Prince, both of Sutton, April 14, 1779
Jonas Collar & Elizabeth Parsons of Spencer, March 4, 1779
Sampson Marven & Ruth Miriam,   March 16, 1779
Moses Nelson & Sarah Hovey,   Aug. 19, 1779
Jesse Merriam & Deborah Pratt,   Nov. 3, 1779
Joseph Rockwood & Martha Shumway,   Nov. 11, 1779
John Pratt & Anna Davis,   Dec. 9, 1779
Tarrant Sibley & Hannah Putnam,   April 22, 1779
Samuel Webster of Upton & Lucy Warren of Dudley,
                                         May 24, 1779
Benjamin Cogswell of Uxbridge, now of Grafton,
   & Susanna Holton of Sutton,   Aug. 29, 1779
Henry Harback & Sarah Prince, both of Sutton,
                                         July 20, 1780
Stephen Ward & Patience Cook, both of Charlton,
                                         Nov. 4, 1780
Lieut. David Putnam, Jr., & Martha Waters, both
   of Sutton,   Jan. 15, 1781
Moses Twiss of Charlton & Sarah Nichols, Jan. 18, 1781
Joseph Davis, Jr., & Jemima Davis,   March 28, 1780
Caleb Fitts of Dudley & Rachel Patch,   Aug. 24, 1780
Nathaniel Carriel of Killingly & Mary Ballard,
                                         March 15, 1781
Jonathan Harris & Huldah Town,   June 14, 1781
Phinehas Kimball of Killingly & Rebeccah Marven,
                                         Oct. 9, 1781
William Smith & Rachel Lewis,   Oct. 11, 1781
Jonathan Corbin of Woodstock & Abigail Wight
   of Gore,   Dec. 24, 1781
Daniel Rawson & Jemima Utter (?), both of Gore,
                                         Jan. 27, 1782
Ebenezer Brown & Bathsheba Conant, both of
   Charlton,   Feb. 11, 1782
George Pike & Mary Sever, both of Charlton, Feb. 27, 1782
Samuel Brown and Hannah Marsh, both of Sutton,
                                         Jan. 2, 1782
Elijah McIntire & Hannah Wilson, both of Charlton,
                                         June 6, 1782

MARRIAGES.

Josiah Wakefield & Molly Putnam, both of Sutton,
  Dec. 31, 1782
Elisha Blandin & Molly Wakefield, June 3, 1783
Thomas Barrett of Woodstock & Elizabeth Smith
  of South Gore, Feb. 13, 1782
Levi Wight, Jr., & Sarah Corbin, both of South Gore,
  Oct. 24, 1782
Jonathan Bixby of Dudley & widow Kezia Allen
  of So. Gore, June 3, 1784
Eleazer Allen & Margaret Harwood, both of Sutton,
  Jan. 21, 1784
Jonathan Harwood & Apphya Woodbury, both of
  Sutton, March 23, 1784
David Coburn of Woodstock & Experience Wyman,
  March 31, 1784
Simeon Fuller & Mary Harwood of Sutton, May 10, 1784
Aaron Carriel & Sally Woodbury, both of Sutton,
  May 11, 1784

CHARLTON.

Nov. 21, 1754, part of Oxford established as the district of Charlton. Prov. Laws, Vol. III, p. 781. A town Aug. 23, 1775. First (Congregational) Church organized 1761. Officiating clergyman mentioned: Rev. Caleb Curtis.

Reuben Comings & Mary Parker, Dec. 2, 1762
John Wymon of Oxford & Anna Town, Dec. 9, 1762
David Allen of Sturbridge & Experience Streeter,
  March 10, 1763
Josiah Blanchard & Elizabeth Hobbs, April 7, 1763
William White & Mary Dressor, April 7, 1763
Elisha Hamilton of Brookfield & Mary Smith, March 3, 1763
Nathaniel Mcintier & Debora Mcintier, April 21, 1763
Ebenezer Lamson & Ruth Phillips, April 28, 1763
Abijah Lamb & Betty Wheelock, Aug. 24, 1763
David Twiss & Esther Town, Oct. 20, 1763
Lemuel Lyon & Hannah Dresser, Nov. 10, 1763
Josiah Robinson & Sarah Twiss, Nov. 17, 1763
Asa Wheelock & Rachel Drury, Dec. 8, 1763

Benjamin Merrit & Elizabeth Smith,	April 19, 1764
Thomas Holland & Hannah Thompson,	Feb. 3, 1764
Joseph Putney & Mary Wakefield,	May 8, 1764
Jonathan Clemons & Hannah Woodard,	Nov. 29, 1764
Benjamin Allton & Susanna Blood,	June 6, 1765
Robert Manning & Abigaill Eustis,	July 11, 1765
Ebenezer Shumway & Comfort White,	Sept. 24, 1765
Amosa Turner & Experience Streeter,	Feb. 27, 1766
Peter Delvey & Lucy Town,	July 10, 1766
Levi Eddy & Sarah Smith,	Sept. 24, 1766
Daniel Elexander & Mehitable McIntire,	Oct. 10, 1766
Lenex Tituss & Rosanna Mory,	Nov. 25, 1766
Lemuel Comes & Rachel Stevens,	Nov. 27, 1766
David Thayer & Joanna Wild,	Feb. 5, 1797
Joseph Streeter & Hannah Dennes,	Feb. 19, 1767
Ebenezer Twist & —— Clemons,	June 5, 1767
Samuel Eustis & Sarah Eustis,	Oct. 14, 1767
Stephen Weld & Elizabeth Thayer,	Oct. 21, 1767
David Hammond & Delight Marit,	Nov. 19, 1767
Richard Blood, Jr., & Mary Thomson,	Nov. 26, 1767
Danield Wild, Jr., & Hannah Swmerton (?),	Jan. 14, 1768
Philip Corban & Mary How,	June 9, 1768
Isaac Taylor & Phebe McIntire,	June 9, 1768
Richard Coburn & Sarah Edwards,	June 16, 1768
Benjamin Wheelock & Elizabeth Thompson,	June 30, 1768
Jonathan Tucker, Jr., & Mary Humphrey,	Sept. 29, 1768
Joseph Thomson & Sarah Wheelock,	Oct. 13, 1768
Nathan McIntire, Jr., & Jemima Ames,	Nov. 25, 1768
Samuel Robinson & Mary Hammond,	Dec. 1, 1768
Jesse McIntire & Martha Lamb,	Dec. 13, 1768
Ebenezer Town & Huldah Wheelock,	Dec. 15, 1768
Jonas Ward & Persis Stow,	March 16, 1769
Samuel Pike & Abigail D——miss (?),	April 4, 1769
Benjamin Goddard of Shrewsbury & Hannah Williams,	Nov. 14, 1769
Jacob Comens & Phebe Converse,	Sept. 14, 1769
Nathan Taylor & Huldah Curtis,	Sept. 14, 1769
Job Marit & Hannah Thomson,	Oct. 18, 1769
Thomas Hall & Anne Milens,	Oct. 26, 1769

MARRIAGES.

Nehemiah Stone & Martha Daggot,	Nov. 16, 1769
Asa Town & Abigail Morey,	Nov. 28, 1769
Elisha Thomson & Abigail Dresser,	Jan. 25, 1770
Thomas Fenton & Charity Dennis,	Dec. 28, 1769
William Polley & Serviah Mower,	March 29, 1770
Zedikiah Drury & Mary Wheelock,	April 17, 1770
Peter Wheelock & Olive Wheelock,	May 24, 1770
Enoch Bigelow & Betty Clemons,	Aug. 28, 1770
Clement Coborn & Dorothy Edwards,	Dec. 26, 1770
Jonas Eddy & Lucy Oak,	Dec. 26, 1770
Ebenezer Harwood & Rebecca Amesbury,	Jan. 3, 1771
Asa Dressier & Abigail Wheelock,	Jan. 10, 1771
Abner Millen & Mary Marith,	May 15, 1771
Isaac Southgate & Eunice White,	June 20, 1771
Joseph Whitemore & Mary Mellen,	Sept. 5, 1771
Stephen Twiss & Mary Needham,	Sept., 1771
Joshua Woodward & Sarah Clemons,	Oct. 24, 1771
John Streeter & Anna Robinson,	Dec. 12, 1771
Eleazer Wheelock & Betty Woodward,	Dec. 12, 1771
Demenicus Davidson & Hannah Twiss,	Aug. 13, 1772
Levi Ward & Hannah Maritt,	Sept. 3, 1772
Elijah Blood & Annis Ward,	Oct. 29, 1772
Jethniel Rich & Elizabeth Davidson,	Nov. 25, 1772
Seth Jones & Mary Dogget,	Feb. 23, 1773
Thomas Lessure & Anna Hall,	April 20, 1773
John Thomson, Jr., & Catherine Town,	July 20, 1773
Jonathan Stow & Mary Twiss,	Aug. 19, 1774
John Dagget & Sarah Jones,	Oct. 19, 1773
Edward Drury & Experience Goodell,	Oct. 20, 1773
Josiah Blanchard & Mary Lamb,	Jan. 26, 1774
Gardner McIntier & Meriam McIntier,	April 9, 1778
John Birchard of Granby & Abigail Curtis,	Jan. 28, 1779
Nathaniel Burden of Sutton & Susanna Sanders,	March 4, 1779
Benjamin Green of Spencer & Mary Streeter,	March 16, 1779
Levi Hicks of Glocester & Hannah Smith,	Oct. 28, 1779
Stephen Goodell & Margaret Evard,	May 7, 1778
Aaron Maret & Prudence Coock,	June 29, 1778

Daniel Convers & Mary Drury,	Sept. 5, 1778
Thomas Stephens & Esther Tucker,	Oct. 13, 1778
Joseph Woodworth & Elizabeth Morey,	Oct. 29, 1778
Nathaniel Green & Esther Bun,	Nov. 13, 1778
John Edwards & Sabra Curtis,	Dec. 30, 1778
Moses Axdel & Tamer Curtis,	March 30, 1779
David Brown & Sarah Duggen,	May 20, 1779
Samuel Streeter & Bathsheba Barton,	July 8, 1779
Paul Wheelock & Beulah Johnson,	Sept. 30, 1779
Jonathan Weld & Ruth Taft,	Dec. 9, 1779
Seth Tucker & Louis Learned,	Dec. 17, 1779
David Dresser & Serviah Polly,	Jan. 13, 1780
Richard Dresser, Jr., & Huldah Taylor,	April 13, 1780
David Daggett & Azubah Wheelock,	June 30, 1774
Elijah Leavens & Rachel Blood,	June 16, 1774
Moses Morey & Persis Baldwin,	Aug. 25, 1774
Eleazer Gleason & Esther Fesley (?),	Dec. 8, 1774
David Powers & Miriam Ward,	Dec. 15, 1774
Joseph Capen Baker & Susanna Foskett,	June 15, 1774
George Needham & Lucy Edward,	Dec. 20, 1774
Isaac Putney & Dorcas McIntire,	March 30, 1775
Nathaniel Blood & Bathsheba Upham,	May 4, 1775
John Dagget & Mary Stephens,	Aug. 22, 1775
John Fitts & Rebecca Dresser,	Oct. 12, 1775
John Stephens & Jerusha Nichols,	Nov. 23, 1775
Abijah Conant & Bathsheba Nickols,	Nov. 29, 1775
Daniel Duggan & Sarah Leath,	Jan. 30, 1776
Elijah Ward & Rachel Nichols,	April 2, 1776
David Rich & Polly Edwards,	May 2, 1776
Capt. Jonathan Tucker & Lucy Livermore,	June 18, 1776
Abijah Clemons & Elizabeth McIntire,	June 18, 1776
Isaiah Blood, Jr., & Martha Upham,	June 27, 1776
Edward Wheelock & Martha Dagget,	July 4, 1776
Caleb McIntire & Elizabeth Herwood,	July 11, 1776
Israil Holton & Isabel Town,	July 23, 1776
William Stodard & Ruth Needham,	Sept. 5, 1776
Reuben Moor & Else Nichols,	Oct. 17, 1776
Ephraim McIntire & Mary Edwards,	June 24, 1777
Jonathan McIntire & Joanna Wiman,	July 10, 1777

MARRIAGES.

Caleb Blood & Sarah Hill of Spencer,	Sept. 2, 1777
David Goodell & Mary Baker,	Oct. 9, 1777
Joseph Grigs of Sturbridge & Presiler Baker,	Nov. 25, 1777
Joseph Chamberlain & Esther Twiss,	Feb. 9, 1778
Thomas Edwards & Susanna Town,	March 5, 1782
Eli Wheelock & Hannah Streeter,	March 14, 1782
Jonathan Clemons & Mary Hopkin,	March 14, 1782
Elisha Ward & Thankful Cook,	April 15, 1782
Rufus Bacon & Eleanor Edward,	April 17, 1782
Daniel Bacon, Jr., & Anna Fay,	May 16, 1782
Samuel Green & Hannah Kenny, both of Leicester,	April 4, 1779
Ithamar Smith & Sarah Wheeler, both of Grafton,	Oct. 7, 1779
Alpheus Coburn & Joanna Edwards,	May 27, 1780
Joseph Blood & Mary Johnson,	May 27, 1780
Eliakim Chamberlain & Anna Stow,	June 18, 1780
Abner Wheelock & Elizabeth Blanchard,	March 26, 1780
Elias Twiss & Lydia Needham,	June 30, 1780
Abel Wheelock of Spencer & Sarah Wyman,	Dec. 19, 1780
Aaron Tucker & Tamenson Stacey,	Dec. 13, 1781
Benjamin Edwards & Marcy Wells,	Dec. 12, 1781
Elijah Thompson & Damaris Wheeler,	March 20, 1781
Bennona Mercy & Huldah Brown,	Jan. 25, 1781
Jonathan Mower, Jr., & Sarah Stephens,	June 17, 1781
John Mower & Elizabeth Edwards,	May 29, 1782
James Lamb, Jr., & Abigail Moore,	May 29, 1782
John Rich & Susannah Putney,	May 29, 1782
Benjamin Dennis, Jr., & Esther Alexander,	May 29, 1782
Jonathan Blanden & Submit Cook, both of Oxford,	Feb. 6, 1783
William Sleeman & Huldah Kinney,	Oct. 9, 1783
David Fisk of Sturbridge & Elenner Jones,	Nov. 13, 1783
Nehemiah Stone, Jr., & Mrs. Lucy Bartlett,	Jan. 15, 1783
Dr. Abel Waters & Mrs. Sarah Davis,	Jan. 15, 1783
Moses Hammond & Mrs. Dorothy Dresser,	April 2, 1783
Ebenezer Stone & Mrs. Esther Lamb,	April 15, 1783

Samuel Lamb, the 3d, & Mrs. Assenah Marsh of Brookfield,	April 15, 1783
James Dresser & Mrs. Irena Hewin,	May 7, 1783
Ezra McIntier, Jr., & Mrs. Mary Hatfield,	May 8, 1783
Ebenezer Wellington & Mrs. Rebecca Leavens,	May 29, 1783
Thomas Wedge, Jr., of Brookfield & Mrs. Margaret Ryan,	June 5, 1783
Jeremiah Barton of Leicester & Mrs. Susannah Dennis,	Oct. 14, 1783
Ebenezer Twiss, Jr., & Mrs. Mary Nichols of Oxford,	Nov. 19, 1783
Josiah Eddy & Mrs. Sarah Dennis,	Jan. 2, 1784
Abijah Oakes & Mrs. Hannah Clemons,	Jan. 22, 1784
John Fargue, a Frenchman, & Mrs. Elizabeth Chubb,	Jan. 22, 1784
Joseph Chubb & Mrs. Mary Freeman,	Feb. 10, 1784
Jonathan Shumway of Belchertown & Mrs. Dorothy Wyman,	March 3, 1784
Robart Edwards & Mrs. Mehitabel Clemons,	April 7, 1784
Aaron Hammond & Mrs. Sarah Bartlett,	May 25, 1784
Nathaniel Wellington & Mrs. Pegge Taft,	June 15, 1784
William O'brine & Mrs. Anna Albee,	June 17, 1784
Thomas Dyer & Mrs. Sibbel Marcy,	July 8, 1784
Solomon Laflin & Mrs. Abijah Woodard,	July 8, 1784
Ripley Merrill & Susannah Gleason,	Nov. 13, 1783
Thomas Wiseman & Abigeal McIntire,	Dec. 11, 1783
Ebenezer Slaton & Rebeckah Hamilton of Brookfield,	Jan. 22, 1784
Peter Wheelock & Lydia Green,	Jan. 22, 1784
Jonathan Harwood & Mrs. Damaris Clemons,	Aug. 18, 1784
Isaiah McIntier & Deborah McIntier,	April 14, 1784
Seth Wheelock & Elizabeth Weld,	April 8, 1784
Israel Morey & Sarah Follett,	April 13, 1785
Adams Wheelock & Lucy Lamb,	April 28, 1785

RUTLAND.

[CONTINUED FROM P. 24.]

Joel Pollard & Mary Maynard,	March 8, 1770
Abraham Wheeler & Jemima Walker,	Aug. 22, 1770
Steven Stone & Marcy Muroe (?),	Aug. 30, 1770
Eli Clark & Lois Stone,	Aug. 30, 1770
Joseph Temple of Dummenston & Lois Hubbard,	Dec. 4, 1770
David Stoel of Guilford & Mary Larrabee,	Dec. 6, 1770
Samuel Dunkan, Jr., & Betty Nurse,	Dec. 11, 1770
Eliphalet White & Dinah McIntyre,	Feb. 28, 1771
Elijah Stone & Eunice Savage,	April 18, 1771
Benjamin Hoit of Hubbardston & widow Stevens,	April 21, 1771
Jonah Smith of Shrewsbury & Elizabeth Browning,	Oct. 15, 1771
Phillip Boyns & Mary McClanathan,	March 6, 1772
William Smith, Jr., & Elizabeth Ames,	Sept. 1, 1772
Thomas Elder of Murryfield & Margaret Moor,	Nov. 26, 1772
Joseph Knap of Spencer & Martha McClanathan,	Dec. 1, 1772
Benjamin Nurse & Marcy Stevens,	Dec. 14, 1772
Eben Lee of Conway & Bethiah Jenkins,	Jan. 11, 1770
Jonas Leonard of Warwick & Sarah Mason,	Feb. 22, 1770
Jonathan Gates & Catey Morse,	May 4, 1770
Elijah Gregory & Jane Carruth,	June 7, 1770
Jonas Carruth of Petersham & Mary Carruth,	June 14, 1770
James Rice & Susanna Cutting,	Sept. 25, 1770
Benjamin Holden & Abigail Bacon,	Nov. 1, 1770
Joseph Wilson of Petersham & Hannah Stone,	Dec. 6, 1770

RUTLAND.

Ebenezer Bodfish of Barnstable & Hannah Child,
                                                          Dec. 27, 1770
Timothy Jenkins & Mary Cunningham,   Jan. 24, 1771
Seth Clark of Keen & Meriam Metcalf,   May 29, 1771
Abijah Jenison & Mary Robinson,   Dec. 5, 1771
Amos Parker of Hubbardston & Lucy Robinson,
                                                        Jan. 2, 1772
Daniel Buxton & Lucy Allen,   Jan 2, 1772
Samuel Carruth & Mary Hamilton,   Jan. 30, 1772
James Laughton of Hardwicke & —— Fuller,
                                                        June 17, 1772
Nathaniel Smith & Sarah Jennison,   March 11, 1772
Abel Davis & Sarah Mendall,   June 18, 1772
Isaac Balcom & Ruth Bacon,   July 9, 1772
Ezra Jones, Jr., & Susanna Stone,   Oct. 15, 1772
Lemuel Osgood & Lydia Merryfield,   Nov. 12, 1772
James Holden & Hannah Bacon,   Nov. 12, 1772
Thomas Richardson & Lois Perry,   Dec. 17, 1772
Jonathan Davis & Hannah Dogget,   Dec. 17, 1772
William Elder of Wor. & Sara Crawford,   Dec. 30, 1772
Enoch Curtis & Sarah Felton,   Jan. 7, 1772
Jeduthan Stone & Elizabeth How of Paxton, Jan. 11, 1773
Caleb Harrington & Anna Laughton,   Jan. 12, 1773
Charles Man & Elizabeth McCobb,   Jan. 24, 1773
Abijah Perry & Grace Locke,   March 18, 1773
John Partridge & Phebe Boyden,   Oct. 7, 1773
Hampton & Kate, (blacks) of Capt. E. Jones, Nov. 4, 1772
John Caldwell & Sarah Caldwell,   Dec. 16, 1773
Hopstill Jenison & Relief Fletcher,   Dec. 16, 1773
Jonathan Hemingway & Martha Resign Wilder of
    Petersham,   April 7, 1774
Thomas Oliver & Hannah Northgate (free blacks),
                                                   May 15, 1774
Noah Leonard & Bethiah Witherel,   May 27, 1772
Nimrod Quameus (negro) & Elizabeth Harris (In-
    dian),   May 17, 1774
Phinehas Perry & (Mrs.) Esther Gates,   May 17, 1774
Barnaba Sears & Rachel Bullard,   May 17, 1774
Micah Boyden & (Mrs.) Phebe Sears,   May 17, 1774

William Choate & (Mrs.) Susanna Church,	May 17, 1774
Elijah Robinson & Sarah Blake,	May 17, 1774
Stephen Johnson of Hardwick & Abigail Rice,	May 31, 1774
Thaddeus Ames & Mercy Rice,	June 2, 1774
John Wit & Priscilla Moxtor,	June 9, 1774
John Chamberlain & Sarah Winslow,	June 16, 1774
Nathan Swift of Rut. District & Mary Willis of Hardwick,	Sept 8, 1774
Thomas Rice & Sarah Nurse,	Nov. 17, 1774

SUTTON.

[CONTINUED FROM P. 104.]

Jonathan Hale & Silence Goddard,	Nov. 22, 1769
Jonathan Kidder & Susannah Dwinel (?) (or Durnel ?),	Jan. 30, 1770
Jonathan Gould & Hannah Singletary,	Jan. 30, 1770
James Leland, Jr., of Grafton & Anne Gale,	Feb. 22, 1770
Capt. Palmer Goulding & Mrs. Rebekah Richardson, both of Worcester,	Oct. 31, 1770
Thomas Eaton of Reading & Abigail Bancroft of Wor.,	Oct. 24, 1770
Joseph Blanchard, Jr., & Mehetable Putnam,	April 10, 1770
Lot Marsh & Abigail Blanchard,	July 5, 1770
Richard Davenport & Anne Buxton,	July 5, 1770
John Woodbury & Mary Chase,	Oct. 17, 1770
Jonathan Robertson & Mary Wood,	Oct. 24, 1770
Moses Park & Hannah Barton,	Oct. 29, 1770
Moses Sibley & Elizabeth Rich,	April 19, 1770
Jonas Jackson & Lucy Cole,	Dec. 5, 1770
David Putnam & Elisabeth Woodbury,	April 12, 1770
Richard Dodge, Jr., & Lois Town,	July 19, 1770
John Safford & Ruth Hayden, both of Worcester,	Dec. 6, 1770
John Kitts & Rebekah Stockwell,	Jan. 15, 1771

SUTTON.

John Kidder & Sarah Dodge,	Feb. 25, 1771
Reuben Barton & Olive Jennison,	June 1, 1770
Reuben Eaton & Abigail Lovell,	Dec. 6, 1770
Samuel Melody of Guilford & Sarah Gale,	Dec. 6, 1770
John Waters & Phebe Goodale,	May 28, 1771
Levi Wesson & Olive Locke,	July 9, 1771
Stephen Harwood & Abigail Streater,	Dec. 10, 1770
Thomas Holman, Jr., & Lydia Bates,	Oct. 17, 1771
Ebenezer Freeman & Mary Frazier of Providence,	Nov. 13, 1771
Francis Dudley & Elizabeth Whipple,	May 21, 1771
Jonathan Elliot, Jr., & Sarah Chase of Uxbridge,	Oct. 17, 1771
Aaron Sibley & Lucy Newell,	Jan. 9, 1772
Isaac Dodge, Jr., & Abigail Morss,	March 19, 1771
John Fuller & Susanna Putnam,	March 26, 1771
Absolom Forbes & Martha Hall,	July 25, 1771
Benjamin Hall & Elizabeth Mossley,	Aug. 22, 1771
Jesse Cummings & Mary Fitts,	Aug. 29, 1771
Stephen Rice & Mary Batchellor,	Sept. 18, 1771
Benjamin Nichols & Lucy Fitts,	Feb. 28, 1772
Ebenezer Sibley & Mary Chase,	Oct. 24, 1771
Samuel Small & Molley Waters,	Jan. 2, 1772
David Sprague of Killingly & Rebecca Wadsworth,	Jan. 2, 1772
Joseph Allen, Jr., of Hardwick & Greely Singletary,	Jan. 15, 1772
Simon Tenney & Sarah Trask,	Jan. 23, 1772
John Bartlett & Rebecca Chase,	Jan. 23, 1772
Jotham Stearns & Mary Roberts,	May 27, 1772
John Davidson & Anna Gould,	Jan. 16, 1772
Isaac Chase, Jr., & Betty Yeates,	Oct. 1, 1772
Daniel Buchnam & Phebe Nichols,	July 1, 1771
Samuel Meriman, Jr., of Northfield & Eunice Severy,	June 11, 1772
Eleazer Stockwell & Ruth Algar, both of Oxford,	Nov. 3, 1772
James Willard of Worcester & Abigail Hayward,	Jan. 5, 1773

MARRIAGES.

Samuel Woodward & Eunice Biglow,	Sept. 8, 1772
Joshua Badger & Ruth Waite,	Sept. 29, 1772
Abijah Tainter & Sarah Small,	Dec. 3, 1772
Abraham Waters & Mehetable Waters,	Dec. 3, 1772
John Waite, Jr., of Worcester & Rachel Case,	Dec. 24, 1772
Samuel Trask, Jr., & Ruth Tenney,	Jan. 21, 1773
Samuel Titus & Martha Steans,	May 14, 1772
Henry King, Jr., & Prudence Dudley,	June 18, 1772
Ezekiel Goldthwait & Anna Adams,	Dec. 3, 1772
Adam Brown, Jr., of Ipswich & Priscilla Putnam,	Dec. 3, 1772
Arthur Dagget, Jr., & Lucy Cutler,	Dec. 10, 1772
Solomon Parsons, Jr., of Glocester & Prudence Dodge,	Dec. 18, 1772
Isaiah Wakefield & Eunice Burdon,	Dec. 24, 1772
Nathaniel Carriel & Bridget Prime,	Dec. 29, 1772
Isaac Hamond of Swanzey, N. H., & Mehitable Prime,	Feb. 16, 1773
Elijah Davis of Oxford & Hannah Rich,	Oct. 29, 1772
Abraham Brown of Salem & Elizabeth Putnam,	March 2, 1773
Hezekiah Hayden & Lois Hayden,	March 4, 1773
Daniel Hayden & Submit Flagg, both of Grafton,	June 9, 1773
Benjamin Carlton & Elizabeth Smith,	June 7, 1773
Samuel Paine of Lebanon, N. H., & Lucy Hall,	Sept. 6, 1773
John Nelson & Elizabeth Kidder,	Oct. 13, 1773
William Chase & Molley Elliot,	Oct. 14, 1773
Joseph Bullen, Jr., & Hannah Morse,	Feb. 11, 1773
Isaac Platts, Jr., of Bradford & Rachel Chase,	Sept. 21, 1773
Jonathan Willard of Worcester & Hannah Putnam,	Nov. 25, 1773
Andrus Waters & Bettey Goodale,	Nov. 25, 1773
David Dudley, Jr., & Lois Whitney,	Dec. 16, 1773
David Grover & Mary Kenney,	Feb. 2, 1774
Thomas Lovell, Jr., & Hannah Gould,	Feb. 9, 1774
John Marble & Lucretia Richardson,	Feb. 24, 1774
Moses Bancroft, Jr., & Sarah Taylor,	Feb. 24, 1774
James Allen of Westboro & Phebe Tenny,	April 21, 1774

Jedidiah Barton & Lydia Peirce,	March 23, 1774
Daniel Bucknam & Abigail Pratt,	April 19, 1774
David Chase & Judith Holman,	April 18, 1774
James Merriam of Country Gore & Eunice Lovel,	May 25, 1774
Anthony Sigourney & Ruth Chase,	June 23, 1774
Jacob Chase & Mary Ingerson,	March 17, 1774
Moody Moorss, Jr., & Abigail Leland,	March 31, 1774
Isaac Gleason & Abigail Dudley,	April 12, 1774
Nathaniel Fry Morss & Hannah Gibbs,	May 18, 1774
Benjamin Stiles & Elizabeth Cutler,	May 22, 1774
Micah Putnam & Anna Carriel,	May 26, 1774
Free Cummings & Ruth Stockwell,	June 16, 1774
Jonathan Rich & Mehetable Dagget,	July 7, 1774
Alpheus Marble & Anna Dudley,	Dec. 15, 1774
Abraham Batchellor, Jr., & Rebecca Dwight,	Dec. 28, 1774
Enos Buxton, Jr., & Mary Dodge,	Jan. 3, 1775
Gideon Woodbury & Abigail Burbank,	Jan. 10, 1775
David Stockwell of Croyden, N. H., & Abial Giles,	Jan. 23, 1775
Timothy Leland & Mary Sibley,	Feb. 9, 1775
Samuel Harwood & Lydia Kenney,	Jan. 5, 1775
Joseph Waters & Elizabeth Dwight,	Feb. 28, 1776
Rev. Daniel Grosvenor of Grafton & Mrs. Deborah Hall,	May 9, 1776
Joshua Willard of Grafton & Phebe Porter,	June 13, 1776
David Putnam, Jr., & Phebe Woodbury,	July 3, 1776
John Couse & Rebecca Sibley,	July 11, 1776
Caleb Putnam & Judith Sibley,	Aug. 21, 1776
Stephen Marble & Betty Putnam,	Nov. 14, 1776
Free Cumming & Alice Gould,	Nov. 14, 1776
John Hall & Dolly Ward,	Jan. 2, 1777
Matthew Lackey & Dorcas Woodbury,	Jan. 28, 1777
Aaron Adams & Sarah Dodge,	Jan. 29, 1777
John Meriam of Concord & Martha Putnam,	Feb. 6, 1777
Samuel Hardy & Judith Garfield,	March 14, 1776
Charles Richardson, Jr., & Susannah Taylor,	March 28, 1776
Samuel Eaton & Joanna Waite,	April 11, 1776
Israel Waters of Charlton & Elizabeth Bartlet,	June 27, 1776

MARRIAGES.

Abel Rowe & Beulah Potter of Upton,	July 8, 1776
Josiah Stiles & Lydia Gale,	July 11, 1776
Jonathan Gould, Jr., & Lydia Jennison,	July 11, 1776
Joshua Waite & Mary Burnap,	Sept. 19, 1776
Ezra Lovell & Mary Jennison,	Sept. 24, 1776
Jacob Snow, Jr., & Betty Marble,	Dec. 18, 1776
Andrew Dodge of Dudley & Jane Carriel,	May 8, 1777
Jonathan Cutler of Oxford & Betty Lillie,	May 8, 1777
Jotham Meriam of Warwick & Sarah Burnap,	July 8, 1777
Moses Hovey & Phebe Jenney,	Aug. 14, 1777
Stephen Fuller & Lydia Putnam,	Nov. 7, 1777
John Bancroft & Anna Waters,	Dec. 1, 1777
John Mellody & Sarah Eastey,	Jan. 20, 1778
Daniel Gould & Mary Gould,	Jan. 22, 1778
Elijah Sibley & Abigail Stone,	Feb. 9, 1778
Daniel Jennison of Oxford & Molly Putnam,	Jan. 29, 1778
Thomas Harbarch & Abigail Gould,	July 8, 1777
Deacon Thomas Holman & Mary Palmer of Mendon,	Feb. 4, 1778
John Childs & Susanna Gould,	March 12, 1778
Daniel Fitts & Chloe White,	April 9, 1778
Benjamin Carter, Jr., & Mary Gale,	March 13, 1777
William Snow & Judith Holman,	Oct. 21, 1777
Timothy Morse of Holden & Hannah Mixer,	Nov. 5, 1777
Joshua Carter & Abigail Nickolas,	Nov. 19, 1777
David Prina Chase & Sarah Greenwood,	Dec. 2, 1777
Jonathan Stone & Chloe Hazeltine,	Dec. 23, 1777
Timothy Sibley, Jr., & Mary Barstow,	Nov. 5, 1778
John Shepard Delyrample of Northbridge & Hannah Elliot,	Dec. 16, 1778
Eli Putnam of Western & Elizabeth Harback,	March 12, 1778
Ebenezer Waters & Susanna Thurston,	May 5, 1778
Samuel Wallis & Sarah Town,	May 7, 1778
Elias Parkman of Braintree & Apphia Putnam,	May 25, 1778
Archelaus Dwinel & Olive Hall,	May 26, 1778
Artemas How of Braintree & Ruth Putnam,	July 4, 1778
Stephen Holman & Mary Jenny (or Tenny),	July 30, 1778

SUTTON.

Jacob Winslow & Elizabeth Knap, both of Northbridge,	Sept. 28, 1778
John Sellen, Jr., of Hardwick & Martha Mosely,	Nov. 26, 1778
Samuel Sibley, Jr., & Sarah Leland,	Dec. 10, 1778
Nehemiah Chase & Oashti (?) Batchellor,	Dec. 17, 1778
Nathaniel Chenney & Mary Harris,	Dec. 31, 1778
Benjamin Snow & Rebecca Gould,	Jan. 7, 1779
Thomas Green & Mary Jacobs,	Jan. 26, 1779
Daniel Tenny, Jr., & Martha Morss,	Jan. 29, 1779
Asa Dodge & Lydia Buxton,	Feb. 9, 1779
Samuel Pain Jones & Rachel Cole,	June 15, 1779
Ezra Mixer & Azubah Haven,	June 21, 1779
William Duncan of Oxford & Sarah Day,	June 22, 1779
Moses Putnam & Mary Allen,	June 24, 1779
Stephen Humes & Mary Hovey,	July 15, 1779
Noah Stockwell & Jemima Town,	July 15, 1779
Bezeleel Gleason & Sarah King,	Nov. 4, 1779
Simeon Blake of Uxbridge & Sarah Wheller,	Nov. 4, 1779
Stephen Sibley & Sarah Collins,	Dec. 9, 1779
Josiah Prime of Swansey, N. H., & Rachel Carriel,	Feb. 20, 1780
William (?) Sarvey (?) & Elizabeth Ward,	March 16, 1780
David Town & Elizabeth Southworth,	March 23, 1780
David Gibson of Fitchburg & Anna Barton,	April 24, 1778
David Copland of Royalston & Martha Putnam,	Sept. 1, 1778
Samuel Leland of Grafton & Abigail Gale,	Dec. 10, 1778
Moses Park & Lydia Bixby,	May 19, 1779
Elias Jenison & Battey Gage,	July 1, 1779
John Cook & Martha Pierce,	July 13, 1779
Eli Whitney of Westboro & Judith Hazeltine,	July 15, 1779
Gershom Wait & Persis Chase,	Sept. 15, 1779
Abel Chase, Jr., & Hannah Bond,	Sept. 29, 1779
Abner Sibley & Mary Studley,	Dec. 9, 1779
Francis Adams & Abigail Taft,	April 11, 1780
Lazarus Le Baron & Mrs. Molly Chase,	March 21, 1786 (?)

BROOKFIELD.

Oct. 15, 1673, Quobauge to be the town of "Brookfield" when forty or fifty families shall have settled there. Mass. Rec., Vol. IV, Part 2, p. 568. A town Nov. 12, 1718. First (Unitarian) Church organized 1754. Congregational, 1756. Baptist, at East Brookfield, 1818. Clergymen mentioned: Rev. Joseph Parsons, Rev. Eli Forbes, Rev. N. Fisk.

Samuel Leach & Rebecca Harris,	June 2, 1755
William Hencher & Ruth Wolcott,	Nov. 6, 1755
Moses Bragg & Sarah Barns,	Oct. 21, 1755
Ebenezer Wright & Thankful Goss,	Dec. 4, 1755
Ez^l (or Er^e) Woodbury & Mary Barns,	Aug. 19, 1755
John Gilburt & Priscilla Walker,	Dec. 23, 1755
Ithamer Wright & Elisabeth Walker,	Feb. 26, 1756
John Peesa (?) & Hannah Ranger,	April 3, 1756
David Bridges of Spencer & Betty Rice,	April 27, 1756
David Brewer & Elizabeth Smith,	May 8, 1763
Jediah Gilbert & Margaret Walter,	Sept. 19, 1764
Nathan Abbott & Mercy Banister,	Nov. 29, 1764
Thomas Brown & Judith Gilbert,	Feb. 7, 1765
James Smith & Sarah Burnet,	March 21, 1765
Beushy Tottle & Priscilla Partridge,	May 30, 1765
Samuel White & Thankful Gilbert,	Aug. 20, 1766
Abraham Patch & Anna Banister,	March 12, 1766
Benjamin Wait & Lois Gilbert,	Jan. 11, 1767
Moses Hamilton & Hannah Felton,	Jan. 15, 1767
John Watt & Martha Brewer,	Feb. 23, 1767
William Dean, Jr., & Lydia Kindrick,	Nov. 8, 1767
Benjamin Felton & Jenna Doroty (?),	Dec. 24, 1767
Abraham Cutler & Huldah Batchellor,	May 25, 1768
Jesse Gilbert & Lucy Barns,	June 30, 1768
James Cunningham & Mary Tuft,	June 9, 1768
Jonathan Bartlett & Anna Mixer,	Dec. 18, 1768
John Bacon, Jr., & widow Mary Olds,	March 25, 1763
Ezra Hamilton & Abigail Crosby,	June 30, 1763
Ephraim Green & Mary Rogers,	Dec. 8, 1763
Martin Ainsworth & Hannah Streeter,	Dec. 13, 1763

BROOKFIELD.

Nathan Richardson & Tamyson Upham,	Feb. 16, 1764
Ephraim Cooley & Lois (?) Walker,	Jan. 23, 1765
Jesse Abbott & Sarah Wakefield,	Dec. 4, 1765
Nathan Hobbs & Lydia Warren,	Feb. 26, 1766
Oliver Wilson of New Braintree & Susannah Walker,	Feb. 27, 1766
John Gilbert, 3d, & Sarah Rich,	March 6, 1766
Josiah Olds & Dorothy Smith,	May 25, 1766
Abraham Walker & Jemima Lovell,	July 17, 1766
Jonas Newton & Mary Woods,	Nov. 19, 1767
Obadiah Cooley, Jr., & Eunice Walker,	Nov. 26, 1767
Benjamin Aldrich & Dorothy Hamilton,	Nov. 27, 1767
Ebenezer Newell & Sarah Banister,	Dec. 3, 1767
Samuel Allen of Wrentham & Hannah Vorce,	Jan. 4, 1768
Jacob Shaw & Mary Hill,	May 6, 1767
William Ayres, 2d, & Rachel Barnes,	May 3, 1753
Obadiah Bartlet & Rebecca Adams,	May 9, 1753
Andrew Kimball & Rebecca Watson,	June 19, 1753
David Barnes & Elizabeth Paterson,	Dec. 11, 1753
Daniel Gilbert & Lucy Barnes,	June 6, 1754
Jer[h] Gould & Hannah Bartlet,	June 5, 1755
Josiah Converse & Mercy Gilbert,	Nov. 18, 1755
Thomas Barnes & Elisabeth Dodge,	Feb. 24, 1756
Rufus Dodge & Elisabeth Dodge,	Dec. 15, 1756
John Germings & Rachel Davis,	June 2, 1757
Josiah Holfield & Hulda Bacon,	July 4, 1757
Timothy Hill & Alice Hinds,	Sept. 26, 1757
Abner How & Sarah Lane,	Sept. 29, 1757
Nathan Gould & Martha Gilbert,	Oct. 31, 1757
Josiah Dwight, Esq., & Elisabeth Buckminster,	Nov. 2, 1757
Samuel Barnes & Mary Bartlet,	Dec. 19, 1757
Jonas Brewer & Mary Jennings,	April 20, 1758
Jonas Hayward & Martha Gilbert,	May 25, 1758
John Lamson & Mary Weeks,	Nov., 1758
Levi Walker & Sarah How,	March 12, 1759
Moses Ayers & Anna Goodale,	Dec. 6, 1759
Gideon Rugg & Dinah Hinds,	July 1, 1760
Jer[h] Gould & Hannah Stevens,	Aug. 21, 1760

MARRIAGES.

Joseph Lane & Rebecca Wit,	June 23, 1760
Asa Bacon & Rhoda Dunkan,	July 3, 1760
Jer[h] How & Lucy Gilbert,	Oct. 30, 1760
Jos. Wolcott & Rebecca Jones,	March 26, 1761
John Watson of Rutland & Thankful Watson,	Nov. 2, 1761
Joseph Gilbert & Hannah Gott,	Dec. 13, 1761
Joshua Draper & Sarah Wright,	May 28, 1762
James Brown & Mary Beacon,	Oct. 7, 1762
Isaac Green & Rachel How,	April 7, 1763
Dan. Wyman & Betty Stone,	Sept. 15, 1763
Jona. Barnes & Dorothy Stow,	Nov. 13, 1763
Reuben Gilbert & Persis Denny,	Dec. 8, 1763
Jesse Barnes & Patience Gilbert,	Dec. 8, 1763
Micajah Ayres & Mary Barnes,	March 14, 1769
Dr. Jos. Stow & Sarah Adams,	May 22, 1765
Rediat Stewart & Lucy Adams,	May 22, 1765
Daniel Bullard & Olive Partridge,	May 29, 1766
Solomon Goodale & Mary Hale,	Nov. 4, 1766
Robert Richmond & Martha Hind,	Nov. 4, 1766
S. Mixter & Betty Bigelow,	May 21, 1767
Henry Spring & Mercy Hamilton,	July 3, 1767
John Berry & Elizabeth Shindle,	Nov. 30, 1769
Phillip Gilbert & Martha Lambson,	Jan. 11, 1770
John Gilbert, 4th, & Bettey Manning,	Oct. 8, 1770
John Cutler & Dorothy Converse,	Nov. 8, 1770
Aaron Willard & Hannah Hamilton,	April 24, 1769
William Gilbert & Rachel Barns,	Dec. 21, 1769
Daniel Watson & Anna Saterley,	March 15, 1770
John Hamilton & Sarah Stone,	March 29, 1770
John Lynds & Sarah Warner,	April 19, 1770
Thomas Cowen & Hannah Rich,	July 23, 1770
Daniel Thomas & Marcy Bartlett,	Aug. 30, 1770
Isaac Robinson & Hannah Collins,	Aug. 30, 1770
Lemuel Gilbert & Ruth Gilbert,	Dec. 6, 1770
Asa Gilbert & Hannah Cutler,	Jan. 3, 1771
Emerson Woolcott & Mary Adams,	Dec. 2, 1767
Samuel Grimes & Mary Hinckley,	May 8, 1768
Abijah Bruce & Hannah Barns,	Aug. 3, 1768

Malacha Maynard & Elizabeth Hinds,	Sept. 6, 1768
John Stevens & Ruth Moor,	Oct. 27, 1768
Jacob McCombs & Anna Richmond,	Dec. 7, 1768
Joseph Belknap & Sarah Walker,	Feb. 15, 1769
Noah Hardy & Hannah Forbes,	March 7, 1769
Daniel Forbes & Sarah Hinckley,	March 22, 1769
William Bowman & Susanna Hinds,	May 23, 1769
Charles Knowlton & Eunice Packard,	Oct. 25, 1769
Eli Gould & Lydia Jennings,	Dec. 21, 1769
John Hamilton & Sarah Stone,	March 29, 1770
James Homer & Mary Stevens,	May 2, 1770
Aaron Putnam & Patience Potter,	June 6, 1770
Samuel Sever & Lucy Biglow,	June 7, 1770
Nathan Bartlett & Ester Child,	June 14, 1770
Thomas Moor, Jr., & Rebecca Harrington,	July 26, 1770
Roger Stevens & Mary Smith,	Dec. 6, 1770
Aaron Bowen & Mary How,	March 20, 1770
Obediah Rice, Jr., & Hannah Hill,	March 21, 1770
John Berry & Elizabeth Kendal,	Nov. 30, 1769
Phillips Gilbert & Martha Lamson,	Jan. 11, 1770
John Gilbert, 4th, & Bettey Manning,	Oct. 8, 1770
John Cutler & Dorothy Converse,	Nov. 8, 1770
Aaron Willard & Hannah Hamilton,	April 24, 1769
William Gilbert & Rachel Barns,	Dec. 21, 1769
Daniel Watson & Anna Saterly,	March 15, 1771
John Lynds & Sarah Warner,	April 19, 1771
Thomas Cowen & Hannah Rich,	July 23, 1771
Daniel Thomas & Marcy Bartlett,	Aug. 30, 1771
Isaac Robinson & Hannah Collins,	Aug. 30, 1771
Lemuel Gilbert & Ruth Gilbert,	Dec. 6, 1771
Asa Gilbert & Hannah Cutler,	Jan. 3, 1771
Emerson Woolcott & Mary Adams,	Dec. 2, 1767
Samuel Grimes & Mary Hinckley,	May 8, 1768
Abijah Bruce & Hannah Barns,	Aug. 3, 1768
Malacha Mainard & Elizabeth Hinds,	Sept. 6, 1768
John Stevans & Ruth Moor,	Oct. 27, 1768
Jacob McCombs & Anna Richmond,	Dec. 7, 1768
John Belnap & Sarah Walker,	Feb. 15, 1769
Noah Hardy & Hannah Forbes,	March 7, 1769

MARRIAGES.

Daniel Forbes & Sarah Hincher (or Hinchen),
                                            March 22, 1769
William Bowman & Susanna Hinds,   May 23, 1769
Charles Knowlton & Eunice Packard,   Oct. 25, 1769
Eli Gould & Lydia Jenings,   Dec. 21, 1769
James Homes & Mary Stevens,   May 2, 1770
Aaron Putnam & Patience Potter,   June 6, 1770
Samuel Chevers & Lucy Biglow,   June 7, 1770
Nathan Bartlett & Esther Childs,   June 14, 1770
Thomas Moor, Jr., & Rebecca Herrington,   July 26, 1770
Roger Stevens & Mary Smith,   Dec. 6, 1770
Aaron Bowen & Mary Howe,   March 20, 1771
Obediah Rice & Hannah Hill,   March 21, 1771
Jason Hamilton & Lydia Hill,   June 27, 1771
Jude Hamilton & Sarah Hoyt,   Oct. 31, 1771
Daniel Brown & Darius (?) Barns,   July 10, 1771
Samuel Palmer & Sarah White,   Sept. 24, 1771
Aaron Barns & Elizabeth Gilbert,   Oct. 3, 1771
Asa Barns & Persis Ross,   Dec. 5, 1771
Peter Lovejoy & Silence Bartlett,   Dec. 25, 1771
Charles Elsworth & Rachel Makepeace,   May 29, 1771
Benjamin Sumner & Martha Clark,   Aug. 29, 1771
William Parke & Mary Leech,   Feb. 6, 1772
Francis Foxcraft & Sarah Upham,   May 5, 1768
Josiah Adams & Nancy Samson of Sturbridge,
                                            July 21, 1768
James Shay & Thankful Walker,   Sept. 21, 1768
Ebenezer How & Sarah Rice,   Sept. 29, 1768
John Marble & Hannah Olds,   Nov. 30, 1768
Reuben Lamb of Spencer & Patience Adams,   Dec. 1, 1768
Elias Brown of Lincoln & Abigail Hobbs,   Feb. 23, 1769
John Nale & Anna Elwell,   May 18, 1769
Abner Cutler & Hannah Peters,   Oct. 24, 1769
Joseph Richardson & Hannah Stevens,   Dec. 7, 1769
Benjamin Bruce & Damaris Gilbert,   March 8, 1770
Nathan Rood & Rachel Streeter,   Aug. 20, 1770
Daniel Ralph & Priscilla Beals,   Aug. 20, 1770
Gideon Gilbert & Lois Crowfoot,   Aug. 30, 1770
Joshua Slayton & Desire Felton,   Aug. 30, 1770

Samuel Barnard, Jr., of Dearfield & Abigail Upham,
                                            Oct. 3, 1770
Moses Hitchcock & Hannah Wilson,   Nov. 28, 1770
Samuel Wood & Abigail Moore,   Dec. 5, 1770
Thomas Wood, Jr., & Abigail Banister,   Dec. 6, 1770
Uriah Fa-e & Hephsibah Dodge,   Dec. 13, 1770
Nathan Hamilton & Abigail Omstead,   Jan. 1, 1771
Simeon Olds & Salley Wright,   Jan. 1, 1771
Benjamin Lynds & Hannah Phips,   Jan. 3, 1771
Benjamin Felton & Ruth Hamilton,   Feb. 3, 1771
William Olds, Jr., & Abigail Hewes,   March 7, 1771
Richard Wait & Susanna Allen,   May 9, 1771
John Rich & Elizabeth Chickley,   April 10, 1771
Thomas Danforth of Tyringham & Lydia Abbot,
                                            May 26, 1771
Josiah Hamilton & Mary Barrows,   June 25, 1771
Jonathan Nutting of Brimfield & Abigail Banister,
                                            June 27, 1771
Simeon Rockwood & Damaris Olds,   July 11, 1771
Solomon Walker & Mary Gilbert,   April 9, 1772
Isaac Barron & Bathsheba Rich,   April 30, 1772
Timothy Wolcot & Miriam Walker,   Dec. 10, 1772
Simeon Olds & Elizabeth Banister,   April 1, 1773
George Bridge & Abigail Williams,   April 9, 1772
John Hinds & Lydia Seager of Spencer,   May 24, 1772
Samuel Parker of Amherst & Sarah Rood of Sturbridge,
                                            July 9, 1772
Jonathan Gilbert & Hannah Converse,   May 27, 1772
Elisha Drake & Mary Richmond,   July 1, 1773
Daniel Edson & Betty Fullen (?),   Aug. 10, 1773
Joseph Draper, Jr., & Mary Pratt of Spencer, Aug. 12, 1773
John Howland & Bulah Bemiss of Spencer,   Aug. 29, 1773
Carley Ward & Caty Graham of Spencer,   Sept. 28, 1773
Ezra Hamilton & Esther Watson,   Dec. 2, 1773
Thomas Dodge, Jr., & Molley Allen,   Dec. 30, 1772
William Terrence of Betshire Town & Hepssibah
    Batchellor,   Jan. 11, 1774
John Reed, Jr., & Martha Richmond,   May 11, 1772
Josiah Partridge & Experience Morse,   Dec. 22, 1772

MARRIAGES.

Isaac Warner & Bulah Hobbs,	Dec. 9, 1772
Zechariah Reddy & Rebecca Warren,	April 7, 1774
Joshua Allen & Susanna Sprague of New Braintree,	April 20, 1774
George Blake & Bethiah Allen of Oakham,	May 19, 1774
Bryant Foster & Thankful Blackwell,	Nov. 21, 1771
Witt Taylor & Lucy Bruce,	Jan. 9, 1772
Moses Rainger & Hannah Ball,	1772
William Dean & Eunice Harrington,	Oct. 15, 1772
Luther How & Elizabeth Watson,	Nov. 19, 1772
William Ayres, Esq., & Mary Woolcott,	Dec. 23, 1772
Thomas Hill & Eleoner Bartlett,	Dec. 24, 1772
John Hill & Rachel Rice,	Feb. 25, 1773
Eli How & Elizabeth Smith,	April 8, 1773
Nathan Gilbert & Jemima Kindrick,	Oct. 14, 1773
Simeon Stone & Dorothy Harwood,	June 2, 1773
Ebenezer Goodell & Anna Newton,	Sept. 3, 1773
Eli Bartlett & Mary Hill,	Nov. 25, 1773
Moses Keep & Hannah Woodbury,	Dec. 2, 1773
Ezra Tucker & Abigail Moulton,	Dec. 9, 1773
Benjamin Adams & Eunice Hale,	Dec. 16, 1773
Moses Woods & Elizabeth Capen,	Dec. 30, 1773
Abel Wilson & Abigail Foster,	Feb. 14, 1774
Thomas Ball & Sarah Woodbury,	Feb. 20, 1774
John Furbush & Kathrine Harper, both of Oakham,	Nov. 22, 1774
Joseph Barns of New Braintree & Merriam Ayers,	March 29, 1775
Samuel Hamilton of Northfield & Molly Tyler,	May 9, 1775
Enoch Bothwell & Sarah Bacon,	June 29, 1775
Samuel Blair & Ann Brown of Westboro,	June 9, 1775
John Bemis & Patience Slayton,	July 4, 1775
Eph. Potter & Susannah Rice,	June 21, 1774
John Burk (?) & Rachel Hair,	Jan. 19, 1775
Thomas Bacon & Hepzibah Boutell,	Feb. 3, 1775
Silas Potter & Tabitha Hersey,	Feb. 3, 1775
Reuben Hendrick & Hannah Jennings,	Feb. 16, 1775
John Whitney & Anna Hamilton,	Feb. 2, 1775

John Wilder of Dummerston & Mary Rice, April 4, 1775
Isaac Beal of Mendon & Prudence Abbot, April 12, 1775
Caleb Rice & Sarah Abbott, June 8, 1775
Thomas Taylor & Dorcas Davis, June 8, 1775
Robert Stevenson of Oakham & Mary Adams,
Jan. 18, 1776
Benjamin Richardson & Alice McCluer, Feb. 15, 1776
John Boyden of Sturbridge & Abigail Brown, Feb. 26, 1776
George Watkins of Sturbridge & Hannah Hobbs,
Feb. 26, 1776
Jonathan Sampson of Belchertown & Sarah Stearns,
March 12, 1776
Asahel Peters & widow Hannah Bartlett, March 14, 1776
Nicholas McCluer & Thankful Kingsbury, May 16, 1776
James Miller, Jr., of Westboro & Mercy Livermore,
June 18, 1776
John Sargeant of Stockbridge & Mary Codner, Jr.,
June 26, 1776
Thomas Draper & Hannah Potter, July 11, 1776
John Hebbert & Dorothy Walker, Nov. 21, 1776
Eli Hitchcock of Weston & Abigail Olds, Dec. 20, 1776
Ezra Torrey & Zilpah Jennings, Jan. 9, 1777
Isaac Lackey of Spencer & Patience Staten, Feb. 15, 1776
Peter Washburn & Sarah Ayres, April 8, 1776
Oliver Hinds & Mary Capen of Spencer, May 2, 1776
Ebenezer Parkman & Sarah Lyscomb, June 6, 1776
Jabez Leath of Grafton & Betty Hall, Nov. 8, 1776
Silvanus Curtis & Mary Phillips of Sturbridge,
Nov. 14, 1776
Moses Ayres & Lucy Cutting, Jan. 1, 1777
Benjamin Higgins & Mary Drury, both of Spencer,
Jan. 14, 1777
Thomas Harbach & Kathrine Beamis, both of Sutton,
Jan. 15, 1777

BARRE.

June 17, 1774, Rutland district established as Hutchinson. Prov. Laws, Vol. V, p. 162. Nov. 7, 1776, the name of the town of Hutchinson changed to Barre. Prov. Laws, Vol. V, p. 592. First (Unitarian) Church organized 1756. Congregational, 1827. Baptist, 1832.

Stepney (servant of George Caldwell) & Mary Warbon,	May 8, 1775
Skelton Felton of Northampton & Silence Pratt,	Aug. 23, 1775
Obadiah Walker & Agnes McCullough,	Aug. 24, 1775
Jacob Wetherel & Ruth Rice,	Oct. 4, 1775
John Lenard & Betty Nurse,	Nov. 15, 1775
Caleb Allen of Conway & Sarah Jenkins,	Nov. 16, 1775
Joseph Farrar & Lydia Stone,	Nov. 23, 1775
Amos Richardson & Martha Dennis,	Nov. 30, 1775
Silas Smith & Eunice Eaton,	Dec. 14, 1775
Doctor Oliver Stickland of Templeton & Mary Low,	May 2, 1776
Jonathan Little & Lydia Nye,	May 2, 1776
Elisha Marsh & Esther Berry,	Aug. 1, 1776
Aaron Ball & Rachel Cheever,	Sept. 26, 1776
Ebenezer Tatman & Dorothy Woodberry,	Nov. 7, 1786
Peter Ripley of Warwick & Abigail Smith,	Dec. 12, 1776
Josiah Bacon of Hutchinson & Polly Tileston (?) of Boston,	Jan. 2, 1777
Joseph Myrick & Ruth Swift,	Jan. 5, 1777
Robert Perkins of Hutchinson & Silence Leach of Pelham,	Jan. 7, 1777
Doctor John Williams of Lebanon & Abigail Jones,	Jan. 23, 1777
Moses Caldwell & Mary Ruggles,	Jan. 29, 1777
James Kennedy of Colrain & Margaret Thompson,	March 18, 1777
Dr. Daniel Rood & Dorothy Robinson,	March 27, 1777
Josiah Parker & Martha Goodell,	April 10, 1777
Reuben Tatman & Margaret English,	June 5, 1777

Andrew Thompson & Hannah Carruth, Sept. 18, 1777
David Richardson & Susannah Bacon, Oct. 2, 1777
Aaron Holden & Rachel Richardson, Oct. 30, 1777
Solomon Bacon & Margaret Forbes, Nov. 13, 1777
Richard Kelley & Hannah Caldwell, Nov. 20, 1777
Thomas Spooner of Hardwick & Mary Haven, Nov. 20, 1777
Jotham Rice, Jr., & Elizabeth Sullen, Jan. 15, 1778
Alexander Thompson of Colrain & Bathsheba Burnet,
 Jan. 28, 1778
William Chamberlain & Elizabeth Winslow, Feb. 24, 1778
Nathaniel Babbet of Athol & Mary Mandell, March 3, 1778
David Hagar & Levinah Holden, March 12, 1778

MILFORD.

April 11, 1780, part of Mendon established as Milford. First (Congregational) Church organized 1741. Clergyman mentioned: Rev. Amariah Frost.

John Kilburn of Mendon (now Milford) & Abigail
 Littlefield of Holliston, June 15, 1780
Joshua Thayer & Sarah Curtis of Holliston, June 15, 1780
Aaron Bullard of Holliston & Lovice Godfrey, Sept. 21, 1780
John Dewing & Patience Sumner, Sept. 21, 1780
John Bullard & Rachel Boynton, Oct. 13, 1780
John Beall & Silence Atwood (?), Oct. 19, 1780
Luther Wheelock & Mary Sumner, Nov. 8, 1780
Richard Hiscock & Sarah Cody, Nov. 16, 1780
Jonathan Hayward & Mary Ballard, Dec. 21, 1780
Artemas Cheeney & Rachel Albee, Feb. 8, 1781
Ebenezer Nelson & Patience Twitchel, March 8, 1781
Nathan Nelson & Jerusha Chapin, March 8, 1781
Jonathan Kimball & Mary Cheeney, July 7, 1781
Isaac Chapin & Rachel Wheeten, Oct. 18, 1781
John Foristell, Jr., of Warwick & Lydia Tenney,
 Nov. 8, 1781
Abner Adams of Northbridge & Ruth Wood, Jan. 16, 1782
John Bowker of Hopkinton & Esther Wedge, March 7, 1782
Stephen Kilburn & Hannah Wight, March 31, 1782

MARRIAGES.

Adam Hayward & Judith Ballard, April 18, 1782
Joshua Bullard of Bellingham & Bethiah Taft,
  April 18, 1782
Ezekiel Jones & Mary Wight, May 9, 1782
Boyce Kimbell, Jr., & Mary Pike of Bellingham, May 2, 1782
Ebenezer Peck & Rachel Lesure, Dec. 7, 1780
Thomas Hiscock & Mary Cody, June 7, 1782
Ziba Holbrook & Rebecca Kimball, Nov. 7, 1782
Nathaniel Flagg of Upton & Mehitabel Cutler, Nov. 13, 1781
John Scammell & Hannah Jones, Nov. 24, 1782
Thomas Twitchel of Westboro & Phebe Pond, Nov. 27, 1782
John Nelson & Bettee Brown, Nov. 28, 1782
Daniel Thompson & Margaret Davison, Dec. 8, 1782
Joseph Johnson & Hannah Albee, Dec. 12, 1782
Asa Jones & Hannah Nelson, Feb. 13, 1783
Jonathan Stearns & Hannah Thayer, May 1, 1783
Stephen Thompson & Phebe Chapin, May 4, 1783
Samuel Hart of Chesterfield & Jemima Warren,
  June 29, 1783
James Hiscock of Hopkinton & Anna Cody, Nov. 13, 1783
Paul Davis & Rachel Chapin, Nov. 29, 1783
Abijah Warfield & Lydia Wheelock, Dec. 11, 1783
Smith Phillips of Holliston & Mary Saunders, Dec. 28, 1783
David Chapin & Martha Bates of Mendon, Feb. 12, 1784
Darius Sumner & Anna Daniels of Mendon, Feb. 19, 1784
Ebenezer Thompson & Abigail Davison, March 11, 1784
Joel Thayer & Susanna Cheeney, April 15, 1784
Nathan Wood & Experience Thayer, April 22, 1784
Oliver Chapin & Mary Jones, April 29, 1784
Abel Albee & Annah Wood, April 29, 1784
Enos Beall & Relief Cheeney, June 25, 1784
James Sumner, Jr., & Mary Jones, July 7, 1784
Jotham Thayer & Bathsheba Wheelock, Aug. 29, 1784
Samuel Thayer & Rachel Nelson, Dec. 9, 1784
Ebenezer Cheeney, Jr., of Warwick & Anna Nelson,
  Feb. 17, 1785
Dick Brattle of Bellingham & Rose Lucy (Africans
  or negroes), May 3, 1785
James Luther & Mary Parkhurst, March 16, 1783

ATHOL.

March 6, 1762, the plantation called Payquage established as Athol. Prov. Laws, Vol. IV, p. 534. First (Congregational) Church organized 1750. Unitarian, 1750. Baptist, 1813.

Elijah Flagg & Elizabeth Comming, both of Templeton,	April 26, 1781
Zaccheus Hasey & Abigail Sergeant, both of Hubbardstown,	May 30, 1781
John Allen & Dolly Dalrymple, both of Northbridge,	July 5, 1781
Zaccheus Rich, Jr., & Lydia Brown,	Nov. 7, 1781
Alpheus Ward & Molly Raymond,	March 7, 1782
Jesse Stockwell & Anna Grought of Templeton,	April 3, 1782
Samuel Duncan & Patience Choat, both of Warwick,	April 13, 1779
David Biglow & Lois Taylor,	June 3, 1779
Willard Varnum & Patty Tompson,	Sept. 9, 1779
Moses Hutchins & Susanna Thayer,	Sept. 9, 1779
Isaac Train & Elizabeth Cummins,	Sept. 14, 1779
Asa Goddard & Lucy Goddard,	Nov. 2, 1779
Daniel Benjamin & Tamason Felton,	Nov. 10, 1779
Charles Baker, Jr., & Anna Jackson,	Nov. 25, 1779
William Young & Keziah Haven,	Jan. 18, 1780
William Straten & Elizabeth Smith,	March 2, 1780
John Fairbank, Jr., & Fanny Kilton,	July 16, 1780
Uriah Rice & Unice Church,	Sept. 7, 1780
Jesse Kendall, Jr., & Elizabeth Raymond,	Oct. 12, 1780
Ruggles Ward & Isabel Oliver,	Nov. 2, 1780
Moses Oliver & Lois Wiswell Humphrey,	Nov. 23, 1780
Solomon Smith & Tabitha Briggs,	Dec. 27, 1780
Willard Varnum & Hannah Walkup,	Feb. 15, 1781
William Raymond & Lydia Ward,	July 6, 1781
Obadiah Janes & Mary Oliver,	Aug. 2, 1781
Elisha Sibley & Elizabeth Twitchel,	Nov. 1, 1781
Levi Fletcher & Jerusha Morton,	March 13, 1783

MARRIAGES.

Asahel Sanders & Afia (?) Rich, May 26, 1783

Thomas Canless (?) & Abigail Sawtell, both of Templeton, Aug. 16, 1783

Edward Raymond, Jr., & Jane Oliver Kindall, Oct. 30, 1783

John Haven & Nabbe Fay, Feb. 10, 1784

John Coalman, Jr., & Susa Shute, of Templeton, March 18, 1784

Thomas Stratton & Thankful Rich, April 5, 1784

Francis Mazrow of Petersham & Anna Frederick, April 12, 1784

Nathaniel Phillips & Mary Baley, April 29, 1784

Ephraham Capron & Sarah Fairbank, May 18, 1784

John Piper & Sarah Willington, both of Templeton, Aug. 1, 1784

David Young & Hannah Lumbard, Sept. 30, 1774

Caleb Thompson of New Salem & Mehitabel Knowles, Nov. 7, 1784

Edward Goddard, Jr., & Ann Death, Nov. 11, 1784

Earll Cutting & Lydia Kendall, Dec. 10, 1784

Asa Lord & Lydia Humphrey, Aug. 15, 1785

Thaddeus Bates (?) & Polly Shattuck, both of Templeton, Sept. 1, 1785

George —— Felton of Petersham & Hannah Oliver, Sept. 12, 1785

Ebenezer Knight, Jr., & Esther Sprague, Jan. 5, 1786

Chester Bingham of Chesterfield & Deborah Rich, Sept. 23, 1786

Levi Kendall & Sally Newell, Oct. 22, 1786

David Pike & Joanne Cheeney, Oct. 26, 1786

Benjamin Powers of Petersham & Anna Raymond, Nov. 1, 1786

NORTHBRIDGE.

July 14, 1772, part of Uxbridge established as the district of Northbridge. A town Aug. 23, 1775. Prov. Laws, Vol. V, p. 419. Friends Society organized 1730. Congregational, 1782. Clergyman mentioned: Rev. John Crane.

Benjamin Powers & Lydia Melandy,	April 16, 1777
Lemuel Powers & Abigail Newland,	April 16, 1777
Lieut. William Park & Mrs. Sally Potter,	Oct. 5, 1780
Abijah Thayr (?) of Douglass & Mrs. Betty Thayr (?),	Aug. 22, 1780
Joel White & Martha Fobes,	Nov. 21, 1780
William Winter & Anna Chamberlain of Grafton,	April 19, 1781
Samuel Cooper & Anna Straight,	May 10, 1781
Jonathan Bacon, Jr., & Molly Adams,	Dec. 13, 1781
Samuel Allbe & Hannah Pratt,	Dec. 20, 1781
Ruben Randal of Richmond & Molly Aldrich,	Aug. 13, 1782
David Winter & Anna Cooper,	Aug. 29, 1782
Nathaniel Fish & Miriam Hamlinton,	April 28, 1783
Enoch Child & Elizabeth Tafts of Smithfield,	July 2, 1783
Israel Thayer & Dolly Hayward,	March 22, 1784
Joshua Slocomb of Franklin & Lucy Dunn,	Nov. 25, 1784
Samuel Lincoln & Mehitabel Thayer,	Jan. 5, 1785
David Batchellor, Jr., & Pattee Hills of Sutton,	Jan. 26, 1785
Wheelock Wood & Lydia Murdock,	March 31, 1785
Jacob Goldthwait & Rachel —— Axtel (?),	April 14, 1785
Samuel Aldrich, Jr., & Sarah Brown,	May 5, 1785
Amos Wheeler of Worcester & Martha Reed,	June 2, 1785
George Aldrich, Jr., of Mendon & Polly Brown,	June 30, 1785
Stephen Trask of Uxbridge & Juda Hunt,	June 13, 1786

ROYALSTON.

Feb. 19, 1765, the tract of land called Royalshire established as Royalston. Prov. Laws, Vol. IV, p. 738. First (Congregational) Church organized 1766. Baptist, at West Royalston, 1768. Clergyman mentioned: Rev. Joseph Lee.

Thomas Thompson & Elizabeth Fry,	March 29, 1769
Abner Ball & Mary Poor,	May 25, 1767
Daniel Brown & Eunice Heminway,	June 28, 1770
Jonathan Woodward & Hepsebah Goddard,	June 19, 1770
Peletiah Metcalf & Lydia Estey,	June 28, 1770
John Wilson of New Braintree & widow Mary Graham,	Oct. 10, 1770
Ezra Prat & Susanna Barton,	Nov. 21, 1771
Jacob Easty & Sarah Chamberlain,	March 19, 1772
James Work & Martha Pierce,	April 28, 1772

BERLIN.

March 16, 1784, part of Bolton and Marlborough established as the district of Berlin. A town Feb. 6, 1812. First (Congregational) Church organized 1779.

James Goddard, Jr., & Keziah Fairbank,	July 28, 1785
Manassah Fairbank & Abigail How of Shrewsbury,	Nov. 3, 1785
Jonathan Fairbank & Perny (?) How,	Jan. 12, 1786
Caleb Fairbank & Moley Goddard,	Nov. 10, 1785
Nahum Houghton & Leovitia How,	Sept. 26, 1786

PAXTON.

Feb. 12, 1765, parts of Leicester and Rutland established as the district of Paxton. Prov. Laws, Vol. IV, p. 734. A town Aug. 23, 1775. First (Congregational) Church organized 1767.

James Sproute & Molly Whittemore,	July 11, 1784
Aaron Morse & Relief Moore,	July 11, 1784
John Pike, Jr., of Sturbridge & Beulah Davis,	Nov. 11, 1784
Samuel Bridgham & Phebe Davis,	Jan. 18, 1785

PRINCETON.

Oct. 20, 1759, part of Rutland and certain common lands adjacent established as the district of "Princetown." Prov. Laws, Vol. IV, p. 266. A town April 24, 1771. First (Congregational) Church organized 1764.

David Averet & Mrs. Susanna Ralf,   Oct. 27, 1767

WORCESTER.

[CONTINUED FROM P. 13.]

Nathan Gleason of Oxford & Rachel Nichols, Jan. 11, 1776
Isaac Knights & Rebecca Cree of Shrewsbury, Jan. 24, 1776
William Stearns, A. M., of Lunenburg & Mary Dana,
      Feb. 26, 1776
John Moore & Mary Gurney,   April 24, 1776
Nathaniel Harrington & Ruth Stone,   July 2, 1776
John Warren of Sudbury & Elizabeth Carson, July 24, 1776
Simon Glasco & Prudence Jone (negroes),   Aug. 1, 1776
John Walker & Mary Willard,   Aug. 7, 1776
Tyler Curtis & Lydia Chamberlain,   Sept. 5, 1776
Micah Johnson, Jr., & Sarah Willard,   Nov. 13, 1776
William Johnson of Westboro & Marcy Taylor, Nov. 25, 1776
Daniel Heywood & Molly Pierce,   Nov. 25, 1776
William Trowbridge & Sarah Rice,   Dec. 12, 1776
Joel Doolittle of Petersham & Tabitha Goodwin,
      Dec. 12, 1776
John Campbell of Oxford & Martha Stevens, Jan. 16, 1777
Phinehas Smith & Eunice Gleason,   Jan. 22, 1777
Paul Gates & Phebe Mahon,   Jan. 23, 1777
Jonathan Stone, Jr., & Mary Harrington,   Feb. 13, 1777
Ebenezer Smith of Sturbridge & Rebecca Knight,
      March 25, 1777
Josiah Perry & Lydia Flagg,   April 3, 1777
Phineas Flagg & Rhoda Stone,   May 25, 1777

Charles White of Peterboro' & Sarah Gray, June 10, 1777
Moses Coolidge of Watertown & Hannah Stowell,
                                                Sept. 25, 1777
Dr. William Walker & Molly Chaddick,   Oct. 8, 1777
Daniel Stone of Charlton & Abigail Jones,   Nov. 5, 1777
John Hair & Elizabeth Bigelow,   Nov. 20, 1777
Vernon Gleason & Lucy Smith,   Dec. 25, 1777
Solomon Willard & Lydia Johnson,   Dec. 25, 1777
James Mcfarland, Jr., & Betty Moore,   Jan. 5, 1778
William Quigley & Thankful Moore,   Jan. 16, 1778
Gideon Griggs & Patty Stevens,   Feb. 10, 1778
Samuel Wiswell & Sally Ward,   Feb. 12, 1778
Cato Walker & Prudence Williams (negroes),   Feb. 26, 1778
Noah Bigelow of Shutesbury (?) & Elizabeth Goulding,
                                                March 18, 1778
Henry Gale & Lucy Knight,   March 19, 1778
Anthony Haswell (?) & Lydia Baldwin,   April 23, 1778
Nathaniel Heywood & Hannah Heywood,   April 23, 1778
David Richards & Rebekah Gates,   May 5, 1778
Samuel Howlet, Jr., & Lucretia Richardson,   May 6, 1778
Silas Henry & Relief Knights,   May 16, 1778
William Cunningham of Spencer & Rebeckah McFarland,
                                                June 4, 1778
Elisha Clark & Mary Bigelow,   June 7, 1778
Elisha Johnson of Southboro' & Sarah Perry,   June 9, 1778
Samuel Whitney & Mary Whitney,   June 24, 1778
David Pierce & Kezia Packard,   July 2, 1778
Ellis Blake & Jane Cook,   Aug. 23, 1778
Josiah Rice & Betty Trowbridge,   Sept. 1, 1778
Samuel Hunt of Charlemont & Eunice Gleason,
                                                Oct. 4, 1778
John Williams of Boston & Hannah Chandler, Nov. 10, 1778
James Blair of Rutland & Martha Young,   Nov. 24, 1778
Thomas Rice, Jr., & Lydia Totman,   Nov. 26, 1778
Juba Williams & Hagar Eveleth (negroes),   Dec. 1, 1778
Nathan White of Uxbridge & Eunice Chapin, Jan. 14, 1779
John Hamilton & Katharine Quigley,   Jan. 27, 1779
Dr. Benjamin Green & Sarah Salisbury,   Feb. 1, 1779
Jonathan Osland & Parnel White,   Feb. 18, 1779

Phineas Gleason & Margaret Keko,	March 31, 1779
Alvin How of Shrewsbury & Mary Willington,	April 21, 1779
Isaiah Thomas & Mary Fowle of Londonderry (mar. Boston),	May 26, 1779
James Trowbridge & Lydia Ward,	June 22, 1779
Samuel Sturtevant & Susannah Packard,	July 6, 1779
Daniel Chaddick & Elizabeth Fisk,	Sept. 26, 1779
William Jones of Westminster & Sarah Curtis,	Oct. 5, 1779
William Brown & Mary Cowden,	Oct. 21, 1779
John Prentice of Ward & Rebeckah Richardson,	Nov. 9, 1779
John Gambel of Northboro & Jane Hambleton,	Nov. 11, 1779
Thomas Pollard of Boston & Betsey Carbet,	Nov. 14, 1779
Thomas Follansbe of Newbury-port & Eunice Stearns,	Dec. 5, 1779
Simeon Dunkin, Jr., & Mary Blair,	April 11, 1780
Abel Heywood & Abigail Chamberlain,	April 27, 1780
John Mahan & Sally Hemingway,	April 27, 1780
Calvin Glazier of North Shrewsbury & Lydia Pierce,	May 18, 1780
Thaddeus Chapin & Lucy Whitney,	June 29, 1780
Josiah Perry & Prudence Harrington,	July 6, 1780
Isaac Flagg & Abigail Baldwin,	Sept. 13, 1780
John Stanton & Sarah Chandler,	Sept. 14, 1780
Joseph Ball & Lucretia Stearns,	Oct. 12, 1780
Joseph Gray & Hannah Millet,	Nov. 2, 1780
Elijah Flagg & Sarah Moore,	Nov. 23, 1780
William Brown, Jr., & Mary Cowdin,	Nov. 29, 1780
Benjamin West, Esq., of Charlestown, N. H., & Mary Maccarty,	Jan. 18, 1781
Jonathan Thayer of Charlemont & Azuba Gleason,	Jan. 31, 1781
James Campbell of Sutton & Anna Gleason,	Feb. 7, 1781
Henry Patch & Hannah Moore,	Feb. 8, 1781
William Johnson & Sarah Baldwin,	Oct 11, 1770
John Taylor & Elizabeth Young,	April 13, 1775
Nathan Lovell of Holden & Anna Inglesbee of Shrewsbury,	April 1, 1781

Noah Jones & Debroah Holbrook, April 25, 1780
Stephen Taylor & Susanna Gates, Sept. 4, 1781
Jacob Holmes & Anne Harrington, April 5, 1781
Amos Singletary, Jr., of Sutton & Mrs. Betty Johnson, Jan. 27, 1777
Archibald McDonald of Chester, Vt., & Mary Moore,
 Feb. 4, 1785
William Seaver, Jr., of Kingston & Polly Chandler,
 Oct. 29, 1785
Nathaniel Paine & Elizabeth Chandler, Dec. 18, 1785
Joseph Trumbell of Petersham & Elizabeth Paine,
 Feb. 14, 1786
John Johnson & Lydia Johnson, March 8, 1786
Alpheus Eaton & Sarah Johnson, April 6, 1786
John Brown & Polly Goulding, Oct. 6, 1786
Benjamin Butman & Susannah Chamberlain, Oct. 22, 1786
Nathaniel Coolidge & Katharine Baldwin, Nov. 14, 1786
Ebenezer Putnam of St. John, N. B., Canada, & Elizabeth Chandler, Dec. 2, 1786
Abraham Lincoln & Nancy Bigelow, Jan. 7, 1787

INDEX.

ADAMS, 2, 7, 8, 11, 16, 17, 25 27. 32, 33, 55, 57, 60, 63, 64, 66, 67, 74, 76, 78, 80, 85, 94, 98, 100, 102, 116, 121, 128, 147, 149, 151, 152, 153, 154, 156. AGAR, 56. ABRAHAM, 75. ABRAM, 75 ALGAR, 145 ADAMS, 146, 157, 159, 163. ABBEE, 76. ARDENAY, 85. ANGELL, 106. AKEN (see Aikens), 120. AVERET, 165. ALLEN, 1, 11, 19, 24, 29, 30, 31, 32, 33, 39, 40, 58, 62, 71, 79, 80, 82, 84, 88, 89, 98, 110, 115, 118, 119, 120, 122, 125, 126, 127, 132, 133, 134, 136, 145, 146, 149, 151, 155, 156, 158, 161. ALEXANDER, 5, 31, 42, 112 (see Elixander). ANDERSON, 6, 81, 94, 118. ANDREWS, 7, 27, 72, 82, 84. ALLBE, 163. ALBEE, 14, 15, 17, 20, 21, 27, 28, 29, 159, 160. AMMEDOWN, 132. AMEDOWN, 16, 17. ATCENSON (?), 92. ARCHER, 20. ALDRICH 163. AMES, 23, 103, 144. AKERS, ACRES, 23. APPLEBY, APPLEBEE, 27, 28. ATHERTON, 43, 44, 46, 48, 52, 53, 54, 55, 56, 57, 96, 114, 115, 117. ALBERT, 44, 109 ALLERD, 107. AMSDEN 45 74. AXTELL, 50, 75, 76. AXTEL (?), 163. ALDEN, 62, 121. AVERY, 68, 108. ALDRICH, 14, 15, 16, 17, 19, 20, 21, 62, 73, 92, 99, 151, 163. ALDRIDGE, 51. AMIDOWN, AMMIDON, AMMIDOWN (see Ammedown), 20, 29, 30, 122, 123, 124, 131, 132, 133, 134. AINSWORTH, 28, 150. ANNIS, 85 ALDIS, 115. AIKENS (see Aken), AIKEN, 118, 121, 122, 123, 124, 126. ALLIS, 123. ABBOT, ABBOTT, 23, 28, 31, 116 117, 118, 119, 150, 151, 155 157. ATWOOD, 16, 26, 29, 30, 117. ATWOOD (?), 159. ARNOLD, 20, 26, 76, 79, 126. ANTHONY, 75. AMORY, 86. AUGER, 2. AULDIS, 16. AUSTIN, 35, 37. AYERS, AYRES, 94, 122, 124, 151, 156, 157. AYNER, 114.

BATTLES, 20, 90, 95. BLANDIN, 136. BARTHOLOMEW, 25. BALDWIN, 58, 59, 61, 62, 63, 65, 66, 80, 83, 87, 95, 104, 130, 166, 167, 168. BARTLETT, BARTLET, 1, 2, 24 59, 71, 73, 89, 98, 99, 101, 115, 125, 145, 147, 150, 151, 152, 153, 154, 156, 157. BASCOM, 1. BARNS, BARNES, 1, 3, 18, 26, 28, 58, 59, 63, 66, 82, 88, 150, 151, 152, 153, 154, 156. BAKER, 2, 9, 17, 18, 31, 46, 47, 79, 80, 85, 87, 109, 127, 134, 161. BACON, 2, 23, 25, 26, 27, 30, 32, 33, 48, 49, 98, 101, 102, 117, 118, 150, 151, 152, 156, 158, 159, 163. BANISTER, 82, 150, 151, 155. BARRET, BARRETT, 2, 22, 26, 27, 40, 42, 44, 45, 46, 48, 57, 136. BRAMAN, 78. BRADISH. 2 12, 50, 85. BATCHELLOR, BATCHELOR, 49, 51, 75, 77, 85, 147, 149, 150, 155, 163. BLACK, 22, 23, 69, 70, 71. BLATCHELER, 49. BLAIR, 4, 5, 61, 70, 71, 72, 94, 156, 166, 167. BARRON, 155. BARUN, 75. BLANCHARD, 31, 32, 33, 49, 60, 62, 66 82, 101, 123, 136, 144. BALL, 6, 8, 10, 17, 22, 23, 36, 40, 46, 49, 62, 63, 64, 69, 73, 74, 75, 76, 84, 85, 88, 89, 109, 110, 113, 114, 115, 156, 158, 164, 167. BALLARD, BALLAD, 29, 83, 91, 107, 114, 115, 116, 117, 128 129, 130, 135, 159, 160. BARBER, 6, 8, 9, 10, 11, 23, 69. BRAGG, 78, 82, 88, 150. BRABROOK, BRAYBROOK, 35, 40, 113. BANCROFT, 8, 11, 13, 19, 35, 82, 144, 146, 148. BARR, 94. BARDINS, 19, 20. BABCOCK, 119. BANKS, 22, 124. BARNEY, 95. BARREL, 23. BATHRICK, 39, 82 BARNARD, 12, 44, 46, 47, 55, 85, 98, 99, 100, 102, 125, 155. BARROW, BARROWS 33, 155. BARRUS, 42. BABCOCK, BADCOCK, 88, 89. BATES, 16, 17, 98, 145, 160, 162. BANGS, 119, 121, 122. BAINS, 93 BRADSTREET, BRADSTREAT, 38, 39, 80. BAL-

12

COM, 17, 73, 91, 92, 93. BARTON, 24, 26, 29, 58, 101, 102, 103, 127, 129, 130, 134, 144, 145, 147, 149, 164. BARSTOW, 18, 27, 97, 148. BUTTERFIELD, 49 BABBITT, 60. 123, 126, 159. BAYLEY, BAYLIES, BAILEY, BALEY, 19, 27, 35, 36, 39, 43, 44, 45, 47, 61, 70, 85, 88, 106, 107, 113, 115, 126, 162. BASSET, 125. BRATTLE, 160. BLAKE, 19, 62, 72, 92, 144, 149, 156, 166. BLACKWELL, 156. BRADISH, 120, 122. BADGER, 24, 146. BRACKETT, BRACKET, 29, 50. BENNET, BENNETT, BENNITT, 4, 34, 36, 54, 68, 69, 70, 82, 83, 87, 95, 104, 105, 106, 111, 112, 113, 114, 115, 117. BEARS, 63. BEERS (?), 128. BELL, 1, 126, BELLOWS, 2, 24, 36, 37, 59, 73, 74, 80. BENJAMIN, 2, 22, 118, 121, 161. BENNEY, 106. BEAL, BEALS, 3, 49, 154, 157. BELNAP, 153. BEAMIS, BEMAS, 157. BENUS, BEMUS, BEMISS, 3, 7, 58, 59, 60, 61, 62, 63, 64, 65, 66, 67, 85, 86, 87, 108, 132, 155, 156, 157. BEAMAN, BEMEN, BEMAN, BEAMON, 3, 7, 34, 39, 84, 90, 91, 104, 105, 106, 108, 109, 113 BREED, 134. BERRY, BEARY, 6, 17, 22, 24, 73, 121, 123, 125, 152, 153, 158. BEALL, 159. BEARD, 9, 10, 59. BELDING, 119. BERNARD, 85. BREWER, 11, 26, 85, 133, 150, 151. BENSAN, BENSON, 14, 16, 18, 21, 92. BENHAM, 21. BEALL, 160. BENT, 22, 24, 73. BEAK, 120. BETTIS, 28. BERNETT (?), 107. BELKNAP, 33, 68, 70, 153. BEACON, 152. BRECKENDRIDGE, 58. BEARNON, 107. BENT, 65. BRIGHAM, 2, 47, 69, 73, 76, 78, 79, 81, 82, 88, 89, 126. BIGELOW, BIGLO, BIGLOW, BIGELO, 5, 7, 9, 10, 13, 35, 45, 53, 56, 59, 67, 68, 70, 75, 76, 79, 80, 81, 82, 83, 84, 85, 87, 92, 104, 108, 115, 116, 146, 152, 153, 154, 161, 166, 168. BIXBY, BIXBEE, 5, 23, 73, 82, 96, 98, 108, 111, 136, 149. BRIDGE, BRIDGES, 6, 25, 36, 53, 56, 63, 64, 66, 73, 74, 117, 150, 155. BINAH, 9. BILLINGS, BILLING, 95, 118, 119, 120, 121, 126 BISHOP, 13. BLISS, 33. BISCO, 63. BRIGS, BRIGGS, 64, 88, 123, 161. BINGHAM, 73, 162. BRITAIN, BRITTAN, 79, 80. BRIANT, 82. BRIDE, 86. BRIAN, 115. BIRAM, 124. BRIMHALL 125. BRIDGEHAM, 164. BROW, 60. BOWEN, 64, 86, 153, 154. BOND, 1, 2, 4, 5, 30, 31, 61, 72, 98, 99, 149. BROWNING, 3, 4, 22, 59. BOSWORTH, BOZWORTH, 83, 115. BROWN, 6, 9, 11, 12, 14, 17, 19, 20, 21, 25, 26, 27, 28, 29, 34, 35, 40, 44, 51, 52, 57, 59, 61, 62, 68, 69, 71, 78, 82, 85, 87, 91, 92, 98, 101, 102, 103, 107, 110, 113, 114, 115, 116, 121, 128, 129, 131, 135, 146, 150, 152, 154, 156, 157, 160, 161, 163, 164, 167, 168. BOUTTELL, BOUTELL, 7, 90, 95, 101, 111, 156 BOON, 77. BOYD, 8, 49, 68. BOYLE, 127 BOGLE, 131. BOYDEN, 9, 10, 11, 81, 103, 134, 157. BONNY, BONNEY, 120, 122. BROOK, BROOKS, 9, 40, 43, 47, 60, 75, 77, 78, 86, 95, 106, 116. BOLTON, 86. BORDEN, 12. BOWMAN, 49, 87, 126, 127, 154. BROCKLEBANK, 106. BOYNTON, 15, 34, 39, 40 96, 107, 108, 111, 113, 159. BOWHER, 17. BOWERS, 20, 57, 86. BLODGET, 53, 112. BOLSTER, 18, 51. BLOOD 18, 27, 34, 44, 45, 46, 65, 127, 131, 132. BOTHWELL, 156. BROCK, 27. BOWING, 51. BROUGHTON, 33. BROPHEY, 38. BOYCE, 50. BLOORS (?), 105. BOWKER, BOUKER, 59, 78, 81, 83, 159. BULLEN, BULLIN, 103, 112, 131, 146. BUCKMINSTER, 1, 151. BUSS, 37, 39, 90, 91, 113. BUTLER, 3, 21, 45, 46, 50, 94. BUTLER (?), 90, 73, 106, 117. BUGBEE, 5, 102. BUSH, 41, 42, 44, 47, 79, 84, 89, 120. BULLARD, 8, 17, 22, 23, 152, 159, 160. BURT, 120. BUXTON, 13, 100, 144, 149, 147. BRUCE, 41, 43, 44, 48, 73, 74, 76, 88, 152, 153, 154, 156. BRUMIL, 14. BUNCRAFT (?), 95. BUSH, 112. BURCH, 14. BUTNAM, 101. BUTMAN, 168. BURNHAM, BURNAM, 17, 34, 37, 44, 46, 99. BURNET, 116, 121, 122, 130, 131, 150, 159. BUCK, 73. BURNEE, 76, 78. BURNAP, 18, 100, 148. BURPEE, 106, 107. BURK (?), 156. BUCHNAM, BUCKMAN, BUCKNAM, 20, 98, 103, 145, 147. BULLEN, 102. BUTTERFIELD, 125. BUT-

RICK, BUTTRICK, BUTTERICK, 23, 53, 70, 113. BURBANK, 101, 147. BURGESS, BURGES, 24, 46, 54, 55, 57. BURLEY, 103. BLUNT, 31. BUCK, 99. BURDON, 100, 103, 146. BURT, 43, 52. BURGE, 44. BYAM, 81, 97, 123.

CHAFEY, CHAFEE, 26, 77. CALL, 59 CARY, 1. CAPEN, 63, 67, 156, 157. CANLESS, 162. CRANSON, 64. CARSON, 165. CHADWICK, 67. CHAFFIN, 70, 72. CHANY, 71 (see Cheney). CLAFLIN, CLAFLIN (?), 98, 128, 130. CLAWLAND, 121. CALEF, 86. CHANDLER, 87, 116. CAPRON, 162. CARRUTH, CARUTH, 88, 97, 159. CARBET, 167. CARTER, 25, 27 29, 30, 36, 37, 39, 40, 53, 90, 91, 97, 101, 103, 105, 106, 108, 109, 110, 111, 112, 113, 114, 117, 148. CANNON, 3. CHAPIN, 12, 13, 14, 15, 16, 75, 77, 159, 166. CARPENTER, 3, 14, 27, 32, 117, 118, 120, 121, 122, 123, 126. CHASE, 20, 74, 75, 78, 91, 92, 94, 97, 98, 99, 100, 102, 103, 144, 145, 146, 147, 148, 149. CRAWFORD, 3, 6, 79, 112. CLAFFORD, 119 CLARK, CLARKE, 3, 4, 5, 9, 11, 12, 16, 17, 18, 20, 22, 23, 31, 32, 35, 51, 57, 58, 61, 63, 64, 66, 78, 97, 121, 122, 123, 126, 154, 166. CALHOONE, 6. CANNON, 93, 94. CHADDICK, 4, 5, 6, 7, 12, 166 167 CANTERBURY, 104. CHAPIN, 81, 160, 167. CAMPBELL, 4, 39, 58, 100, 127, 128, 131, 133, 165, 167. CRAIGUE, CRAIGE, 22, 70, 94. CARLYLE, CARLISLE, CARLILE, CARLYL, 5, 37, 59, 77 (see Corlisle). CHANDLER, 6, 9, 10, 11, 23, 24, 26, 57, 107, 125, 166, 167, 168. CRANE, 163. CRAWFORD, 8. CASE, 101, 117, 146. CARGILL, 30. CAMERON, 9. CASWELL, 94. CARRYL, CARRIL, CARRIEL (?), 21, 83, 98, 100, 101, 102, 103, 134, 135, 136, 146, 147, 148, 149 CALDWELL, 9, 22, 24, 99, 123, 158, 159. CHAPLIN, CHAPLAIN, 37, 40. CHAPMAN, 10 (see Chipman). CHARLTON, 39. CARLTON, 35, 36, 54, 146. CHAMBERLAIN,

CHAMBERELAIN, CHAMBERLIN, 10, 11, 12, 24, 25, 27, 29, 32, 57, 73, 74, 92, 101, 122, 123, 127, 128, 144, 159, 163, 164, 165, 167, 168. CHAMBAIN, 26. CATO, 11. CHAPLIN, CHAPLAIN, 36, 38, 97. CHEKEYS, 1. CHENNEY, CHENEY, CHEENEY, 13, 17, 31, 32, 33, 69, 125, 149, 159, 160, 162 (see Chany). CUFF, 19. CLEVELAND, CLEAVELAND, 21, 28, 122. CLELAND, 54. CREIGHTON, 21. CLERK, 23. CLEMENS, CLEMONS, 28, 63, 73, 85. CHENERY, 69. CREE, 72, 165. CHESTNUT, CHESTNUTS, 79. CHEVERS, 154. CHEEVER, 158. CHILD, CHILDS, 3, 4, 7, 8, 12, 22, 31, 35, 50, 52, 68, 75, 81, 85, 101, 124, 134, 148, 153, 154, 163. CHILSON, 18, 21, 51, 62. CHICKERING, 69. CLIFORD, 74. CHIPMAN, 119 (see Chapman). CHILES, 121. CHICKLEY, 155. COLMAN, 37, 39. COBB, 119, 120, 121, 122, 123, 124, 126. COTTINGHAM, 84. CONVERSE, CONVERS, 1, 25, 26, 60, 67, 151, 152, 153, 155. COLLINS, COLLENS, 2, 74, 76, 120, 149, 152, 153 COLLAR, COLLER 64, 78, 129, 131, 133, 135. COWDIN, COWDEN, 4, 22, 35, 51, 95, 167. CHOATE, 61, 79, 144, 161. CONDON, 51. CONGUERETT, 107. COMINGS, COMMINS, COMMINGS, COMMING, 19, 62, 98, 102, 136, 161 (see Cummings). CROSBEY, CROSBY, 5, 12, 44, 49, 60, 69, 78, 115, 118, 120, 150. CROWFOOT, 154. CROWELL, CROWL, 121, 130. COOK, 5, 9, 10, 15, 18, 19, 20, 61, 80, 92, 103, 115, 130, 133, 135, 149, 166. COMAN, 67. CODY, 159, 160. CROOKS, 14. CROSIEL, 97. COPLAND, 149. COLSON, 15. COLE, 52, 55, 144, 149. COBLEIGH, COBLEY, 53, 109. CORBETT, CORBITT, 15, 93. CONN, 52, 54, 55, 56, 89. CROSE, 125. CONKLIN, 58, 64. COLLIE, 19. COLBURN, 37, 91. COWEL, 66. COVEL, 129. CORBIN, CORBAN, 24, 25, 26 27, 28, 31, 32, 33, 101, 135, 136. COGSWELL, 135. COBURN, COBORNE, 26, 31, 55, 107, 131,

INDEX.

136. CONANT, CONONT, 25, 26, 35, 36, 48, 85, 87, 122, 129, 134, 135. COWEE, COWEY, 87, 106. COALMAN, 162. COTTON, 29. COOLIDGE, COOLEDGE, 41, 44, 45, 90, 116, 166, 168. CROSSET, 80, 81. CROMP, 30. CROUCH, COUCH, 47, 55. COX, 122, 124, 125. COREY, 32, 34, 44, 54, 66. COWEN, 152, 153. COOPER, 55, 56, 107, 163. CROSMAN, 33, 92, 114. CODNER, 157. CORLISLE, 36. COHE, 87. COMBS, 46. COOLEY, 58, 151. CUTTER, 3, 94. CUTTING, 5, 6, 68, 69, 70, 71, 78, 80, 83, 86, 87, 104, 157, 162. CURTIS, 5, 6, 9, 11, 21, 24, 25, 27, 29, 47, 50, 66, 83, 84, 100, 106, 120, 127, 128, 129, 136, 157, 159, 165, 167. CUNNINGHAM, 6, 22, 72, 94, 150, 166. CUMBERLAND, 9. CUTLER, CUTTLER, 16, 44, 49, 66, 75, 88, 94, 98, 146, 147, 148, 150, 152, 153, 154, 160. CUMINGS, CUMMINS, CUMMINGS, CUMINS (see Comings), 19, 20, 37, 38, 59, 73, 86, 92, 102, 103, 117, 128, 131, 145, 147, 161. CUFF, 19. CUTTEN, 25. CHUBB, 32. CHURCH, 43, 96, 111, 112, 121, 144, 161. CUSHING, 78, 81. CULVESON (?), 93. CHURCHILL, 109.

DAVIS, 1, 12, 20, 22, 23, 24, 26, 28, 29, 35, 37, 38, 39, 46, 52, 53, 56, 57, 60, 68, 69, 70, 71, 72, 76, 88, 91, 98, 113, 128, 129, 130, 131, 132, 133, 134, 135, 146, 151, 157, 160, 164. DANNELL, 7. DRAKE, 155. DAVENPORT, 3, 5, 7, 9, 80, 99, 100, 101, 103, 144. DRAPER, 10, 11, 19, 20, 21, 64, 66, 67, 152, 155, 157. DAMON, 13, 82. DANIELS, 14, 16, 17, 18, 19, 20, 78, 99, 160. DARLING, 14, 16, 17, 20, 21, 34, 37, 93, 96. DALRYMPLE, 28, 29, 161. DAY, 96, 98, 131, 149. DARBY, 42, 87, 106, 109, 131. DABY, 54, 90. DAVISON, DAVIDSON, 28, 66, 92, 145, 160. DAVID, 76. DANA, 128, 130, 165. DASCHET, 89. DANFORTH, 95, 122, 155. DAGGET, 98, 99, 146, 147. DRESSER, DRESSOR, 1, 27, 28, 31, 32, 107,

110, 136. DENISON, 2. DENNY, DENY (?), 3, 59, 60, 62, 75, 152. DEXTER, 24, 77, 118, 119, 120, 124, 125, 126. DENNIS, 28, 29, 158. DEAN, 43, 67, 94, 121, 122, 124, 126, 150, 156. DREWRY, 60. DEMONS, 68. DEERING, 86. DWELLY, 56. DEPUTRON, 105. DENSMORE, 119 (see Dunsmore). DELANEY, 134. DELYRAMPLE, 148. DEWING, 159. DEATH, 162. DIDO, 11. DINAH, 19. DILLINGWORTH, 12. DIX, 17, 61, 71, 95. DIVOLL, DIVOL, 34, 36, 37, 39, 90, 91, 105, 110, 116. DICKENSON, DICKINSON, 43, 110, 119. DICKERSON, 56, 117. DIGINS, DIGENS, 44, 112. DRIDEN, 71 (see Dryden). DIKE, 87, 102, 103, 133. DWIGHT, 85, 98, 147, 151. DIXON, 134. DWINEL, 144, 148. DOOLITTLE, 6, 9, 165. DODGE, 24, 25, 27, 33, 34, 35, 36, 37, 38, 39, 40, 57, 59, 60, 97, 98, 99, 100, 129, 144, 145, 146, 147, 148, 149, 151, 155. DORMAN, 34. DOWNE, DOWNES, 38, 39, 95. DOOR, 48. DOPSON, 57. DODS, DODDS, 68, 69. DOWNING, 94, 118. DORCHESTER, 108. DOLE, 110, 117, 131. DOTY, DOTEY, 118, 123. DOAN, 119. DOROTY, 150. DURNEL, 144. DUDLEY, 3, 10, 48, 97, 99, 100, 101, 103, 130, 145, 146, 147. DUNCAN, DUNKAN, DUNKIN, 8, 12, 13, 22, 149, 152, 161, 167. DUNSMORE, DUNSMOOR, 18, 37, 63, 79, 105, 106, 107, 111, 113, 118, 120 (see Densmore). DUNN, DUN, 21, 22, 65. DUGEN, 32. DUTTON, 34, 35, 36, 46. DUNSTER, 38, 85. DUPEE, 45, 105. DRURY, 50, 67, 73, 78, 79, 80, 81, 83, 136, 157. DUNBAR, 61, 65. DUNNELL, DUNIL, 64, 98. DUNTON, 73. DUNLAP, 88. DUELLEY, 92. DUNKLEE, 97. DUNN, 163. DYER, 1, 7. DRYDEN, 68, 70 (see Driden).

EAGER, EAGUR, 3, 82, 83, 87, 88, 109, 114. EATON, 4, 5, 12, 61, 71, 117, 144, 145, 147, 158, 168. EARL, EARLL, 6, 7, 9, 58, 62, 70, 124, 126. EPHRAIM, 13. EDWARD, EDWARDS, 40, 45, 46, 128, 129. EASTABROOK, 74, 83,

84 (see Esterbrooks). EARCY (?), 131. EASTEY, EASTY, 148, 164 (see Estey). ELDER, 8, 9 114. EMERSON, 18, 20, 21, 25, 131 (see Emmorson). ELWELL, 26, 30, 121, 154. EVERETT, 39, 87. EDES, 53. ESTERBROOKS, ESTABROOKS, ESTABROOK, ESTHERBROOKS, 67, 71, 72, 86 (see Eastabrook). EDGEL, 72. EVENS, 85. EVERDAN, 103. EVELETH, 105, 108, 166. EDSON, 119. ESTEY, 164 (see Eastey). ELLIS, 13, 16, 18, 33, 58, 82, 90, 97, 125. ELLISON, 20, 50. ELIOT, ELLIOT 28, 100, 101, 103, 145, 146, 148. ENDICOTT, 36. EDMINSTER, 64. EHLICH, 78. ENIRDON, 92. ELIXANDER, 92 (see Alexander). ELDRIDGE, 93. ENGLISH, 158. EDMONDS, 3 (see Edmunds). EMMORSON, 86. EMMONS, 117. EMMONDS, 118. ELSWORTH, 154. EDSON, 155. EDMUNDS, 25, 26, 27, 28, 59. EUSTICE, 63. EDDY, 65, 127, 130, 131, 132, 133, 134.

FAY, 1, 23, 31, 32, 47, 73, 74, 78, 79, 84, 88, 94, 118, 119, 120, 123, 124, 126, 133. FRAME, 1. FARR, 2, 12, 53, 57, 73, 118, 119, 134. FLAGG, 4, 9, 10, 11, 12, 38, 50, 52, 68, 69, 71, 72, 77, 78, 81, 84, 104, 109, 146, 160, 161, 165, 167. FAIRFIELD, 3, 97. FA—E, 155. FARNSWORTH, FARNWORTH, 9, 53, 54, 55, 56, 57, 59, 86, 91, 113, 117. FAIRBANK, FAIRBANKS, FRAIRBANK, 17, 25, 40, 41, 45, 46, 47, 48, 52, 54, 55, 56, 76, 78, 89, 92, 105, 106, 109, 110, 113, 114, 115, 116, 117, 122, 161, 162, 164. FARNUM, 18, 20, 21. FARROW, FRARROW(?), FARRAR, FARRER, 25, 79, 77, 107, 158. FAULKNER 31, 43. FARWELL, FAREWELL, 35, 37, 38, 44, 53, 54, 55, 56, 95, 112. FARLEY, 37. FARMER, 54, 57. FAY, 162. FARCE, 97. FARRINGTON, 113. FASSET, 118. FRAZIER, 145. FRENCH, 15, 16, 17, 41, 45, 51, 77. FLETCHER, 22, 28, 38, 49, 50, 53, 60, 68, 69, 86, 96, 100, 104, 118, 161. FESINDEN, FESSENDEN, 23, 87. FELTON, 24, 150, 154, 155, 158, 161, 162. FREEMAN, FREEMON, 26, 32, 33, 35, 36, 118, 120, 124, 145. FENNER, 29. FELLOWS, 53. FELCH, 68. FENTON, 94. FELING, 99. FREELAND, 130, 133. FREDERICK, 162. FISK, 4, 13, 14, 15, 18, 31, 32, 33, 49, 50, 51, 69, 70, 71, 72, 73, 81, 99, 102, 103, 118, 119, 120, 121, 122, 131, 133, 150, 167. FITTS, 12 28, 30, 97, 100, 101, 130, 132, 133, 134, 135, 145, 148. FISH, 15, 19, 20, 21, 51, 84, 92, 99, 118, 133, 163. FIFE, 45, 46. FISHER, 17, 50, 51, 63, 94, 96. FRIPHEL, 20. FRINK, 23, 61. FITCH, 35. FINNEY, 56, 119, 123. FRISSELL, 79 (see Friphel). FLINT, 84, 86, 122. FINTON, 94. FIELD, 117. FORBUSH, 4, 6, 9, 38, 48, 49, 50, 52, 58, 60, 71 76, 77, 118, 121, 122, 126 (see Furbush). FOSTER, 10, 16, 25, 28, 31, 34, 35, 37, 39. FORSTER, 40, 44, 46, 56, 58, 70, 96, 101, 114, 117, 119, 121, 125, 132, 156. FROST, 13, 71, 95, 128, 129, 159. FORBES 24, 50, 70, 124, 145, 150, 153, 154, 159. FOBES, 51, 163. FORBUS, 58. FOSKET, 26, 42, 43, 44. FOWLER, 38. FOSS, 39. FLOOD, 42. FOSGATE, 47, 85, 86, 89. FLOYD, 70. FORCE, 93. FOWL, 112. FOWLE, 115, 117, 167. FORD, 124. FOTHERGILL, 124. FOXCRAFT, 154. FORISTELL, 159. FOLLANSBE, 167. FULLERTON, 11. FULTON, 22. FULLER, 34, 35, 36, 37, 41, 90, 91, 97, 120, 123, 124, 128, 136, 145, 148. FULLAM FULLOM 56, 57. FURBUSH, 66, 78, 115 124, 156 (see Forbush). FURNAS, 124. FULLEN, 155. FRY, 164.

GATS, 66 (see Gates). GALE, GAIL, 3, 4, 10, 13, 24, 27, 69, 70, 82 98, 99, 100, 102, 144, 145, 148, 149 166. GATES, 4, 5, 9, 10, 11, 12, 13, 23, 36, 40, 43, 45, 47, 52, 53, 57, 59, 83, 90, 91, 106, 109, 114, 165, 166, 168 (see Gats). GRAY, 4, 6, 7, 8, 9, 11, 12, 13, 37, 58, 71, 91, 130, 166, 167. GRAHAM, 6, 12, 31, 66 67, 155, 164. GAMBELL, GAMBLE, 9, 105, 167. GAY, 14, 25, 71, 72. GAYER, 85. GAUSE, 14. GLASCO, 165. GAGE, 21,

89, 149. GLARIS, 79. GRATON, 27. 58. GRAFIELD, 57. GRANT, 72, 109, 132, GANES, 31. GASCHET, 88, 89. GARY, GAREY, 35, 85, 97, 106, 107, 110. GRANGER, 119. GARDINER, GARDENER, GARDNER, 36, 71, 74, 96. GLAZIER, 41, 46, 68, 69, 70, 72, 81, 85, 111, 120, 121, 167. GRAVES, 41, 74, 80, 84, 85, 87, 91, 113, 123. GARFIELD, 55, 58, 59, 62, 64, 65, 66, 78, 91, 100, 101, 103, 147. GLEASON, 2, 4, 5, 8, 9, 10, 13, 16, 25, 26, 33, 61, 62, 64, 67, 69, 83, 98, 101, 102, 103. GLEZEN, 70, 72, 108, 127, 128, 130, 131, 133, 147, 149, 165, 166, 167. GREEN, 2, 3, 5, 6, 7, 9, 14, 16, 25, 47, 48, 58, 59, 60, 62, 64, 65, 67, 87, 88, 96, 112, 115, 116, 118, 119, 149, 150, 152, 166. GREENWOOD, 5, 39, 69, 80, 99, 100, 148. GREGGS, 12, 41. GREENLEAF, 41, 110. GREATON, 62. GREGORY, 73. GEARY, 113, 116. GERRISH, 113. GLEAZER, 122. GERMINGS, 151. GILBERT, 118, 119, 121, 124. GILBURT, 1, 2, 23, 47, 60, 61, 93, 94, 150, 151, 152, 153, 154, 155, 156. GIBBIN, 2. GRIGGS, 13, 76, 166. GILES, 50, 100, 147. GIBBS, 18, 41, 46, 63, 85, 99, 100, 108, 117, 147. GILL, 22, 39. GILSON, 34. 36. GIBSON, 36, 37, 39, 56, 75, 95, 149. GRIFFIN, GRIFFEN, 37, 60, 121. GRIMES, 38, 114, 152, 153. GILCHRIST, GILCREST, 38, 94. GILLHAY, 59. GINNE, 118. GIFFEN, GIFFIN, 118. 125. GRIFFETH, 134. GOULD, GOOLD, 2, 9, 10, 17, 28, 33, 34, 37, 38, 43, 54, 72, 75, 93, 96, 97, 98, 99, 100, 101, 102, 103, 104, 135, 144, 145, 146, 147, 148, 149, 151, 153, 154. GOSS, 2, 3, 40, 41, 43, 47, 48, 109, 111, 115, 120, 150. GROSVENOR, 102, 147. GOULDING, 4, 5, 6, 71, 72, 76, 78, 144, 166, 168. GOODWIN, 6, 11, 61, 110, 165. GROUGHT, 161. GROUT, 10, 11, 35. GROSS, GROS, 113, 131, 132, 134. GORE, 27, 49, 51. GOTT, 152. GOODRIDGE, 35, 36, 37, 38, 39, 40, 96, 114. GORDAN, 84. GROTON, 36. GROVER, 146. GOODELL, GOODALE, 39, 42, 43, 69, 76, 78, 80, 82, 86, 98, 100, 101, 103, 113, 145, 146, 151, 152, 156, 158. GORHAM, GHORAM, 118, 126. GOODENOUGH, GOODNOUGH, 42, 80. GOLDTHWAID, GOLDTHWAIT, 50, 146, 163. GOODFREY, GOODFREE, GODFRY, 53, 106, 107, 110, 115, 159. GOODSPEED, 60, 119, 120. GODARD, GODDARD, 70, 76, 79, 80, 81, 83, 84, 85, 97, 102, 103, 144, 161, 162, 164. GOOLDSBURY, 77. GOWING, 78, 90. GOODANOW, GOODENOW, 79, 82, 89, 107, 110, 118, 120. GUEST, 32. GUN, 62, 112. GURNEY, 165.

HARPER, 22, 34, 52, 56, 105, 156. HAZON, 37. HAWES, HAW, HAWS, 1, 2, 93, 94, 98. HARDING, 1, 30, 31, 32, 33. HAMILTON, 1, 6, 8, 60, 63, 66, 121, 136, 150, 151, 152, 153, 154, 155, 156, 163, 166. HASCALL, HASKEL, HASKELL, 23, 27, 30, 40, 42, 53, 54, 55, 56, 57, 106, 107, 112, 114, 115, 116, 117, 119, 121, 122, 123, 125. HATFIELD, 2. HAZELTINE, HASELTINE, 3, 19, 49, 54, 57, 99, 103, 148, 149. HARDY, 49, 74, 76, 147, 153. HARRY, 51. HARRINGTON, 5, 6, 8, 9, 10, 11, 12, 13, 35, 38, 39, 46, 50, 58, 59, 64, 70, 71, 72, 73, 76, 77, 78, 81, 83, 85, 89, 104, 108, 114, 115, 117, 153, 156, 165, 167, 168 (see Herrington). HATCH, 31, 61, 65, 66, 120, 126. HARRIS, 3, 4, 8, 9, 42, 46, 54, 69, 71, 89, 90, 105, 124, 125, 128, 129, 135, 149, 150. HART, 5, 9, 12, 36, 128, 133, 134, 160. HASWELL, 166. HASTINGS, 6, 10, 36, 43, 44, 45, 54, 62, 79, 83, 84, 88, 110, 112, 116, 119, 123, 124. HARKNESS, 34, 39. HARTHION, 8. HAPGOOD, 24, 52, 54, 55, 57, 81, 82, 86. HATHAWAY, 51, 126. HAIR, 9, 13, 156, 166. HAVENS, HAVEN, 27, 75, 100, 101, 149, 159, 161, 162. HAGER, HAGOR, HAGAR, 41, 73, 85, 102, 159. HAMOND, HAMMON, HAMMOND, 9, 21, 33, 61, 63, 112, 118, 124, 125, 146. HARRIMAN, 35, 124. HARD, 9. HAMANT, 31, 32. HAYWORD, HAYWOOD, HAYWARD, HARWOOD, HAWOOD, 2, 14, 15, 16, 17, 18, 19, 31, 34, 49, 50, 59, 60, 61, 63, 65, 69, 88,

92 98, 100, 101, 103, 110, 113, 120, 121, 128, 134, 136 145, 147, 151, 156, 159, 160 163 (see Heyward, Heward). HARTWELL, 37, 39, 57, 68, 86, 95, 133. HALL, 19, 20, 23, 24, 49, 50, 52, 55, 56, 76, 77, 78, 88, 91, 93, 94, 97, 99, 100, 102, 104, 129, 145, 146, 147, 148, 157. HADLOCK, 19. HANNAH, 44. HAFFRON, 22. HAWKINS, 20. HAMBLETON, 167. HAIL, HALE, 20, 23, 31, 38, 47, 52, 54, 56, 57, 70, 84, 87, 90, 99, 112, 113, 144, 152, 156. HAIDEN, HAYDEN, 28, 30, 51, 74, 78, 88 144, 146. HARBRIDGE, 132. HADLEY, 86, 87. HAILD, 57. HARBARCH, HARBACH, HARBACK, 98, 99, 101, 102 103, 135, 148 157. HARROD, 59. HANCOCK, 94, 111, 133 HASEY, 60, 161. HAMAN, 65, HAWKES, 122. HARR—TON, 70 HARON, 75. HANMER, 126. HARDY, 79. HASKINS, 125. HATSHORN, 82. HARVEY, 85, 107, 109, 111, 112, 126 (see Hervey). HAWKS, 95. HAINES, 85. HENDERSON, 64, 82, 89. HAWOOD, HEYWARD, HEYWOOD, 1, 5, 9, 10, 11, 16, 37 60, 69 70, 71, 72, 79, 82, 83, 105, 108, 114 165, 166, 167. HEDGE, 119, 123. HERRING, 8, 71. HEARD, 68 71 (see Hurd). HEYDEN, 8, 12 23. HENRY, 8, 9, 34, 35, 40, 55, 166. HENNY, 84. HEARNS, 10 122. HERVEY, 74 (see Harvey). HEARSAY, HERSEY, 11, 117, 156. HERRINGTON, 86, 154 (see Harrington). HENLY, 11. HEWES, 124, 155. HECTOR, 78. HEATH, 18, 28. HEWARD, 87 (see Hayward). HERENDEEN, 92. HEFFRON, 22. HEBBERD, HEBBERT, 129, 157 (see Hibberd). HEALEY, 27, 28, 29. HENCHER 150. HEDGES, 29, 32. HENDRICK, 156. HEALD, 38. HEMENWAY, HEMMENWAY, HEMINWAY, 46 47, 70, 71, 80, 83, 164, 167. HENSHAW (?), 60, 61 (see Hinshaw). HIDE, 1, 4. HINDS, HIND, 1, 4, 31, 79, 80, 151, 152, 153, 154, 155, 157. HILL, HILLS, 1, 14, 16, 28, 48, 49, 52, 61, 92, 93, 101, 104, 109, 131, 151, 153, 154, 156, 163. HILYARD, 16. HICKS, 20, 99, 101, 102. HIBBARD, HIBBERD, HIBBERT, 25, 26, 29, 78, 129 (see Hebberd). HILTON, 34, 36. HINSHAW, 60, 62 (see Henshaw). HISCOCK, 67, 102, 103, 159, 160. HILT, 110. HIGGINS, 118, 119, 121, 157. HINKLEY, HINCKLEY, 120, 123, 125, 126, 152, 153. HINCHER, HINCHEN, 154. HITCHCOCK 155, 157. HOWLAND, 67, 155. HOLDIN, HOLDEN, 2, 4, 22, 34, 37, 43, 46, 54, 56, 82, 85, 86, 87, 111, 127, 159. HORTON, 45. HOLTON, 5, 37, 100, 103, 135. HOLT, 38, 39, 44, 54, 69, 81, 97, 107, 113, 115. HOMES, HOLMES, HOLMS, 7, 8, 43, 123 154, 168. HOUGH, 41. HOSLEY, 86, 131. HOLLAND, 7, 17, 80, 81, 82, 83, 97, 102. HOLBROOK, 10, 12, 13, 14, 15, 16, 17, 19, 21, 29, 49, 51, 75, 78, 92, 160, 168. HOW, HOWE, 10, 11, 12, 21, 22, 23, 25, 28, 40, 42, 48, 49, 61, 62, 63, 67, 68, 69, 70, 71, 76, 78, 79, 82, 83, 85, 88, 91, 98, 106, 125, 132, 148, 151, 152, 153, 154, 156, 164, 167. HOWARD, 11, 26, 28, 31, 32, 69, 86, 102. HOUSE, 105, 114. HOPKINS, 21, 34 124. HOAR, 86, 87 106 116. HOOKER, 25, 32, 119. HODGE, HODGES, 123, 124. HOVEY, 25, 26, 38, 129, 131, 134, 135 148, 149. HOMER, 153. HOSMER, 89. HOBBS, 31, 32, 136, 151, 154, 156, 157. HOWELL, 93. HONN, 105. HOUGHTON, 34, 35, 36, 40, 41, 42, 43, 44, 45, 46, 47, 48, 52, 53, 54, 57, 82, 83, 84, 90, 104, 105, 106, 107, 108, 109, 110, 111, 112, 113, 114, 119, 129, 164. HOUGHT, 40. HODGSKINS, HODGSKIN, 35, 36, 56, 96. HOLFIELD, 151. HOOD, 131. HOLMAN, 36, 42, 48, 97, 98, 99, 100, 101, 102 116, 127, 145, 147, 148. HOWLET, 166. HOLL, 38, 131. HOPPING, 74. HOIT, HOYT, 77, 78, 154. HUNTLEY, 1. HUBBARD, HUBBURD, 4, 5, 6, 7, 23, 68, 69, 71, 72, 82. HULL, 6, 8, 20, 21, 99, 124. HUTCHINSON, 9, 42, 75, 98, 99, 100, 101, 103. HUNT, 10, 16, 22, 26, 27, 53, 67, 108, 112, 119, 120, 122, 124, 126, 130, 163, 166. HUTCHINS, 24, 36, 46, 52, 53, 161. HUMPHREY, 25, 28, 126, 129, 130, 161, 162. HUKER, 25. HUMPHY, 128. HUZZA,

51. HURD, 53 (see Heard). HUDSON, HUTSON (?), 73, 88, 96, 97, 105, 124, 131, 133, 134. HUMES, 92, 149. HUNTER, 94. HUSE, 103. HUSK, 106. HUNKINS, 127. HYLARD, 20. HYLE, 55. HYSCOM, 73.

INMAN, 26, 27. INGRAHAM, 31. IRELAND, 35, 37. IVES, 133. INGERSON, 147, INGLESBEE, 167. INGOLSBEE, 84.

JAMES, 2. JACKSON, 19, 23, 51, 53, 59, 62, 64, 66, 86, 87, 97, 106, 109, 144, 161. JACKMAN, 35. JAMESON, 126. JACOBS, 149. JANES, 161. JENNINGS, JENINGS, 2, 26, 60, 151, 153 154 156, 157. JENNISON, JENISON, 8, 24, 36, 102, 103, 116, 133, 145, 148, 149. JEPPARDSON, 17. JEPERSON, 92. JENKINS, 24, 39, 122, 158. JEFFERDS, 24. JEWETT, JEWET, JEWITT, 24, 37, 45, 47, 48, 107, 111, 113. JEWELL, 25, 27, 28, 132. JENNEY, JENNY, 49, 126, 148. JESEPH, 83. JENNIS, 117. JENNY, 148. JINNEY, 124. JOHNSON, 1, 6, 7, 8, 9, 24, 31, 32, 33, 38, 44 45, 47, 52, 61, 73, 74, 80, 82, 83, 89, 90, 91, 94, 102, 108, 110, 113, 118, 119, 120, 122, 123, 124, 125, 126, 134, 144, 160, 165, 166, 167, 168 (see Joneson). JOSLIN JOSLYN, 26, 41, 72, 73, 84, 90, 93 94, 96, 105, 112, 115, 116, 117, 126. JONES, 3, 9, 10, 11, 17, 18, 24, 25, 42, 44, 46, 61, 64, 65, 76, 86, 90, 107, 113, 128, 149, 152, 158, 160, 166, 167, 168. JOHNSTONE, 71. JONESON, 92. JONUS (?), 114. JORDEN, JORDAN, 119, 121, 122. JONE, 165, JOYNER, 39.

KATHERIN, 43. KATHAN, 59. KNAP, 65, 73, 101, 149. KELSO, 6. KELLY, KELEY, KELLEY, 10, 12, 54, 88, 159. KENT, 16, 43, 61, 83. KEITH, 17, 20, 21, 27, 102, 125. KEYES, KYES, KEYS, 21, 40, 51, 78, 79, 80, 81, 82, 84, 86, 88, 99, 131. KENNEDY, 34, 158. KENDALL, KENDAL, KENDEL, 38, 39, 40, 55, 70, 83, 85, 91, 96, 105, 106, 107, 108, 110, 111, 112, 113, 114, 115, 116, 131, 153, 161, 162 (see Kindall). KELCEY, 45. KNEELAND, 53. KEEP, KEEPE, 54, 56, 57, 156. KEZER, 85, 86. KENNEY, 99, 100, 101, 146, 147. KELLOG, 118. KEKO, 167. KINDRICK, 150, 156. KILLAM, KILLUM, 2, 102. KING, 5, 47, 97, 98, 102, 103, 130 146, 149. KILLEY, 6. KILTON, 161. KNIGHT, KNIGHTS, 8 9, 10, 12, 13, 34, 44, 45, 46, 54, 56, 65, 71, 72, 82, 107, 108, 109, 110, 114, 116, 162, 165, 166. KIMPTON, 19, 20. KIDDER, 24, 26, 27, 28, 30, 49, 100, 101, 144, 145, 146. KIMBALL, KIMBELL, 37, 38, 75, 77, 78 81, 94, 95, 135, 151, 159, 160. KILBOURN, KILBURN, 40, 104, 113, 115, 159. KINGMAN, 57. KINGSLY, 62. KINNEY, KINNY, 66, 98, 102, 103, 123. KINT, 83. KITTERIDGE, 110. KINGSBURY, KINGSBERY, 128, 130, 131, 133 157. KITTS, 144. KINDALL, 162 (see Kendall). KNOX, 8, 11. KNOWLAND, 29, KNOWLTON, KNOLTON, 42, 76, 81 82, 83, 119 121, 125, 153, 154. KOREY, 126. KNOWLES, 162.

LAWRENCE, LARRANCE, 5, 53, 55, 73, 84, 117, 118, 119, 121, 125. LAMSON, LAMBSON, 130, 133, 136, 151 152, 153. LATHORNE, 18. LAMB, 28, 58, 62 63, 64, 65, 66, 67, 70, 97, 128, 129, 130, 132, 136, 154. LARNED, LARNARD 28, 29, 30, 49 (see Learned). LACE, 32. LARRABEE, 33. LAW, 36, 55, 104. LAUGHTON, LAWTON, 46, 58, 64, 122, 126. LOCKEY, 49, 50, 92, 147, 157. LAZELL, 52, LAMON, 58 LAMMOND, 58. LAMBERT, 88. LAGGET, 106. LARKINS, LARKIN, 109, 116. LAFFLIN, 128, 129. LANE, 151, 152. LEACH, LEECH, LEITCH, 1, 31, 61, 112, 150, 154 158. LEWIS, 2, 61, 113, 135. LEE, 2, 7, 24, 29, 32, 74, 81, 93, 121 164. LEONARD, 12 22 23, 122. LEGG 13, 15, 17, 49. LESUER, LESURE, LEISURE, 13, 16, 17, 18, 19, 49, 160. LEALAND, LELAND, 48, 75, 76, 77, 78, 100, 101, 103, 144, 147, 149. LEASON, 55, 122. LE-

VEAR, 55. LEW, 114. LEARNED, LEARNARD, LEARNED, 127, 128, 129, 130, 131, 133, 134 (see Larned). LEVINS, 129 130. LE BARON, 149. LEATH, 157. LENARD, 158. LINCOLN, 2, 45, 90, 91, 93, 94, 105, 123, 124, 163, 168. LITTLE, 4, 34, 37, 40, 93, 158. LIVERMORE, 13, 30, 53, 60, 62, 65, 69, 88, 122, 157. LIBRET, 25. LINGLEY, 41. LINTON, 92. LITCH, 94. LILLIE LILLEY, 99, 100, 102, 103, 130, 148. LIPUNWELL, LIPINWELL, 104, 105 (see Lyppenwell). LITTLEJOHNS, 106. LINDS, 121. LITTLEFIELD, 159. LOVEL, LOVIL, LOVELL, 5, 8, 31, 63, 68, 69, 71, 92, 97, 132, 145, 146, 147, 148, 151, 167. LOW, 7, 37, 95, 158. LOVIS, 10. LYON, 14. LOVETT, LOVITT, 15. LOVEJOY, 34, 35, 154. LONGLEY, 41, 46, 48, 89, 107, 112, 114. LOCK, LOCKE, 47, 95, 105, 108, 110, 111, 113, 115, 116, 127, 145. LONG, 50. LOVING, 65. LORD, 162. LUMBIRD, 31. LUMBARD, 162. LUCE, 121. LUCY, 160. LUTHER, 160. LYSCOMB, LYSCOM, 2, 73, 119, 157. LYCETT, 70. LYNDS, LYND, LYNDE, 8, 10, 58, 59, 61, 63, 64, 68, 80, 81, 123, 152, 153, 155. LYMAN, 13. LYMONDS, 54. LYON, 24, 30, 31, 32, 61, 62, 77, 78, 101, 108, 136. LYPENWELL, 116 (see Lipinwell).

MASON, 1, 2, 24, 30, 31, 32, 33, 113, 125. MASCROFT, 1. MARCY, 1, 28, 29, 30, 31, 32, 33. MARSH 2, 17, 22, 31, 33, 78, 92, 93, 97, 98, 99, 100, 101, 102, 105, 117, 119, 130, 135, 144, 158 (see Mersh). MARCH, 62, 100, 127. MATHEWS, MATHEW, 3, 72, 73, 85, 93, 108. MAHAN, MAHON 5, 8, 13, 31, 34, 165, 167. MAYNARD, MAINARD, 11, 76, 79, 80, 81, 82, 84, 88, 89, 107, 153. MARSHALL, MARSHAL, 15, 28, 68, 69, 71. MARUDE, 18. MANDELL, 120, 123, 159. MAN, 23, 31, 63. MAZROW, 162. MAY, 26, 28, 60, 63, 106. MAYA (?), 128. MAYO, 27, 131, 132. MASTERS, 59. MANSFIELD, 30, 92, 96. MANNING, 152, 153. MARTIN, MARTYN, MARTEN, 31, 32, 36, 37, 38, 39, 40, 42, 82, 95, 132. MACKENTIER, MACKINTIRE, 33, 127 (see McIntier). MAHANAY, MAHONEY, 45, 81. MAKEPEACE, 33, 154. MARVIN, 128, 135. MARBLE, 41, 46, 50, 52, 75, 97, 101, 120, 126, 146, 147, 148, 154. MARSTASS (?), 75. MARSTON, 59. MENDALL, 7. MELVIN, MELVEN, 10, 72, 76, 95. MELLET, 12. MERRIAM, MERIAM, MERIUM, MERIMAN, 14, 17, 42, 44, 47, 57, 75, 85, 86, 112, 127, 128, 129, 130, 131, 132, 133, 135, 145, 147, 148. METCALF, 23, 69, 164. MEBROW, 41. MEEDS, MEAD, MEADS, 52, 55, 56, 125. MERRIT, MERRITT, 59, 60, 61. MERCY, 66. MELLEN, 70, 104, 113. MEARS, 90. MERSH 92 (see Marsh). MESSER, 93. MELLADY, 99. MERRICK, 118. MEIGS, 125. MELODY, MELLODY, 145, 148. MELANDY, 163. MIRICK, 1, 2, 23, 72, 118, 126. MILLS, 1, 7, 71, 87, 132. MILLET, 7, 8, 167. MILLER, 8, 11, 12, 69, 77, 85, 86, 87, 134, 157. MITCHEL, 8, 35, 108. MILES, 24, 54, 80, 81, 83, 84, 87. MIX, 32. MIRIAM, 42, 43, 87, 128, 131, 135. MIXER, MIXOR, 63, 73, 80, 81, 148, 149, 150. MIXTOR, MIXTER, 89, 131, 152. MOORSS, MORE, MOOR, MOORS, MOORE, MOORES, 1, 3, 4, 5, 6, 7, 8, 9, 10, 11, 12, 13, 22, 23, 35, 40, 42, 43, 44, 45, 47, 48, 62, 71, 73, 74, 80, 95, 102, 106, 107, 109, 110, 111, 112, 113, 116, 120, 128, 129, 130, 131, 132, 133, 147, 153, 154, 155, 164, 165, 166, 167, 168. MORSE, MORSS, 2, 11, 19, 21, 24, 25, 29, 31, 32, 49, 62, 69, 72, 73, 74, 78, 81, 82, 83, 84, 85, 92, 99, 101, 103, 145, 146, 147, 148, 149, 155, 164. MOWER, 4, 5, 12, 61, 99, 116, 127. MORRIS, MORRISS, 9, 25, 30, 32, 50, 106. MORY, MOREY, 16, 17, 33, 63, 65, 66. MORGAN, 17, 50, 63, 64, 66, 118, 126. MOSELY, MOSELEY, MOSSLEY, 21, 97, 145, 149. MONTOR, 24. MOFFAT, MOFFIT, MOPHIT, 32, 37, 52, 130. MOULTON, 42, 156. MON-

INDEX.

ROW 64 (see Munroe). MOSTMAN, 85. MOSEMON, MOSMAN, 107. 116. MORTON, 161. MOXTOR, 144. MULLENS, 10. MURDOCK, 19, 21. 163. MUNROE, MUNROW (see Monrow), 50, 57, 89, 117. MUZZY, 62, 63, 64, 65, 66, 79, 81. MUNYE, 65. MUNJOY, 84. MULLICKEN, 98. MUNDELL, 120. MUNDEN, 121. MUNEIL, 129. MYRICK, 158. MacCARTY, 4, 109, 167. McFARLAND, 4 6, 8, 12, 22, 53, 166. McCRACKIN, McCRACKEN, 6, 36. McFADDEN, McFADIN, 8, 10, 41. McNAMMAR, 16. McMAINE, 22. McCLANATHAN, 29. McCALLEN, 30. McWAIN, 44, 45, 46. McFARLING, 104, 109. MACCLEWAIN, McCLEWAIN, 4, 41, 42, 44, 58. McPHESON, 6. McCLELLAN, McCLALLAN, 6 8, 18, 76. McKINSTRY, 2, 33. McINTIER, McINTYER, McINTYRE, McINTIRE, 22, 28, 64, 122, 123, 128, 135, 136. McBRIDE, 42, 44 46. McKNIGHT, 101, 129. McMICHAELL, 118. McCOMBS, 153. McDONALD, 168. McKLURE, McCLURE, McCLUER, 31, 63, 157. McMULLEN, 69, 71. McCULLOUGH, 158.

NALE, 154. NEWTON, 2, 3, 7, 16, 60, 66, 69, 72, 73, 74, 76, 79, 80, 81, 84, 87, 102, 103, 111, 113, 120, 123, 124, 126, 151, 156. NELSON, 14, 15, 18, 49, 50, 51, 73, 102, 107, 135, 146, 159, 160 NEWCOMB, 19. NEWELL, 24 25, 27, 28, 29, 30, 32 33, 59, 62, 100, 103, 145, 151, 162. NEWHALL, 58, 60, 61, 62, 63, 73, 85, 113. NEWLAND, 163. NICHOLS, NICKOLS, 1, 7, 9, 10, 11, 12, 17, 41, 48, 61, 64, 68 71, 91, 96, 100, 104, 105, 108, 109, 112, 122, 128, 129, 130, 133, 134, 135, 145, 165. NICKLESS, 39, 97. NIXON, 80. NIMS, 110, 122. NICHOLAS, 148. NOBLE, 3. NORCROSS, 36, 39, 111, 112, 113. NOE, 87. NOWELL, 116. NURSE, NURSS, 23, 41, 43, 44, 47, 48, 74, 144, 158. NUTTING, 155. NYE, 91, 92, 93, 94, 120, 121, 122, 124, 125, 126, 158.

OAK, OAKS, 7, 8, 26, 28, 42, 43, 45, 47, 53, 69, 88. ONTHANK, 74. OSLAND, 166. OREL, 17. OBER, 50, 85. OVERLOOK, 56. ORMES, 63 64. OLMSTEAD, 118, 155. OLIPHANT, 3. OLIVER, 9 24 41, 126, 161, 162. OBRIAN, 17. OSGOOD, 6, 22, 23, 43, 81, 87, 90, 91, 105, 106, 107, 108, 109, 110, 111, 112, 116, 117. OSBORN, 42, 44. OLDS, 80, 150, 151, 154, 155, 157. OSBURN, 4.

PARSONS, PARSON, 44, 58, 60, 100, 106, 108, 135, 146, 150. PAGON, 1, 25. PAIGE, PAGE, 2, 3, 33, 37, 40, 51, 54, 104, 109, 114, 119, 121, 122, 123, 124, 126. PARMENTER, 3, 5, 46, 79, 89, 90, 109, 111. PARMETER, 124. PLATTS, PLAT, 33, 37, 146. PAINE, PAIN, 5, 9, 12, 30, 38, 62, 123, 146, 168 (see Peine). PARKS, PARK, 7, 19, 52, 54, 55, 66, 98, 99, 101, 102, 123, 125, 144, 149, 163. PARKE, 154. PARKER, 7, 10, 11, 26, 27, 28, 34, 42, 47, 59, 61, 66, 67, 70 73, 80, 84, 86, 92, 93, 106, 130, 136, 155, 158. PATCH, 8, 38, 125 134, 135, 150, 167. PARKMAN, 88, 148, 157. PATRICK, PARTRICK, 12, 23, 94, 118. PACKARD, 121, 153, 154, 166, 167. PRATT, PRAT, 14, 29, 36, 41, 42, 47, 49, 52, 60, 78, 84, 101, 110, 114, 116, 117, 118, 120, 124, 128, 129, 131, 132, 133 134 135, 147, 155, 158, 163, 164. PARKHURST, 15, 16, 17, 53, 57, 105, 160. PAUL, 59. PALMER, 17, 49, 148, 154. PALEY, 59. PATTERSON, PATERSON, 63, 151. PASMORE, 18, 21. PAYSON, 95. PARCAS, 21. PARTRIDGE, 21, 31, 70, 150, 152, 155. PARKHILL, 37. PERKINS, 68, 94, 98, 99, 121, 123, 158. PETERS, PETER, 1, 15, 154, 157. PERRY, 1, 5, 26, 66, 70, 165, 166, 167. PEIRCE, 5, 10, 19, 37, 39, 43, 44, 68, 69, 80, 84, 90, 129, 132, 133, 147, 166 (see Pierce). PEARSE, 101. PERSE, 87. PHELPS, 11, 22, 54, 82, 95, 104, 109, 110, 112, 113, 114, 115, 116, 117. PENNIMAN, PENNYMAN, 15, 16, 18, 19, 21,

87. PEPPER, 117. PRENTICE, 18, 19, 77, 78, 104, 105, 113, 115, 167. PRESTON, 19, 27. PREIST (see Priest). PRESCOTT, 69, 87, 115, 116, 117. PERSONS, 23. PEARSONS, 96. PERMENTER, 23. PERRIN, 25. PEASE, 25, 50. PEABODY, 34, 39. PERHAM, 48, 49, 51, 78. PEESA (?), 150. PECK, 49 160. PETERSON, 51, 108. PEINE, 62, 73 (see Paine). PERUN, 92. PIKE, 2, 3 20, 29, 32, 40, 60, 62, 67, 72, 79, 82, 135, 160, 162, 164. PHILLIPS, 7, 74, 87, 90, 117, 128, 129, 134, 136, 157, 160 162. PRINCE, 10, 28, 135. PIERCE, 32, 36, 37, 38, 40, 48, 53, 55, 64, 87, 91, 95, 100, 126, 149, 164 165, 167 (see Peirce), PLIMPTON, 32. PRIEST, 35, 41, 45, 46, 48 52, 54, 55, 57, 108, 111, 114, 115. PRICE, 37. PI—ES, 41. PIPER, 41, 44, 113, 162. PITT, 48. PIERKS, 83. PHIPS, 91, 155. PRIME, 146, 149. POWERS, POWER, 2, 19, 20, 43, 46, 52, 72, 108, 111, 112, 117, 119, 120, 125, 162, 163. PORSON, 3. POTTER, 4, 35, 50, 70, 148, 153, 154, 156, 157, 163. PROCTOR, 8, 54, 112, 113. POFFER, 14. POPE, 14. POOR, 36, 96, 112 114, 164. POND, 16, 160. POLLEY, 25, 95. POLLIS, 32. POOL, POOLE, 35, 36, 39. POLLARD, 41, 44, 46, 47, 48, 56, 80, 167. PORTER, 61, 62, 96, 147. PROUTY, PROUTEE, 63, 64, 65, 66, 67, 107, 113. PUTNAM, 3, 6, 11, 13, 25, 26, 34, 36, 39, 41, 51, 54, 77, 96, 98, 99, 100, 101, 102, 112, 122, 129, 131, 132, 135, 136, 144, 145, 146, 147, 148, 149, 153, 154, 168. PULCIPHIR, 14. PUTNEY, 24, 27, 28, 29, 30, 131. PLUMMER, 29. PUFFER, 32 45, 56. PUSLIA (?), 96. PURRINGTON, 125. PLYMPTON, 30, 31.

QUIGLEY, 166.

RANDAL, RANDALL, 4, 40, 52, 56, 80, 84, 121, 163. RAWSON, 15, 18, 19, 20, 21, 49, 51, 76, 77, 134, 135. RAMSDELL, RAMSDEL, 17, 125. RAYLEY, 39. RAND, 52 53, 77, 80, 81, 86, 111, 131. RAYMOND, 68, 69 70, 109, 121, 161, 162. RAA, 84. RAMOR, 87. RAINGER, 94, 156. RAYMENT, 122. RAINHEART, 125. RACKIT, 130. RANGER, 150. RALPH, RALF, 154, 165. READ, REED, 13, 19, 20, 21, 22, 36 37, 38, 52, 53, 59, 70, 71, 74, 77, 88, 89, 92, 93, 97, 105, 128, 133, 155 163. REXFORD, 15 REMINGTON, 31, 35. REVERA, 62. REDDY, 156. RICE, 1, 3, 4, 5, 6, 7, 8, 9, 10, 11, 22, 23, 31, 32, 35, 40, 44, 46, 49, 58, 59 (?), 60, 61, 64, 65, 66, 67, 69, 70, 71, 72, 76, 78, 79, 80, 81, 82, 84, 87, 88, 89, 94, 98, 100, 102, 103, 105, 106, 107, 112, 115, 119, 120, 121, 122, 123, 124, 125, 144, 150, 153, 154, 156, 157, 158, 159 161, 162, 165, 166. RICHARDS, RICHARD, 2, 27, 30, 35, 54, 56, 73, 77, 101, 108, 166. RICHARDSON, 3, 7, 11, 15, 17, 23, 32, 42, 43, 45, 46, 60, 83, 85, 87, 90, 91, 98, 99, 101, 104, 105, 106, 107, 108, 109, 110, 111, 112, 113, 114, 124, 144, 146, 147, 151, 154, 157, 158, 159, 166, 167. RICHMOND, 9, 94 119, 152, 153, 155. RICKEY, 10. RIST, 20. RIPLEY, 23, 158. RION, 31. RITTER, 39, 40. RIGHT, 64 (see Wright). RICH, 65, 92, 97, 99, 103, 129, 131, 144, 146, 147, 151, 152, 153, 155, 161, 162. RIXFORTH, 124. ROGERS, ROGER, 1, 26, 41, 53, 62, 68, 71, 72, 90, 104, 113, 118, 119, 129, 150. ROBBINS, ROBINS, 1, 33, 45, 47, 56, 77, 84, 91, 92, 106, 107, 110, 111, 113, 115, 127. ROBERTS, ROBERT, ROBARTS, 2, 5, 42, 63, 76, 77, 101, 119, 145. ROOD, 3, 24, 30, 154, 155, 158. ROBINS, ROBBINS, 128, 130, 131, 133. ROYS, ROYS (?), 3, 79. ROLENS, ROWLIN, 4, 42. ROSS, 8, 25, 46, 47, 93, 107, 111, 116, 154. ROCKWOOD, 13, 14, 77, 78, 134, 135, 155 ROBERTSON, 82, 133, 144. ROBINSON, 15, 23, 24, 25, 26, 28, 29, 71, 76, 118, 119, 120, 121, 122, 123, 125, 127, 132, 133, 136, 144, 152, 153, 158. ROBERSON, 40. ROWE, 148. ROLF, 60. ROWE, 71, 113. ROZER, 71, 125. ROCKETT, ROCKET, 128. ROFF, 85 (possibly Ross). ROWELL, ROWEL, 98, 134. ROUTELL, 111. RUE, 1. RUGGLES,

RUGLES, 3, 94, 118, 119, 120, 121, 122, 123, 125, 126, 158. RUSSELL, RUSSEL, 5. 35, 37, 42, 43, 44, 45, 54, 56, 112, 115. RUTTER, 16, 17, 93. RUD, 37. RUGG, 38. 104, 105, 106, 107, 110, 113, 114, 115, 116, 151. RUSS, 111. RYAN, 66.

SPARHAWKE, SPARHAWK, 36, 96, 129, 133, 134. SWANSEY, 109. STACEY, STACY, 1, 2, 30, 31, 32, 33, 76. SABINS, SABEN, 1, 25, 27, 32, 33, 44. SARGENT, SARGEANT, 58, 59, 60, 61, 62, 65, 70, 157, 161. SADLER, SADDLER, 6, 18, 49, 50, 77, 78. SPAULDING, 73. STRAIGHT, 163. SPAFFORD, 33. SMALL, 95, 145, 146. STADE, 7. SANDERS, SAUNDERS, 86, 160, 162. STARNS, 38 (see Stearns). SAWIN, 7, 8, 42, 61, 63, 86. STANTON, 76, 167. STATEN, 157. SHAPLY, 33. SHAY, 154. SANDERSON, 8, 54, 55, 57, 60, 61. SATERLEY, 152, 153. SALMON, 34. SWAN, 13, 34, 42, 61, 80, 90, 101. SACKWELL, 116. SAWINE, 85. SAMPSON, 45, 54, 56, 154, 157. SPRAGUE, SPRAIGE, 13, 27, 60, 61, 65, 66, 97, 145, 156, 162. STANLEY, 77. SALISBURY, 166. STAPLES, 14, 16, 93. SANDERSON, SAUNDERSON, 55, 62, 65, 67, 89. SHATTUCK, 25, 162. STANFORD, 16, 124. STANHOPE, 46, 47. SLARROW, 22. SCARBOROUGH, 16, 17. SAFFORD, 55, 56, 117, 118, 119, 123, 144. SLAYTON, 63, 64, 154, 156. SCAMMELL, 17, 160. SAWYER, 41, 42, 43, 44, 45, 46, 47, 52, 53, 55, 56, 79, 85, 86, 88, 90, 96, 97, 104, 105, 106, 107, 108, 109, 110, 111, 113, 114, 116. SANGER, 20, 24, 29. STRATEN, 161. STRATTON, 44, 68, 71, 118, 162. SALEM, 21. SAWTELL, SAWTEL, 41, 56, 97, 162. SARVEY (?), 149. SHAW, 22, 60, 85, 114, 123, 124, 151. SALES, 28. SHERTLIFF, 72. STREETER, STREATER, 1, 29, 32, 92, 99, 100, 102, 127, 128, 129, 133, 136, 145, 150, 154. SHERMAN, 75, 76, 77, 78, 79, 81, 85, 93, 120. STERNE, STERNS, STEARNS, 4, 5, 6, 8, 9, 10, 11, 12, 13, 17, 18, 25, 33, 34, 36, 38, 44, 45, 47, 53, 55, 61, 68, 78, 86, 91, 111, 115, 117, 123, 145, 146, 157, 160, 165, 167. STEVENS, STEVEN, STEVANS, 6, 7, 10, 22, 37, 63, 68, 75, 86, 101, 134, 151, 153, 154, 165, 166. SEAGER, SEAGUR, 7, 58, 61, 89, 155. SPENCER (?), 128. SPENCE, 8, 11. SEVER, SEVERS, 86, 89, 135, 153. STEDMAN, 11, 36, 85, 87, 131. SELLEN, SELLON, 123, 149. SHEPPARD, SHEPARD, 12, 72. SEECOMB, 52. SWEETLAND, 96. SHEFFIELD, 14, 29, 49, 61. SHEAPCOTT, 75. STELES, STEEL, STEAL, 15. 34, 39, 51, 93, 94, 96. STEBINGS, STEBBINS, STEBINS, 59, 63, 86, 122. STEWART, STEWARD, 18, 35, 37, 38, 90, 96, 108, 113, 117, 120, 152 (see Stuart). SEAVER (?), 97, 113, 168. STEVENSON, 22, 23, 157. SWEETSER, 90. SERLS, SEARLS, 32. SWEETSER, 23. STETSON, 120, 124. SEVERY, 49, 97, 145. SEARS, 23, 93, 118, 119, 121. SENIOR, 86. SWEENEY, 23. SHEAD, SHED, 87, 105, 111, 114. SPEAR, 25. SLEVANT (?), 119. SIMPSON, SIMSON, 1, 129. SPRING, 3, 49, 86, 152. SWIFT, 144, 158. SMITH, 5, 6, 7, 8, 9, 10, 12, 13, 15, 16, 17, 21, 23, 24, 25, 27, 28, 30, 31, 32, 33, 34, 36, 38, 41, 47, 58, 60, 61, 64, 65, 66, 67, 68, 69, 70, 71, 72, 77, 78, 79, 80, 81, 82, 83, 84, 87, 91, 105, 107, 108, 110, 112, 113, 115, 120, 125, 126, 128, 132, 133, 134, 135, 136, 146, 150, 151, 153, 154, 156, 158, 161, 165, 166. SIBLEE, SIBLEY, SIBLY, 19, 21, 98, 99, 100, 101, 102, 103, 104, 123, 126, 130, 131, 133, 134, 135, 144, 145, 147, 148, 149, 161. STRICKLAND, 23. SIMONS, SIMEONS, 30, 85, 120. SIMONDS, 34, 82, 123 (see Symonds). STILES, 34, 35, 38, 39, 42, 46, 147, 148. STICKNEY, 36, 38, 69. STRICKLAND, 158. SIGOURNEY, 147. SINCLAIR, 65. STIMPSON, STIMSON, 75, 96. SINGLEBURY, SINGLETURY, SINGLETARY, SINGLETARRY, 97, 100, 102, 103, 134, 144, 145, 168. SHINDLE, 152. SWINNERTON, 104. SCOTT, 1, 25, 28, 43, 59, 62. STOW, 2, 8,

55, 57, 67, 71, 73, 75, 76, 77, 88, 152. STONE, 4, 9, 22, 23, 25, 28, 29, 36, 38, 47, 52, 53, 56, 57, 60, 61, 62, 68, 72, 74, 79, 80, 81, 83, 84, 91, 97, 100, 103, 104, 120, 127, 128, 130, 131, 132, 133, 134, 148, 152, 153, 156, 158, 165, 166. STOWELL, 4, 7, 87, 166. STODDARD, 21, 60 62, 63, 66. SOLLNE, 31. STORER, 60. SOUCHEE, 35. STOCKWELL, 35, 36, 93, 98, 99, 100, 101, 102, 104, 127, 132, 144, 145, 147, 149, 161. SNOW, 36, 37, 40, 41, 44, 48, 53, 59, 62, 66, 67, 69, 74, 82, 86, 102, 106, 107, 109, 111, 112, 121, 124, 125, 132, 148, 149. SOUTHWICK, 47. SOUTHWORTH, 91, 99, 149. SOMES, 53. SLOCOMB, 163. SCOLLAY, 57. SPOONER, 112, 118, 124, 126, 159. STOWERS, 58, 60. SOUTHGATE, 60, 65, 84, 122. SPROWL, 61. SLOPER, 63. SPROUT, SPROUTE, 69, 124, 125, 164. SPOFFORD, 90. SULLIVAN, 8. STURMAN, 14. SLUEMAN, 14. SUMNER, 18, 66, 78, 105, 154, 159, 160. SHUMWAY, 31, 33, 127, 128, 129, 131, 132, 133, 134, 135. STUN (?), 45. STUART, 106 (see Stewart). STUDLEY, 149. SULLEN, 159. SHUTE, 162. STURTEVANT, 167. SYMONDS, SYMONS, 2, 39, 52, 57, 91 (see Simonds). SLY, 27, 28. SYLVESTER, 59.

TAFT, TAFTS, 3, 14, 16, 17, 18, 19, 20, 21, 28, 45, 50 51, 52, 71, 78, 103, 134, 149, 160, 163. TATMAN, 4, 5, 8, 11, 130, 158. TRACY, 6. TAYLOR, 6, 24, 25, 31, 32, 33, 34, 39, 40, 45, 53, 55, 56, 57, 58, 60, 73, 74, 76, 77, 78, 84, 85, 86, 87, 88, 93, 100, 103, 104, 122, 128, 146 147, 156, 157, 161, 165, 167, 168. THAYER, 13, 14, 15, 16, 17, 18, 19, 20, 64, 91, 125, 129, 159, 160, 161, 163, 167. THAYR (?), 163. TAMPLING, 20. THALD, 23. TARBELL, TARBILL, TARBALL, 31, 32, 34, 40, 53 90. TAINTER, 72. 146. THRASHER, 94. TRASK, 100, 145, 146, 163. TALLE, 134. TRAIN, 161. TEMPLE, 2, 11, 12, 51, 52, 76, 78, 79, 81, 82, 84, 100, 114, 117. TENNY, TENNEY, 15, 49, 50, 61, 88, 145, 146, 149, 159.

TREADWELL, 97, 134. TERRANCE, TERRENCE, 104, 155. TERRY, 125. TENISON, 127. TEWEL, 132. TENNY, 148. TWITCHELL, TWITCHEL, 15, 20, 32, 51, 159, 160, 161. THWING, 21. TITUS, TITAS, 25, 92. 108, 122, 130, 134, 146. TINKLER, 58. TIMTON, 93. TINNEY, 113. TWISS, 129, 135, 136. TWIST, 98. 127. TIMSDELL, 130. TILESTON (?), 158. TOMPSON, THOMSON, THOMPSON, 3, 14, 15, 19, 20, 21, 22, 28, 59, 63, 68, 84, 94, 113, 117, 119, 123, 158, 159, 160, 161, 162, 164. TROWBRIDGE, 6, 9, 12, 165, 166, 167. THOMAS, 6, 8, 32, 41, 59, 105, 120, 121, 122, 127, 130, 152, 153, 167. TOLMAN, 11, 58. TOWN, 12, 28, 76, 97, 98, 100, 101, 102, 127, 128, 129, 131, 132, 133, 134, 135, 136, 144, 148, 149. TORREY, TORRY, 14, 15, 17, 51, 157. THOUGHT, 41. TOWNSEND, 42, 48, 83, 84, 88, 105, 111, 114. TONY, TONNEY, 49, 51. TOBE, 51. THROOP, 81. TOOZER, 89. TORRENCE, 94. TORNER, 96. TOOKER 111 (see Tucker). TOTTLE, 150. TOTMAN, 166. TUCKER, 1, 8, 18, 59, 62, 63, 65, 80, 81, 82, 83, 105, 155 (see Tooker). TRUMBLE, TRUMBELL, 2, 60, 168. TURNER, 8, 56, 57, 71, 78, 109, 116. THURSTON, THURSTIN, 11, 15, 38, 51, 83, 85, 95, 97, 109, 133, 134, 148. TURTELOT, 29. TUTTLE, 43. TUFTS, TUFT, 120, 150. TYLER, 3, 19, 21, 48, 73, 156.

UPHAM, 3, 6, 24, 27, 29, 33, 61, 65, 67, 94, 134, 151, 154, 155. UNDERWOOD, 48, 67, 84, 133. UTTER (?), 135. UIALL, 51. UPTON, 95.

VARNUM, 161. VERRY, 7. VICKERY, 16. VINTON, VINTEN, 26, 30, 59. VORCE, 151.

WATT, 81, 150. WARNER, 2, 44, 48, 55, 56, 57, 69, 90, 93, 105, 110, 118, 119, 120, 121, 122, 152, 153, 156. WALKER, 2, 5, 8, 9, 11, 13, 19, 20, 21, 31, 32, 39, 43, 47, 48, 50,

INDEX.

51, 60, 63, 69, 73, 74, 77, 79, 85, 86, 94, 97, 99, 101, 102, 103, 112, 120, 121, 122, 150, 151, 153. WANSON, 37. WARD, 3, 5, 6, 7, 9, 10, 11, 12, 13, 15, 19, 20, 30, 43, 49, 50, 60, 62, 68, 73, 74, 80, 86, 89, 127, 128, 135, 147, 149, 155, 161, 166, 167. WALLIS, WALLACE WALLES, WALLAS, 4, 6, 21, 34, 61, 92, 117, 148. WAIT, WAITE, 5, 7, 15, 59, 61, 62, 70, 77, 83, 97, 99, 121, 146, 147, 148, 149, 150, 155. WATER, WATERS, WARTERS, 5, 8, 25, 62, 100, 101, 135, 145, 146, 147, 148. WARRIN, WARREN, WARRAN, 5, 11, 24, 25, 26, 27, 28, 30, 46, 49, 50, 51, 62, 63, 65, 66, 75, 80, 85, 86, 94, 110, 117, 121, 122, 131, 135, 151, 156, 160, 165. WALKUP, WALCUP, 7, 50, 51, 161. WALCOTT, 47, WARE, 75, 93, 94, 95. WADSWORTH, 75, 103, 145. WATKINS, 85, 157. WATTEN, 86. WASHBURN, 94, 121, 124. WALLINGSFORD, 109, 112. WARDEN, 126. WALTER, 150. WALKER, 154, 155, 157, 158, 165, 166. WARBON, 158. WHARFIELD, WARFIELD, 15, 18, 77, 160. WASHBURN, 17, 62, 120, 157. WAKEFIELD, 28, 29, 101, 103, 132, 136, 146, 151. WALDRON, 30. WART, 128. WALTON, 39. WALLEY, 40. WAND, 49. WATSON, 59, 60, 61, 62, 64, 65, 66, 67, 133, 134, 151, 152, 153, 155, 156. WHELLER, 149. WELD, WELDS, 1, 30, 31, 33, 87, 129. WHEELOCK, 2 5, 14, 15, 16, 17, 21, 35, 51, 59, 75, 79, 80, 84, 89, 90, 91, 106, 116, 136, 159, 160. WELLS, 2, 116, 118, :19. WHEELER, WHEELOR, 7, 8, 15, 22, 23, 40, 43, 46, 48, 52, 60, 65, 68, 69, 72, 76, 79, 80, 81, 82, 83, 84, 85, 87, 97, 99, 101, 107, 110, 119, 121, 122, 123, 163. WESSON, 8 10, 76, 145. WELLINGTON, 12. WHEET, WHEAT, 14, 66, 122. WHETCOMB, 44, 45, 46, 47, 48, 91 (see Whitcomb). WEBB, 19, 72. WETHERILL, WETHERELL, WEATHERELL, WETHEREL, 25, 26, 29, 102, 158 WEST, 25, 167. WESTON, 94. WEBSTER, 27, 122, 124, 135. WELLMAN, 97, 98. WETHERBEE, WEATHERBEE, 34, 38, 40, 52 53, 54, 55, 56, 57, 74, 80, 85 (see Witherbee).

WELCH, 41. WENTWORTH, 54, 95 (see Wintworth). WEDGE, 60, 159, WHEATON, WHEETEN, 69, 85, 159. WEEKS, 94, 121, 123, 125, 151. WELLIS, 121 (see Willis). WILLIAMS, 20, 26, 28, 31, 33, 71, 74, 83, 85, 86, 88, 102, 107, 111, 112, 115, 155, 158, 166. WHITTELL, 33. WITT —, 62. WITT, 2, 45, 88. WITHERBY, WITHIRBEE, WITHERBE, 2, 40, 73, 90, 94, 96 (see Wetherbee). WITHERILL (see Wetherell). WHIPPLE, WHIPLE, 2, 8, 75, 76, 77, 98, 99, 104, 118, 119, 122, 124, 128, 146. WIMAN, 87 (see Wyman). WHITCOMB, WHITCOM, WHETCOMB, 3, 40, 41, 42, 43, 44, 45, 54, 55, 56, 90, 93, 97, 105, 107, 110, 111, 115, 118, 119, 120, 123. WHITE, WIGHT, WITE, 3, 13, 14, 15, 16, 17, 18, 19, 20, 21, 26, 31, 34, 38, 43, 48, 49, 50, 53, 56, 58, 62, 63, 64, 67, 72, 77, 86, 90, 91, 93, 98, 100, 102, 104, 108, 114, 115, 116, 117, 119, 121, 122, 123, 126, 132, 133, 134, 135, 136, 159, 160, 148, 150, 154, 163, 166. WILLARD, 3, 10, 12, 13, 24, 28, 29, 30, 35, 52, 53, 54, 55, 56, 57, 76, 77, 86, 104, 105, 107, 109, 110, 112, 113, 114, 116, 117, 145, 146, 147, 150, 153, 165, 166. WINTER, 19, 26, 29, 30. WHITNEY, 3, 5, 6, 7, 10, 14, 15, 34, 36, 37, 38, 42, 44, 45, 46, 49, 50, 51, 52, 53, 54, 55, 56, 57, 63, 66, 67, 68, 70, 72, 75, 77, 79, 80 81, 82, 83, 85, 86, 88, 91, 92, 93, 97, 98, 99, 106, 113, 128, 133, 146, 149, 156, 166, 167. WHITAKER, 22, 113. WINCH, 3, 7, 22, 68, 69, 71. WINCHET, 46. WHITING, WHITEING, 6, 40, 74, 109. WINSLOW, 88, 118, 119, 122, 125, 144, 149, 159. WRIGHT, 6, 23, 26, 35, 49, 50, 56, 66, 80, 81, 84, 96, 104, 113, 118, 119, 120, 122, 123, 132, 150, 152, 155. WISWELL, WISWALL, 7, 49, 166. WILMON, 40. WILD, 40. WILDER, 7, 10, 23, 28, 41, 42, 43, 44, 45, 46, 47, 84, 89, 90, 104, 105, 106, 107, 108, 109, 110, 111, 112, 113, 114, 115, 116, 117, 157. WILBER, 44. WILLIGNTON, 9, 10, 11, 13, 68, 162. WINN, 116 (see Wynne). WILEY, WILLEY, 10, 12, 13, 127, 129 (see Wyley). WHITTEMORE, WHITEMORE, WHITTIMORE, WHIT-

MORE, 54, 55, 60, 61, 65, 66, 67, 69, 75, 76, 79, 90, 97, 98, 100, 164. WISOR, WISER, 13, 32. WIZEL, 54. WILCOX, 29. WILLSON, WILSON, 14, 18, 21, 27, 35, 36, 37, 39, 41, 42, 43, 45, 46, 58, 60, 61, 65, 66, 67, 71, 78, 79, 87, 88, 89, 91, 93, 94, 103, 109, 116, 128, 129, 133, 151, 155, 156, 164. WHITMAN, 16. WIT, 144, 152. WILLINGTON, 167. WINTER, 163. WILES, 55. WILLS, 113. WILKINS, 97, 102. WINTWORTH, 56 (see Wentworth). WILLIS, 56, 57, 64, 121, 122, 123, 125, 144 (see Wellis). WICKER, 60, 86, 126. WING, 122, 126. WINCHESTER, 75, 76, 118, 124. WITHINTON, 85. WINSHIP, WINCHOP, 43, 86, 87. WOODS, WOOD, 1, 2, 3, 14, 18, 19, 20, 28, 29, 30, 35, 36, 37, 38, 39, 43, 46, 48, 49, 50, 51, 60, 64, 73, 75, 76, 79, 86, 87, 89, 91, 93, 94, 95, 106, 111, 112, 115, 116, 144, 151, 155, 156, 159. WOOLCOT, WOLCOTT, 1, 128. WOODBURY, WOODBERY, 1, 3, 98, 100, 102, 121, 136, 144, 147, 150, 156, 158. WOODWARD, 7, 8, 12, 20, 22, 51, 58, 66, 85, 87, 92, 102, 103, 123, 124, 125, 146, 164. WHOATE, 18. WORK, 23, 62, 164. WOTT, 38, 43. WORSTER, WOOSTER, 43, 54, 58, 62, 63. WOODARD, 63, 64, 67. WOODDY, 77. WOOLSON, 93, 101. WOODCOCK, 112. WOLCOTT, WOOLCOTT, WOLCOT, 150, 152, 153, 155, 156. WOOD, 160, 163. WYMAN, WYMON, 23, 26, 37, 45, 83, 84, 89, 91, 104, 107, 115, 117, 128, 136, 152 (see Wiman). WYNNE, 116 (see Winn). WYLEY, 128 (see Wiley).

YEATS, YEATES, 17, 145. YOUNG, 8, 9, 12, 21, 71, 161, 162, 166, 167.

ZWIER, ZWEAR, 55. Z—RED (?), 110.

www.ingramcontent.com/pod-product-compliance
Lightning Source LLC
Chambersburg PA
CBHW030552080526
44585CB00012B/350